Conscience and Corporate Culture

Foundations of Business Ethics

Series editors: W. Michael Hoffman and Robert. E. Frederick

Written by an assembly of the most distinguished figures in business ethics, the Foundations of Business Ethics series aims to explain and assess the fundamental issues that motivate interest in each of the main subjects of contemporary research. In addition to a general introduction to business ethics, individual volumes cover key ethical issues in management, marketing, finance, accounting, and computing. The volumes, which are complementary yet complete in themselves, allow instructors maximum flexibility in the design and presentation of course materials without sacrificing either depth of coverage or the discipline-based focus of many business courses. The volumes can be used separately or in combination with anthologies and case studies, depending on the needs and interests of the instructors and students.

Conscience and Corporate Culture

Kenneth E. Goodpaster

To Lindsay —
With respect and
appreciation for your
work in developing
ethical corporate cultures.
Best,

Ken Goodpaster
3/2010

Blackwell
Publishing

© 2007 by Kenneth E. Goodpaster

BLACKWELL PUBLISHING
350 Main Street, Malden, MA 02148-5020, USA
9600 Garsington Road, Oxford OX4 2DQ, UK
550 Swanston Street, Carlton, Victoria 3053, Australia

The right of Kenneth E. Goodpaster to be identified as the
Author of this Work has been asserted in accordance with
the UK Copyright, Designs, and Patents Act 1988.

First published 2007 by Blackwell Publishing Ltd

2   2008

Library of Congress Cataloging-in-Publication Data

Goodpaster, Kenneth E., 1944–
Conscience and corporate culture / Kenneth E. Goodpaster.
p. cm. — (Foundations of business ethics)
Includes bibliographical references (p.   ) and index.
ISBN: 978-1-4051-3039-4 (hardback : alk. paper)
ISBN: 978-1-4051-3040-0 (pbk. : alk. paper)
1. Business ethics.
2. Corporate culture—Moral and ethical aspects. 3. Conflict of interests.
4. Conscience. I. Title. II. Series.

HF5387 G658 2007
174′.4—dc22
2006007479

A catalogue record for this title is available from the British Library.

Set in 10.5/12.5pt Plantin
by Graphicraft Limited, Hong Kong
Printed and bound in Singapore
by C.O.S. Printers Pte Ltd

The publisher's policy is to use permanent paper from mills that
operate a sustainable forestry policy, and which has been manufactured
from pulp processed using acid-free and elementary chlorine-free
practices. Furthermore, the publisher ensures that the text paper
and cover board used have met acceptable environmental
accreditation standards.

For further information on
Blackwell Publishing, visit our website:
www.blackwellpublishing.com

I would like to dedicate this book to my wife Harriet who made it possible for me to get away to do much of the writing – and to my children, Beth, John, and Kate, children-in-law, Rick and Mindi, and grandchild Alice.

Contents

List of Figures

Foreword

The publication of this book is important and timely. Business and academic communities are in need of a bridge between ethical reflection and corporate decision-making. Its author, Kenneth Goodpaster, is eminently qualified to build this bridge. He reaches doers and thinkers on a subject that is as difficult as it is important.

I have been fortunate to work with Professor Goodpaster. After a career as a lawyer and as a CEO, I joined the faculty at the University of St. Thomas. For 20 semesters we team-taught MBA students using the case method. His approach from the perspective of a trained ethicist and mine from the perspective of a general manager, often but not inevitably, found congruence. I have also been a participant as student in his leadership forums for management development at Medtronic, Inc.

He is a master teacher. As I read this book, I hear his voice and visualize him in the classroom. He is tireless as he moves around the room pulling from the participants their definition of the elements of a business case – always insistent, always requiring student precision in analysis. His voice is gentle, but unrelenting. Frequently, he retreats to the white board to jot down a position or illuminate an inconsistency. At session end he has recorded the essence of the discussion with its conclusions and its ambiguities. His summations are brilliant. And I have seen him engage business executives in this same manner. Executives are entranced, as are students with the breadth of his knowledge.

He does understand business. To him the classroom and the executive suite have similar needs. He recognizes that the corporation is a business school in real time, needing to have its values defined and applied. His linkage in Great Books forums for managers and students flawlessly ties the wisdom of timeless writing with the immediacy of tomorrow's decision. He is unique. His professional experience has been focused on linking ethical understanding with application in the workplace.

He has co-authored a widely used casebook, *Business Ethics: Policies and Persons*, now in its fourth edition. Numerous managements have assisted his business case writing by trusting him with sensitive documents and interviews. His many discussions with a variety of executives have given him rare perspective on their business dilemmas, triumphs, and failures. With insight, his cases reveal a chain of decisions putting the student, often with discomfort, in the shoes of one compelled to decide. These skills of insight, provocation, organization, and presentation are evident in this book. With care it moves one from the call of conscience to operational courage.

There is need for *Conscience and Corporate Culture*. While the vast preponderance of corporations are ethical and well-managed, we nevertheless, are faced with a constant news stream of trials, convictions, televised perp walks, and news releases from federal agencies and state attorneys' general.

All public companies must face the impact of legislation, stock exchange rules, and pronouncements of best practices by a variety of shareholder representatives. Clearly the public's lack of confidence in the accuracy and transparency of balance sheets and profit and loss statements has negatively affected the attitude of investors. But we the public have our own inconsistency. As shareholders we demand maximization of value in the securities we own directly or through our 401(k) accounts while as citizens we demand ethical corporate behavior. These dual demands do not inevitably converge on the same behavior.

Goodpaster recognizes that there is ambivalence about business ethics in American and European society. It begins with skepticism about the moral credentials of the profit-driven market system. The ambivalence becomes evident, he writes, when we recognize our reluctance to prescribe a cure by legislating moral criteria to balance managerial decision-making. He is a realist by recognizing that both our laws and our social norms caution managers and boards of directors against thinking that strays too far from a strict duty of care to shareholders.

The book is divided into two parts. The goal of Part I, "Conscience: Response to a Pathology" is to clarify the hazard to which business ethics is a response and to identify the idea of conscience in relation to corporate culture. This Part is grounded in Goodpaster's lifetime of study, writing, and teaching. It is direct and thought-provoking. In an opening quotation he recognizes that treatises on ethics can be voluminous and may in some respects be abstract and vague. This, the book is not. It holds the reader as it presents concepts verified by experience and common sense.

In this Part he examines the role of moral reflection (conscience) in the lives of each of us as individuals and the corresponding role it plays in the culture of an organization. Conscience, he believes, is a primary check on the unbalanced pursuit of goals and purposes.

Through a series of examples drawn from public events and from thoughtful observers, he describes a syndrome for which a label is convenient. In 1986 he referred to this malaise as teleopathy, combining the Greek roots for "goal" and "disease." He writes, "If there were manuals for character disorders in ethics as there are in physical and emotional disorders in medicine, I submit that teleopathy would be as central in its manual as heart disease and depression are, respectively, in theirs." Teleopathy is the unbalanced pursuit of goals or purposes by an individual or an organized group.

With great insight he describes its principal symptoms:

- Fixation or singleness of purpose under stress; leading to
- Rationalization; leading to
- Detachment.

In its most extreme form it may suspend ethical awareness in the decision-making process. Different criteria take over our thoughts and actions as we struggle with meeting the quarterly earnings goal, winning the game, or gaining the promotion.

Goodpaster illustrates the unbalanced pursuit of purpose directly, in decision-making, and indirectly, in the form of loyalty to a role or function such as "breadwinner," "doctor," or "employer." In these contexts, our purposes are implied in the background – supporting a family, healing the sick, keeping the company going – but such purposes may be pursued with or without balance. Thus, corporate conscience is not in the end a matter of external compliance or competitive advantage; it is a matter of internal assessment and improvement. But even though internal moral compasses are more reliable than external sanctions – legal or economic – compasses are inert without the courage to act.

The power of his thoughts requires me from time to time to put the book down – to close my eyes and mentally drift over times in my past when unfortunately his definitions may have fit me. He has given all decision-makers a new set of standards, new measurements with which to judge conduct, and (thankfully) a reminder to employ more frequently the power of conscience.

Having examined issues of conscience and teleopathy, he shifts to operational questions. It is the leader who must display ethical awareness when the values and behavior of an organization are at stake. She or he is the person most responsible for giving substance to the moral agenda of the organized group.

While Part I sets the table, Part II, "The Moral Agenda of Leadership," provides the feast. The chapters of Part II apply the conceptual foundations laid in Part I. While concepts of leadership from *Good to Great* by Jim Collins and *Authentic Leadership* by Bill George are drawn upon to provide valuable insights into the responsibilities of ethical leadership, the impact of Part II comes from Goodpaster's extensive experience.

He offers practical advice to leaders. He recommends an agenda for shaping corporate culture with three broad imperatives: orienting, institutionalizing, and sustaining conscience in the organization. His definitions are explicit:

- *Orienting*: Giving direction, setting a course, getting there from here. He illustrates his point with several corporate mission statements, with the procedures for discerning dominant ethical values and with methods of attaching importance to them.
- *Institutionalizing*: Making the company's values a part of its operating consciousness. The process of relating ethical values to operations at every turn and reinforcing with symbols, ceremonies, and celebrations. And, developing an incentive and reward program that moves away from a total reliance on self-interest. He asks how corporate conscience can become "second nature" if the "first nature" of the corporation is economic.
- *Sustaining*: Extending and sustaining shared ethical values over time. Constant renewal. Organizational character can have a tendency to wear down. Ongoing attention must be given to the next generation of leadership, but also to the external forces that influence the values of the company. Again the author relies on

his considerable experience. He illustrates using a broad variety of practices used by companies large and small.

Always the realist, Goodpaster recognizes that business leaders are the principal architects of corporate conscience. They must manage the challenges of pursuing profit while maintaining integrity. Delivering on the moral agenda is their responsibility. Enlightenment and courage must walk hand in hand.

Goodpaster argues that there must be another – supplementary – item on the moral agenda. He invokes the classical question from Plato's dialogues – "Can virtue be taught?" If business leaders are to avoid defaulting on the moral formation of future leaders there must be continuing educational support structures. He postulates "three academies" as essential.

First, the modern business school, which must squarely face the question, "Can ethics be taught?" He argues that the three imperatives of corporate leadership (orienting, institutionalizing, and sustaining shared values) must be mirrored in the administration of business schools and in their curricula. Yet ethics education needs to continue beyond graduation. Second, corporate management's education and leadership development programs must address the moral agenda – both in general and as it relates to the institutionalization of company-specific values. Third, associations of leaders that oversee and set global standards for corporate ethics must be specific, forthright, and culturally encompassing. He describes several such organizations and opines that such structures are as essential to professional management as their counterparts in medicine and law.

For most of his professional life he has interacted with and counseled corporate executives. Some of the most-used cases in MBA curricula are based on his extensive corporate studies. He is a prized moderator at the Aspen Institute and is frequently drawn upon by executives with complex and daunting problems. For many years he has actively conducted intense sessions with several layers of Medtronic executives in leadership development and ethics reinforcement. He understands the pressures, the complexity, and the urgency implicit in decision-making. And he understands the dilemmas of the women and men who are called upon to make those decisions.

To study and write about the ethics of business is indeed valuable. But to carry study and writing forward to application is often missed or avoided. Goodpaster concretely shows the way to the practice of improved business ethics. He is there for us who ponder difficult decisions in the classroom, the boardroom, the office, or in the wee hours of the night.

"Application" for Goodpaster has a broader meaning than for most. His goal is to create ethical corporate cultures. He points the way to institutionalizing an awareness that leads to moral judgments that are pervasive rather than singular. This is indeed ambitious. The book is a gem. It is a profound and riveting read. It should be a standard in the business school and a regularly consulted source in the manager's office. It will be a classic. I highly commend it to you. May you, as I have, emerge with a heightened conscience and with a host of sensible options for its application in forming and sustaining ethical business cultures.

Thomas E. Holloran JD[1]
Senior Distinguished Fellow, University of St. Thomas School of Law, Professor Emeritus, University of St. Thomas College of Business and Former President, Medtronic, Inc.

Preface

The philosopher is just like the rest of us non-philosophers, so far as
we are just and sympathetic instinctively, and so far as we are open to
the voice of complaint. His function is in fact indistinguishable from
that of the best kind of statesman at the present day. His books upon
ethics, therefore, so far as they truly touch the moral life, must
more and more ally themselves with a literature which is confessedly
tentative and suggestive rather than dogmatic – I mean with novels
and dramas of the deeper sort, with sermons, with books on statecraft
and philanthropy and social and economic reform. Treated in this way,
ethical treatises may be voluminous and luminous as well; but they
never can be final, except in their abstractest and vaguest features;
and they must more and more abandon the old-fashioned, clear-cut,
and would-be "scientific" form.

(William James, 1891)

This book is written in the spirit of this passage from William James.
It is in some ways a report on more than three decades of professional
evolution. And it is rooted in a conviction that management can
"profit" in a deeper-than-ordinary sense from the self-scrutiny that
ethics affords. Most importantly, the reader will find here a vision
of ethics in business that emphasizes the crucial role of leadership
as the real-world bridge between the values of the individual and the
shared values of the organized group. This means leadership at the
top, certainly, but just as certainly leadership at every key position
of managerial responsibility throughout the corporation.

Genesis of this Book – From Harvard Business School . . .

When I joined the Harvard Business School faculty in 1980, a wayward philosopher seeking to connect ethical theory with management education, I confronted an enormous intellectual and cultural gap between the discipline of ethics and the discipline of management. Cognitive dissonance, some call it. I discovered that philosophers were trained to think differently from professional managers. They usually *zigged* when managers *zagged*. They *ascended* the ladder of reflection toward premises and assumptions when managers *descended* the ladder toward pragmatics and action; they often insisted on *examining* a goal or purpose while managers were more concerned with *implementing* it.

This experience was, at first, exasperating. Both the substance and the style of my training ran counter to the distinctive practical orientation of business administration. Despite the dissonance, however, I was convinced that philosophy – specifically *moral* philosophy or *ethics* – had much to offer and much to gain from a "joint venture" with management education.

On the *gain* side, there was practicality and pedagogy. Moral philosophy in the twentieth century had been preoccupied with conceptual analysis. Questions about the meanings of terms like "right" and "good" had dominated the philosophical landscape to the exclusion of questions about what actions *are* right and what things *are* good. Conceptual analysis had run amok and a return to "applied" ethics was needed.

What philosophy had to *offer* were an inheritance and a talent. The inheritance was a body of thought about ethics and the human condition that had developed over more than two millennia. The talent was an eye and an ear for distinguishing cogent reasoning from its counterfeits. At a time when the ethical aspects of professional management were coming under increasing scrutiny, this seemed like a valuable resource.

Efforts had been made at many academic institutions during the 1970s for management and philosophy departments to "team teach" business ethics. The belief was that the two sides of the house – management and ethics – needed somehow to be joined. Most of these efforts met with limited success, however, because the integration that was needed was simply *reassigned* to the students rather than *modeled* by the faculty. The marriage of management and moral philosophy would take more than this if it were not to end as so many marriages do today.

I was convinced, and remain so, that a deeper kind of integration is needed. The natural tendency in our society of professionals is to call in the experts when we experience some degree of dissonance over a problem. When the problem is how to relate ethics to business decision-making, that tendency leads us to call in ethics specialists much as we would call in specialists in international relations when faced with a question about the US balance of trade. But in business ethics, it doesn't work that way. The kind of understanding needed to integrate ethics and management is of a different kind. Professor Donald A. Schön of MIT once suggested an image that may have special meaning in this context:

> In the varied topography of professional practice, there is a high, hard ground which overlooks a swamp. On the high ground, manageable problems lend themselves to solution through the use of research-based theory and technique. In the swampy lowlands, problems are messy and confusing and incapable of technical solution. The irony of this situation is that the problems of the high ground tend to be relatively unimportant to individuals or to society at large, however great their technical interest may be, while in the swamp lie the problems of greatest human concern. The practitioner is confronted with a choice. Shall he remain on the high ground where he can solve relatively unimportant problems according to his standards of rigor, or shall he descend to the swamp of important problems and non-rigorous inquiry?[1]

I found myself departing the high ground and entering the swamp. In the process, I came to believe that if the field of business ethics was to have a future, a new kind of discipline would have to be formed that did not yet exist. A generation of educators was needed that could think and teach using the skills of management *and* the skills of moral philosophy at once. It was necessary to get both mindsets in the same body.

On the advice of several Harvard colleagues, therefore, I learned business policy by the case method. Never mind that I was on the instructor's side of the desk. I considered myself a learner. I had to relinquish my "expertise" to learn. It was like starting a second career after having become established in a first. But my students and faculty colleagues helped.

I learned the hard way and the only way: *from teaching and from practice*. At first, I could not appreciate the so-called administrative point of view – how competent managers think about problems; the way they identify issues, formulate and implement strategy, generate action plans. This appreciation was neither part of my experience nor part of my background in moral philosophy. I had to walk in the moccasins of the general manager. I had to puzzle over the strategic, organizational, and interpersonal challenges that general managers face. And I had to do it *case by case*.

In the process, I gained an appreciation for the *vocation* of the manager, charting a course amidst the uncertainties of physical events and human nature: motivating others, remaining loyal to providers of resources, setting goals, imposing new structures, monitoring progress and performance, achieving purposes through cooperation and the exercise of authority.[2] I listened and I learned just how different was the mind of the manager from the mind of the philosopher. Not better or worse. *Different*.

There were challenges on the other side of the desk too. My first classes in business ethics, using the case method, were no small challenge to my students. On some days, looks of glazed incomprehension were a relief from looks of irritation. What had Plato or John Stuart Mill to do with this marketing strategy and these accounting practices? What was the point of comparing and contrasting utilitarian and social contract theories of justice? But they learned, often in spite of their professor, that questioning *ends* was healthy and that questioning *means* to ends was healthy too; that moral reasoning was more than shooting from the hip; and that their fellow students were actually following certain tried and true patterns in the way they joined their realism with their idealism.

The "joint venture" eventually began to happen. It happened as I acknowledged that the frameworks and concepts that are the stock-in-trade of philosophy often blush in the face of the complexity and concreteness of management decisions. What was needed was an ethical *point of view*, not an ethical *algorithm*. I had believed this many years ago, but had forgotten it. I began to change, to think differently. Outer dialogues became inner dialogues. A case-method teacher had joined the philosopher in me, and slowly the case-method teacher was being joined by a manager. There were *different kinds of wisdom* here, not just different occupations.[3]

... to the University of St. Thomas

I joined the University of St. Thomas faculty at the end of the 1980s after coming to know students, faculty, and administrators in this energetic Minnesota institution over several years. A university with over 10,000 students, half undergraduate and half graduate, St. Thomas had grown dramatically during the previous two decades. Its graduate programs in business were third largest in the nation with over 3,000 students. I was honored with an endowed chair that provided generously for teaching innovations, curricular initiatives, research assistance, and community involvement.

The Twin Cities business community had a special attraction for me because of an executive initiative then called the *Minnesota Center for Corporate Responsibility*. Today it is called the *Center for Ethical Business Cultures* and it is formally affiliated with the University of St. Thomas. Founded in the mid-1970s, CEBC was unique because it was undertaken not by academics or government programs, but by an honest desire on the part of business leaders to enlighten and encourage themselves in the realm of corporate social responsibility. Today CEBC member companies number over 130 across Minnesota.

Despite these attractions, I have been asked more than once why I would leave a stable position at the Harvard Business School, arguably the best business school in the country, to join a less well-known institution in the Midwest – especially in a part of the Midwest that is well-known for its severe winters! To this question, my reply must invoke the title of a book by Rabbi Harold Kushner, *When All You've Ever Wanted Isn't Enough*. While I continue to value my ten years at Harvard, I value as much the opportunity that the University of St. Thomas has given me to experience and explore themes higher on its list of priorities than on the lists of many more "elite" business schools.[4] The mission of the College of Business at the University of St. Thomas is to educate *"highly-principled global business leaders."*

This book is born, therefore, from more than a philosopher's desire to combine ethical reflection with business education and corporate decision making (my Harvard mission). It also comes from a desire to place these aspirations in the context of the wider *spiritual* journey that grounds them (my St. Thomas mission). By using the word *spiritual*, I do not mean to suggest a hidden religious agenda in any denominational sense, but I do wish to affirm a source of both personal and institutional motivation that is often ignored (because unspoken) in conversations and classrooms that address themes like leadership, corporate culture, conscience, and morality.

During my 15 years at St. Thomas, I have not only been active in course design and case-based research, but alongside these essential activities, I have been part of curricular innovations in business policy, the development of a Great Books course for MBA students in the style of the Aspen Institute Executive Seminar, an elective course on "Spirituality and the Modern Manager," and a set of guidelines for global business ethics now widely known as the *Caux Round Table Principles of Business Conduct*.[5] I have also had the opportunity to develop relationships with some of the most respected companies in corporate America, including 3M, Honeywell, Cargill, H. B. Fuller, and especially Medtronic, Inc.

Emory University president James T. Laney observed in *Harvard Magazine* (Fall 1985) that many academic disciplines have retreated from including values and wisdom – and I would add *spiritual conviction* – in what is being taught. "Not long ago," he wrote, "Bernard Williams, the noted British philosopher, observed that philosophers have been trying all this century to get rid of the dreadful idea that philosophy ought to be edifying." Then Laney added, "Philosophers are not the only ones to appreciate the force of that statement . . . How can society survive if education does not attend to those qualities which it requires for its very perpetuation?"[6]

As the field of business ethics develops, it is my hope that philosophical and empirical research will be joined by a spiritual understanding of ethical awareness.[7] This can only happen if business schools are willing to serve as a bridge.[8] In the words of the poet David Whyte, "Whatever strategy we employ, or whoever we choose to speak with, we are eventually compelled to bring our work life into the realm of spiritual examination. Life does not seem to be impressed by our arguments that we can ignore our deeper desires simply because we happen to be earning a living at the time."[9]

Two Audiences

I write on the theme of conscience and corporate culture with two audiences in mind: educators in the field of business ethics and practicing corporate executives. These are the groups I have come to know best professionally, and I believe that both have an important voice in the conversation about business ethics. Executives are on the firing line daily, formulating and implementing policies that have significant effects on the lives of many people, including their own. In the end, they are the *architects* of conscience in corporate culture. Business educators are the teachers of tomorrow's managers through professional school curricula. They are the group best trained in the methods and history of ethical reasoning. Often dialogue between these groups is frustrated by language barriers and occasionally by mistrust of motives.

Writing for two audiences, however, is risky. I understand and appreciate the warnings of colleagues, publishers, and editors who doubted the possibility of a book that could successfully speak to both groups. My decision not to accept their advice is based on my conviction that work in business ethics cannot and will not go forward unless constructive dialogue *between* these audiences increases dramatically. And we must remember that executive education is a form of life-long learning continuous with the education of undergraduate students and MBA students. The two audiences do eventually come together. A *common* language and a *common* literature are needed. The chapters that follow represent a step in that direction.

Kenneth E. Goodpaster
Minneapolis & St. Paul, Minnesota
Spring 2006

Acknowledgments

Special thanks go to many who have served as guides along my journey, including John B. Matthews and Thomas Piper at Harvard Business School, and Michael Evers, Theodore Fredrickson, Thomas Holloran, Michael Naughton, David Nimmer, and Ron James, President of the Center for Ethical Business Cultures at St. Thomas. Merci beaucoup to Professor Henri-Claude deBettignies at INSEAD. Invaluable support has come from T. Dean Maines, Research Associate, collaborator, case writer extraordinaire. I am enormously indebted to many on the staff of the University of St. Thomas, but to no one more than Nancy Bruggeman, my Administrative Assistant and guiding light throughout the manuscript preparation process. Jeff Dean and Danielle Descoteaux at Blackwell Publishing were patient and enthusiastic facilitators of the book-in-process. And I must add thanks to over 300 executives of Medtronic, Inc. all around the world who have taught me more than they will ever know about joining idealism to realism in business decision-making.

I would like to thank the following publishers and individuals for permission to use selections from my previous work:

B. Magazine
Kenneth E. Goodpaster, "Conscience and the Corporate Culture," from *B. Magazine*, Spring 2005 (University of St. Thomas), pp. 18–21. Reprinted with permission.

ACKNOWLEDGMENTS

Blackwell Publishing
Kenneth E. Goodpaster, "Teaching and Learning Ethics by the Case Method," from Norman Bowie (ed.), *The Blackwell Guide to Business Ethics* (Oxford: Blackwell, 2002), pp. 117–41. Reprinted with permission.

Business Ethics Quarterly
Kenneth E. Goodpaster, "Business Ethics and Stakeholder Analysis," *Business Ethics Quarterly*, Vol. 1, No. 1 (January 1991), pp. 52–71. Reproduced with permission.

Kenneth E. Goodpaster, "Conscience and its Counterfeits in Business Life: A New Interpretation of the Naturalistic Fallacy," *Business Ethics Quarterly*, Vol. 10, No. 1 (January 2000), pp. 189–201. Reproduced with permission.

Greenwood Publishing Group
Kenneth E. Goodpaster, "Examining the Conscience of the Corporation," from Marc. J. Epstein and Kirk O. Hanson (eds.), *The Accountable Corporation, Volume 2: Business Ethics*. Copyright © 2005. Reproduced with permission of Greenwood Publishing Group, Inc., Westport, CT.

Ivey Management Services
Kenneth E. Goodpaster, "Ethics or excellence? Conscience as a check on the unbalanced pursuit of organizational goals," 9B04TB07 (Reprint Number), *Ivey Business Journal*, Volume 68, Number 4 (March/April 2004). Copyright © 2004 by Ivey Management Services. One time permission to reproduce granted by Ivey Management Services, July 20, 2005.

Opragen Publications
Kenneth E. Goodpaster, T. D. Maines, and Arnold M. Weimerskirch, "A Baldrige Process for Ethics?" from *Science and Engineering Ethics*, Vol. 10, No. 2 (April 2004), pp. 243–58. © 2004 by Opragen Publications. Reprinted with permission.

The SAIP Inventor Group
Kenneth E. Goodpaster, Clinton Larson, T. D. Maines, and Arnold M. Weimerskirch. "SAIP Executive and Board Survey and Scorecard."

I would also like to thank the following publishers and companies for permissions to use their copyright material:

The New Directions Publishing Corporation
"The Woodcarver" by Thomas Merton, from *The Way of Chuang Tzu*. Copyright © 1965 by The Abbey of Gethsemani.

M. C. Escher Company
M. C. Escher's "Fish and Scales." Copyright © 2005 The M. C. Escher Company – Holland. All rights reserved. www.mcescher.com.

Faber and Faber (World rights excluding US)
Choruses from "The Rock" 1934, excerpt from *Collected Poems 1901–1962*, by T. S. Eliot, copyright © 1936 by Harcourt Inc., copyright © 1964, 1963, by T. S. Eliot.

Harcourt, Inc. (US rights)
Choruses from "The Rock" 1934, excerpt from *Collected Poems 1901–1962*, by T. S. Eliot, copyright © 1936 by Harcourt Inc., copyright © 1964, 1963, by T. S. Eliot.

University of Illinois Press and David Wagoner
"Lost," by David Wagoner, from *Traveling Light: Collected and New Poems*. Copyright © 1999 by David Wagoner.

DeMello Spiritual Center
"Presence – Where Shall I Look for Enlightenment?" by Anthony DeMello, from *One Minute Wisdom*. Copyright © 1985 by Anthony DeMello, S. J.

Medtronic Inc.
The Medtronic Medallion and Mission Statement.

Pollinger Limited
"The Woodcarver" by Thomas Merton, from *The Way of Chuang Tzu*. Copyright © 1965 by Abbey of Gethsemani.

Introduction

Capitalism in Crisis

Everything seemed to change in the fall of 2001. Why? Partly because we found we were living in illusion, like the prisoners in Plato's famous *Allegory of the Cave*. We were shocked on September 11 to discover realities that threatened not only *individual lives* – but our entire *way of life*.

The Enron/Arthur Andersen scandals, which we can date from October and November 2001, also revealed to us that we were living in an illusion, only this time an illusion related to shadowy financial reporting – misrepresentation to employees and shareholders of the realities on which their security was based.

Throughout 2002 we were reminded of our illusions again and again: Tyco, WorldCom, Adelphia, Global Crossing. And on February 1, 2003, our illusions were dealt another blow when the Space Shuttle *Columbia* disintegrated on re-entry, killing all seven of its crew members.

The collapse of the financial towers of Enron and Andersen – like the collapse of the World Trade Center towers – revealed our vulnerability in the face of certain kinds of fanaticism. And our public institutions made aggressive responses to these crises. In the case of 9/11, it was Afghanistan and eventually Iraq. In the case of Enron/Andersen (and World Com and Tyco and Adelphia and others), it was the Sarbanes-Oxley Act of 2002.

The crash of the *Columbia* space shuttle also revealed our vulnerability – and the aggressive public response came through the

1

Columbia Accident Investigation Board (CAIB). In its report in August 2003 the Board stated:

> NASA's organizational culture and structure had as much to do with this accident as the external tank foam. Organizational culture refers to the values, norms, beliefs, and practices that govern how an institution functions.[1]

Illusions and vulnerabilities take many forms.

Tempting Responses

Now, one type of response to these heartbreaking events that is tempting – almost instinctive, but wrongheaded – is to adopt draconian measures to combat such crises wherever we find them, measures so extreme that the cure becomes worse than the disease:

- Terrorizing the terrorists (blaming Islam and attacking innocents in the process);
- Wiping out corporate corruption by replacing the free market with government regulation (blaming innocent companies in the process);
- Eliminating the NASA Space Program (blaming its mission, rather than its culture, in the process).

These tempting measures have in common a strategy of "fighting fire with fire," "meeting insanity with insanity," and in general *embracing* the very pathology that we seek to avoid! These defenses do not transform the world, they simply reinforce the insanity. And in the process, they lead to the loss of great assets – religious tolerance, free markets, and space exploration.

No, our responses have to be more enlightened – and they may ask more of our institutions and of ourselves than we expect. We will need *knowledge* and *discernment*, to be sure, but also certain *habits of the heart*, which corporations and business schools rarely make the focus of their educational efforts.

We need to understand that there is a common pattern underlying these tragic events and we need to develop an ethical response to that pattern. This will be the theme of the chapters in Part I of this book. The chapters in Part II will take up the *moral agenda* that this understanding presents (a) to practicing executives, and (b) to business educators.

Part I – Conscience: Response to a Pathology

In Chapter 1, I argue that the pattern behind the tragic events mentioned at the outset is this: Take an organizational culture that is *fixated* on certain goals *whatever the cost*; combine it with the group's *rationalization* of its behavior in the name of those goals, and repeat this behavior again and again until the protesting consciences of the participants become detached, anesthetized. These are the symptoms of a pathology that can infect our most treasured institutions, including not only those in the private and public sectors, but also the moral-cultural sectors of religion, the media, and education.[2]

- We see these symptoms in the *fanatical* behavior of terrorists;
- but we also see these symptoms in the *obsessive* behavior of corporate executives; and
- in the *driven* behavior of NASA decision-makers.

Fixation, rationalization, and detachment are symptoms of an occupational hazard of professional life – a hazard to which both individuals and groups can succumb. Objectives become idols; obstacles become threats; second-thoughts are not allowed – and eventually, second thoughts disappear.

In Chapter 2, I discuss the pathology in cultural terms, offering a construct that will help relate it to its antidote, corporate conscience. The idea of a "mindset" is introduced to provide some structure to the conversation about corporate culture.

Despite the behavior of individual decision-makers, the larger reality is a cultural reality, and this viewpoint has been characteristic of diagnosis after diagnosis of corporate wrongdoing in recent years. From Enron and Andersen to WorldCom and Tyco, and from healthcare giants like HealthSouth to government giants like NASA (with the *Challenger* and *Columbia* shuttle disasters).

Warren Bennis, Professor of Management at the University of Southern California wrote in the *New York Times* (2/17/2002) that:

> Mr. Lay's failing is not simply his myopia or cupidity or incompetence. It is his inability to create a company culture open to reality, one that does not discourage managers from delivering bad news. No organization can be honest with the public if it is not honest with itself.

Others have commented in more detail on the Enron culture. Malcolm Gladwell in an article in the *New Yorker* entitled "The Talent Myth" observed that:

> This "talent mind-set" is the new orthodoxy of American management. It is the intellectual justification for why such a high premium is placed on degrees from first-tier business schools, and why the compensation packages for top executives have become so lavish. In the modern corporation, *the system is considered only as strong as its stars*, and, in the past few years, this message has been preached by consultants and management gurus all over the world. None, however, have spread the word quite so ardently as McKinsey, and, of all its clients, one firm took the talent mind-set closest to heart. . . . *The company, of course, was Enron.* [Emphasis added.]

In Chapter 3, I describe the role played by moral reflection (conscience) in the lives of each of us as individuals and suggest that it may offer helpful clues for understanding the corresponding role to be played by conscience in the culture of an organization. Conscience is our primary check on the unbalanced pursuit of goals and purposes. Here the anatomy of conscience is explained in relation to a typology of decision-making patterns (self-interest, market competition, and the law) and the principal avenues of ethical analysis are described and illustrated.

Many have remarked about the limitations of law and competition when it comes to effecting changes in the *cultures* that gave rise to the tragedies. Laws and markets can change behavior by adjusting incentives and sanctions for those covered by them, but both have a difficult time reaching core ethical values – individual and corporate *consciences*. The reason is that corporate conscience is not in the end a matter of *external* compliance or competitive advantage; it is a matter of *internal* self-assessment and improvement. It is a matter of what we as persons – and corporations as organizations – *stand for*. Our responses to crises, then, need to be discerning – if they are not

4

to land us in bigger problems. As Jeffrey Garten, Dean of Yale's School of Management put it:

> Regardless of the current direction of the United States, September 11, 2001, and the Enron-Andersen fallout constitute powerful strategic inflection points. Alone, either would easily qualify as being a critical discontinuity in our lives. But, for many reasons, their combined effect on the balance between government and business could constitute an earthquake in American society.[3]

What the scandals and shocks have drawn our attention to are the profound challenges of *remediation* – and the importance of individual and organizational consciences as forms of *prevention*. Internal moral compasses can be much more reliable than external sanctions – legal or economic.

Chapter 4 addresses a series of objections and replies to "the very idea" of corporate conscience. I argue that surrogates for conscience are insufficient and conclude that the moral agenda of management is neither dispensable nor redundant. This chapter also addresses *legitimacy* questions raised by the special duty of loyalty owed by managers and directors to stockholders. How are we to understand the force of this obligation in relation to the conscientious manager's duties to other stakeholders? Unless we are prepared to place limits on the duty of loyalty, the idea of corporate conscience cannot be defended. Ethics cannot amount to blind compliance – either with the demands of law or with the demands of stockholders.

Ambivalence

Part I reveals a strange ambivalence about corporate conscience in the American ethos, ambivalence that is less prevalent in the European Union, for example. There is, of course, widespread *skepticism* about the moral credentials of the profit-driven market system. As Irving Kristol wrote: "Two cheers for capitalism!" In business, as in campaign politics, we witness too often *an unbalanced pursuit of goals and objectives*. Over the past 35 years we have seen this pathology at work from Watergate to WorldCom. We have seen it in the career crashes of inside-traders like Ivan Boesky, in the corporate crashes of Enron and Andersen, and in the literal crashes of the World Trade Center and the space shuttles *Challenger* and *Columbia*. Call

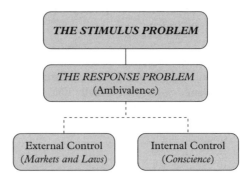

Figure I.1   The stimulus problem

this the *stimulus* problem: a business system that lends itself to certain kinds of excess (see Figure I.1).

The *ambivalence* emerges when we recognize our reluctance to prescribe the most obvious cure for the stimulus problem: the use of moral criteria (beyond economic and political competition) to balance managerial (and political) decision-making. Both our laws and our social norms, for example, caution managers and boards of directors (as agents of shareholders and the corporation as a whole) to *suspend* their ethical judgment – literally to *alienate* it. We fear that incompetence might parade as virtue, or that ethical judgment might mean moral fanaticism. Either way, we seem to resist our most obvious alternative to amorality. This could be called the *response problem*.

We preach about the need for ethics in business and in politics, but are intimidated by the thought that chief executives and politicians might actually take our advice! We want ethical leaders and ethical organizations, but we are reluctant to trust in anything but (flawed) competitive systems to help us find and replace them. We tether our leaders to constituencies and atomize constituencies into countable votes and measurable interests.[4]

Is there a way to overcome – or at least mitigate – this approach-avoidance conflict with conscientious decision-making? I believe that even if there is not a *complete* resolution of the conflict, there is a way to mitigate the problems posed by it. The way lies in trusting more in a shared moral consciousness, trusting that we can tell integrity from its counterfeits – and wisdom from misguided zeal. In an age in which the credentials of democratic capitalism are actually being taken seriously by its former adversaries, we owe it to ourselves *and* to newly interested parties around the world, to resolve any ambivalence at its core.[5]

Some may argue that the *very idea* of a moral agenda for management is unrealistic, unnecessary, or even dangerous. For such readers, my hope is that their skepticism can be challenged by an honest look at the problematic alternatives. This is the objective of Part I of this book. Others may applaud the idea of a corporate moral agenda or corporate conscience, but may be puzzled about its *practical* implications. For them, Part II will be especially important.

Part II – The Moral Agenda of Leadership

In Part II, the focus shifts from conceptual questions like "What?" and "Why?" to operational questions like "Where?" and "How?" It is the *leader* who must ultimately make ethical awareness "happen" when the values and behavior of the *organization* are at stake. The leader is the principal architect of corporate conscience and the one who must manage the stimulus–response paradox. He or she is the person most responsible for giving substance to the moral agenda of the organized group.[6] That agenda includes three broad imperatives: *orienting*, *institutionalizing*, and *sustaining* conscience in the corporate culture. Associated with each imperative, there are potential barriers. The imperatives and their corresponding barriers are taken up in the second half of the book.

Chapter 5 explains that orienting means giving direction, setting a course. "Getting there from here," however, is impossible if "here" is a mystery. Some leaders fail to appreciate that they must understand where their organizations are, ethically, to begin with. Orienting (or reorienting) shared values in a culture is like orienting (or reorienting) corporate strategic planning. A thoughtful teacher once observed some years ago that "the question that has not been asked cannot be answered." As the orientation of a culture becomes clear in relation to a company's current position, however, questions about the *legitimacy* of that orientation may arise. What we called in Part I the "response problem" may be felt as an operating challenge requiring special attention.

In Chapter 6, I show how an organization can align its ethical aspirations with its incentive and reward systems. *Institutionalizing* means making the company's value orientation part of its operating consciousness. This process includes communication, motivation, and discipline, relating ethical values to operations at every turn. It also means reinforcing them with symbols, ceremonies, and celebrations. A conundrum in this domain may be that conventional management incentives and rewards often appeal more to self-interest than to other motives.

Chapter 7 takes up the third item on the agenda, extending and sustaining shared ethical values over time. This means continually renewing corporate conscience in the face of a kind of "entropy." As with individual character, organizational character can weaken with the passage of time and under pressures to compromise. Like physical processes in nature, social processes such as orienting and institutionalizing values have a tendency to wear down. This means ongoing attention not only to the next generation of leadership, but to the forces in the outside social environment that influence the values of the company. A potential barrier appears in this context: Can corporate conscience be sustained without "imposing values" on others?

Finally, in Chapter 8, I discuss the importance of educational support structures for the moral agenda of management, what I call the "three academies." The *first academy*, the modern business school, must come to terms affirmatively with the classical question "Can ethics be taught?" if it is to avoid defaulting on the moral formation of future leaders. Here I argue that the three imperatives of corporate leadership (orienting, institutionalizing, and sustaining shared values) have a mirror image that is rarely present in business schools: the need to initiate, integrate, and continue ethics education.

The *second academy*, corporate management education programs, must also address the moral agenda – both in general and as it relates to the institutionalization of company-specific values. The corporation is a business school in its own right, and needs to incorporate ethics education just as the first academy does.

The *third academy* – associations of distinguished leaders to oversee and set global standards for corporate ethics – may not yet exist, although there are candidates in the offing. I have in mind the Caux Round Table and other organizations that offer transcultural ethical principles and a self-assessment and improvement tool analogous to the Baldrige process for quality management. Such an institution is as essential to professional management as are its counterparts in medicine and law. The moral agenda of the corporation requires scrutiny and stewardship from the generation of leaders most experienced with its possibilities and challenges.

It is my hope that these reflections will serve as a platform for communication between doers and thinkers on a subject that is profoundly difficult and profoundly important. For managers, reflecting on their moral agenda affords an opportunity for self-understanding. For business educators, it can stimulate dialogue on conventional academic definitions of managerial competence. For philosophers, it displays a way of "doing ethics" that may help renew the practical, Socratic foundations of the discipline.

The field of business ethics must focus on ways to discourage moral blindness and thoughtlessness in the competitive environment of corporate decision-making. The stakes are high, for defaulting on this moral agenda could mean, and arguably should mean, the erosion of the corporation itself, as we know it. As my former Harvard colleague Kenneth Andrews once put it, "If organizations cannot be made moral, the future of capitalism will be unattractive – to all of us and especially to those young people whose talents we need." We should perhaps ask no *more* of corporations than we ask of ourselves morally, but neither should we ask *less*.

Part I

Conscience: Response to a Pathology

The claims of morality, as they operate in human life, present on the face of it a very different appearance from the claims of policy or purpose. They come as a recognized obligation to do or not to do, which is often seen to involve the temporary surrender or restriction of a desire in itself innocent, of a perfectly legitimate purpose. All serious moralists have had to recognize this very obvious and familiar contrast.

(J. L. Stocks, 1930)[1]

As a society, we are starving ourselves of ethical leadership. It appears to be *essential, yet somehow both dangerous and perhaps even illegitimate, to guide business decision making by moral values* – values that go beyond not only pure self-interest, but also conventional economic, legal, professional, and other external frameworks. This fits the classic definition of a *paradox*.[2]

Business ethics appears to be *essential* because the requirements of business life are often so intensely goal-directed that they blind individuals and organizations to the ethical aspects of what they do. Yet business ethics appears to be *illegitimate* because the market and our legal system place significant limitations on management discretion when it comes to decision-making criteria. Managers who appeal to ethical values, if they are not looked upon as questionably sincere are often looked upon as going beyond their authority. Lynn Paine formulates the point this way in her 2003 book, *Value Shift*:

By what authority can managers recognize the claims of third parties? To these skeptics, corporate ethics sounds a little bit unethical, especially if it means incurring costs or foregoing opportunities for profit. This objection – let's call it the "fiduciary objection" – has often been used to rebut moral claims advanced on behalf of nonshareholder constituencies.[3]

We urge attention to health and safety in relation to consumer products and environmental protection, but shareholders will sue or Wall Street analysts will punish companies that go farther down this road than their competitors – or even farther down this road than the law requires. Because of this, calls for integrity and responsibility in business life – often in the wake of corporate scandals like those experienced in recent years – tend to lose energy and effect. Entropy sets in. Like pebbles in a pond, their initial splash dissipates and seldom results in very much structural or cultural change. David Sanger in a *New York Times* article "Inertia and Indecision at NASA," wrote:

> To those who remember the Challenger investigation, it was an echo of the suppressed memorandums that the commission uncovered, when engineers sent out urgent warnings that it was too cold to launch the Challenger, and were ignored.
>
> "It's the same damn thing," said Gen. Donald Kutyna of the Air Force, retired, a gadfly on the Challenger panel along with the physicist Richard Feynman. "They didn't learn a thing. We had nine O-rings fail, and they flew. These guys had seven pieces of foam hit, and it still flew."[4]

Business as usual is reinforced by the system itself in many ways. Ethics is more easily *invoked* than *institutionalized*. Efforts to reduce the risks of the "stimulus problem" are muted by assertions of risks associated with the "response problem." As we move from rhetoric to reality, the economic and social architecture of business life presents formidable challenges to ethically motivated reformers.

Managing in the face of this paradox is not easy. Certainly the ideas in this book will not make the problem disappear. They may lead the reader to appreciate the *power* of the paradox, however, so that the vision and strength needed to *manage it* can be found. Conscience, as will become clear, is a form of vision and strength in a culture, not a merely subjective *sentiment* as it is sometimes portrayed.

In the four chapters of Part I, I explore the paradox discussed above – the stimulus problem – which I call "teleopathy," the significance

12

of the idea of a "mindset," the meaning of "conscience" as a way to address the stimulus problem, and the response problem, challenging "the very idea." Without an understanding of these issues as they relate to the lives of individuals and the cultures of organizations, business ethics is devoid of content. These chapters build progressively toward a discussion of the crucial role of leadership in managing the paradox.

1

Teleopathy:
The Unbalanced
Pursuit of Purpose

There is a hazard in business decision-making against which ethical awareness offers protection. It is the stimulus to which conscience in both personal life and corporate culture is a response. This is a useful way to start our journey because if urging the importance of business ethics is not a response to a real world problem, it will go the way of rhetorical fads and fashions.

There may not be one stimulus and one response; but there is a *pattern* among the stimuli and, therefore, among the best responses. In this chapter, using case illustrations, I will describe the main features of this hazardous pattern and, in the next chapter, the corresponding features of an ethical response. Both the individual decision-maker within the organization and the organization itself as a decision-making entity will need our attention; for I hope to show that the hazardous pattern applies to both.[1] I begin, by considering two cases from the past.

Two Tragic Events in 1986 –
An Individual and an Organization

I remember 1986 at the Harvard Business School. It was the year when, with my students, I began to see a pattern that I had never noticed before. I have seen this pattern frequently since then – frequently enough to justify having coined a word to describe it. But first, some background.

In 1986, two unrelated events took place that eventually unraveled into national scandals. One involved an individual, Wall Street investment banker Martin Siegel, who told arbitrageur Ivan Boesky in January that he was moving from Kidder Peabody to Drexel Burnham Lambert. He was trying to extricate himself from a relationship that eventually led, in November of that year, to the tragic collapse of a brilliant career. A *Wall Street Journal* article described the scene:

> 38 year-old Martin A. Siegel, one of Wall Street's leading investment bankers, was spending the afternoon in the Park Avenue offices of Martin Lipton, an eminent takeover lawyer and a man Mr Siegel had come to regard almost as a father. Suddenly a federal marshal burst in upon the two men, thrusting a subpoena into Mr Siegel's hand. When Mr Siegel read the subject matter of the investigation – Ivan F. Boesky – and the accompanying list of his own takeover deals at Kidder Peabody & Co., in the 1980s, he knew his career was over. He began sobbing, as a horrified Mr Lipton rushed to comfort him.[2]

The second event involved an organization. It was the decision taken by the National Aeronautics and Space Administration (NASA), despite the cautionary advice of one of its key suppliers, Morton Thiokol, Inc., to proceed with the launch of the space shuttle *Challenger*. On January 28, 1986, a shocked nation witnessed the launch and explosion of the rocket off the Florida coast. All seven persons on board perished.

There are lessons in these two stories from 1986 that take us beyond the judgments and actions of the specific situations – lessons not only about the ethical awareness of individuals, but about the cultures of organizations. As we reflect on these lessons, we will also learn about the role of leadership in molding institutional values and giving them substance.

The individuals involved were certainly not what we would call "evil" people. Martin Siegel was a talented and ambitious executive, a man whose career was described as "one of the most spectacular success stories on Wall Street."[3] Yet he ended up pleading guilty in federal court to two felony counts for his role in the Boesky scandal.

Siegel apparently could see no harm in his actions. He embraced the use of inside information "for personal gain, to advance his career, and to benefit his firm." His life at the time was apparently dominated by a need for security and a drive to achieve success, power, influence, and wealth as a means to that goal. In his first meeting with Ivan

Boesky, he communicated his insecurity. As one reporter put it, this was "like placing red meat before a lion."

> "I'll make some investments for you," Mr Boesky volunteered, and one thing led to another. By the end of that conversation, the two had forged an agreement: In return for information furnished by Mr Siegel, Mr Boesky would pay him an unspecified percentage of Mr Boesky's own profits from trading on the information.[4]

The focus for Siegel was on achieving certain career goals, not on wrongdoing as such. He thought of the money as a "consulting fee."

In connection with the *Challenger* disaster, one attorney, Robert Levin, remarked that:

> None of these folks that decided to fly the Challenger (at NASA and Morton Thiokol) wanted those people to die. None of them in their hearts would acknowledge that they were doing something stupid, evil, or rotten. We're not talking about murderers. We're talking about people who took a desperately high risk with other people's money, other people's property, other people's lives – hoping like hell that the good luck that had always attended NASA activities would hold.[5]

No one alleged intent to harm, any more than they did in the case of Boesky and Siegel. But many alleged a failure of individual and organizational *judgment*. The priorities or values of key individuals as well as NASA's organizational culture were said to be *reckless* and *out of balance*.

In November 1986, the same month in which Siegel was served with his subpoena, the US House of Representatives' Committee on Science and Technology concluded its hearings on the *Challenger* case and observed that "meeting flight schedules and cutting costs were given a higher priority than flight safety" at both NASA and Thiokol. There was speculation about the economic, media, and political pressures around the time of the launch decision. The nation still struggled to understand the tragedy amidst wrenching sadness over the fate of the victims.

At NASA, there was an overarching goal of great magnitude. There were problems and pressures along the way in an enormously complex undertaking. There was a strong tendency – ultimately apparently decisive – to ignore or minimize information that threatened the achievement of that goal. In the words of NASA's Lawrence Mulloy, one of the key decision makers on the launch, "You make a commitment and you try your damnedest to meet it. It's probably self-imposed professional pride – doing what you, by God, said you were going to do."[6]

Two Tragic Echoes in 2003 –
An Individual and an Organization

There are, of course, current "echoes" of these 1986 events, lest we think 1986 too remote in time. The collapse of Enron was the largest bankruptcy in American history. And the story of Andrew Fastow, Enron's former Chief Financial Officer, resembles the story of Martin Siegel in a number of ways: "[T]he federal task force investigating Enron's collapse filed a criminal complaint . . . accusing Mr Fastow of defrauding investors by persistently falsifying financial statements through the use of a series of complex partnerships."[7]

Like Siegel, Fastow was a corporate climber whose ambition linked him to a "mentor" who could help him realize his dreams: "At Enron, Mr Fastow, then 29, became known as one of 'Skilling's boys,' a group of young energy marketers and financiers who seemed destined to lead the company."[8] As Boesky mentored Siegel, Skilling seems to have mentored Fastow.[9] And like Siegel, his life was dominated by a drive to achieve power and influence for a kind of security. "People who grew up with him judged him as extremely ambitious and recall how he quarreled with high school teachers over his grades. Former Enron colleagues have called him prickly and a bully."[10] No one alleged "evil" intent on Fastow's part, any more than for Siegel 17 years earlier, but a distortion of judgment seems clear in both cases.

On February 1, 2003, the Space Shuttle *Columbia* disintegrated on re-entry after completing its mission, killing all seven astronauts aboard.[11] The echo of the 1986 NASA *Challenger* disaster was unmistakable. Indeed, the report of the *Columbia Accident Investigation Board* (CAIB), released in late August 2003 used this very language. Board member Dr Sally Ride, who also served on the commission investigating the *Challenger* disaster, "observed that there were 'echoes' of *Challenger* in *Columbia*."[12] And the news analysis of the report was unequivocal: "The same keep-it-flying culture found to have disregarded ample evidence of a fatal flaw in the O-rings in the *Challenger* case failed again to heed warning signs that foam debris could cause deadly damage to the aging, fragile *Columbia*."[13]

The CAIB was more pointed than the public might have expected in attributing the *Columbia* disaster to a persistent cultural malaise at NASA:

> In the board's view, NASA's organizational culture and structure had as much to do with this accident as the external tank foam. Organizational culture refers to the values, norms, beliefs and practices that govern how an institution functions. At the most basic level, organizational culture defines the assumptions that employees make as they carry out their work. It is a powerful force that can persist through reorganizations and the reassignment of key personnel.[14]

NASA's culture in 2003, as in 1986, was driven by an overarching goal, including an "ever more compressed" launch schedule for a critical section of the space station by February 19, 2003. NASA Administrator Sean O'Keefe was firm about respecting schedule deadlines. "The date seemed 'etched in stone,' the report said, and NASA employees had a sense of being 'under the gun.'"[15]

Discerning the Pattern: Moral Projection

There are differences between and among the stories of Martin Siegel, Andrew Fastow and the NASA disasters involving the *Challenger* and *Columbia* shuttles. The first two are primarily about individuals and their "mentors," while the second two are about an organization (at two points in its history) and its culture. Two involve illegal conduct without loss of life; the other two involve legal conduct with fatal results. But despite the differences, I believe that there is a common pattern.

Once clarified, the root of the problem is as compelling in relation to organizational decision-makers (like NASA) as it is in relation to individual decision-makers (like Siegel and Fastow). The idea that there is a parallel between the decision-making dynamics of individuals and of organizations is a central message of this book. It is an old insight, as old as Plato, and yet it is rich in significance for modern business life.

The idea is that organizations are in many ways macro-versions (projections) of ourselves as individuals – human beings writ large. Because of this, we can sometimes see more clearly in organizations certain features that we want to understand better in ourselves. And the reverse is often true as well. Sometimes the management of organizations can profit from what we understand about ourselves as individuals.

The dynamics of goal-directed motivation and ethical values are present in both arenas and present us with fruitful comparisons. I have referred to this analogical approach in the past as the "moral projection" principle and will explore its ramifications here and throughout this book. Formally, it can be stated as follows:

> *Moral Projection Principle.* It is appropriate not only to describe organizations and their characteristics by analogy with individuals, it is also appropriate normatively to look for and to foster moral attributes in organizations by analogy with those we look for and foster in individuals.[16]

As we explore the occupational hazard of business life represented by the Siegel, Fastow, and NASA cases, the fact that our case illustrations involve both individuals and an organization will help clarify the analysis. First we examine the symptoms of the "hazard."

The First Symptom

The cases of Martin Siegel, Andrew Fastow, and NASA typify the hazard. Reflective observers from a variety of backgrounds – psychoanalysis, philosophy, business administration, and management practice – offer us several illuminating "windows" on the problem.

The first such window comes from Bowen H. McCoy, former managing director of Morgan Stanley & Co. McCoy's essay "The Parable of the Sadhu" was the first winner of an award established in 1982 by the *Harvard Business Review* for the best original article written by a corporate manager that would "inform and expand executives' consideration of ethical problems in business."[17]

The essay described a mountain-climbing experience in which a group of climbers that included McCoy, intent on reaching a summit in the Himalayas, faced a painful decision. A day before reaching their goal, they came upon an Indian holy man, a sadhu, who had somehow got lost and was in serious danger of dying from exposure. The group had to decide whether to take the sadhu to safety or continue toward the summit. Time and circumstances did not permit both. McCoy described his passion and rationalization under stress, and his group's eventual continuation toward the summit. He pointed to his main "excuses" but knew they were not adequate:

> I felt and continue to feel guilt about the sadhu. I had literally walked through a classic moral dilemma without fully thinking through the consequences. My excuses for my actions included a high adrenaline flow, *a superordinate goal*, and a once-in-a-lifetime opportunity – factors in the usual corporate situation, especially when one is under stress.[18]

McCoy applied his parable to individual managers and their pursuit of goals – *but also to groups and their leadership*. He saw in his mountain-climbing experience a symptom and a symbol of an ethical challenge in business life:

> Had we mountaineers been free of physical and mental stress caused by the effort and the high altitude, we might have treated the sadhu differently. Yet isn't stress the real test of personal and corporate values? The instant decisions executives make under pressure reveal the most about personal and corporate character.[19]

Like McCoy and his party, Martin Siegel and Andrew Fastow fixated on "superordinate goals" and lost their balance.[20] So did the decision-makers at NASA (both the *Challenger* team and the *Columbia* team). Under stress they ignored certain higher values (like honesty and concern for safety) in favor of lesser values (like security and efficiency).[21] Their "superordinate goals" became like gods.

A Second Symptom of the Hazard

Another, very different "window" on the stimulus problem reveals a second symptom of the hazard we have been exploring. It comes from Saul Gellerman, author of a classic article in the *Harvard Business Review* entitled "How 'Good' Managers Make Bad Ethical Choices." Gellerman pointed to the practice of "rationalization" as a principal source of unethical conduct in business. He focused on a number of well-publicized cases from the 1980s: the Manville asbestos lawsuits (worker and consumer safety), the Continental Illinois Bank failure (imprudent loan acceptances risking depositors' money), and E. F. Hutton (massive check kiting on more than 400 banks). Gellerman wrote:

In my view, the explanations go back to four rationalizations that
people have relied on through the ages to justify questionable conduct: believing that the activity is not "really" illegal or immoral; that
it is in the individual's or the corporation's best interest; that it will
never be found out; or that because it helps the company the company
will condone it.[22]

Granting that executives have "a right to expect loyalty from employees against competitors and detractors," Gellerman immediately
added "but not loyalty against the law, or against common morality,
or against society itself." Some kinds of loyalty, like the loyalty of
Martin Siegel to Ivan Boesky, of Andrew Fastow to Jeff Skilling,
or the decision-makers at NASA to cost controls and scheduling (in
2003 as in 1986), cause people to lose their balance. These invocations of loyalty are excuses for "selective perception" and therefore
"narrowed" judgment. They limit the full context of a situation in
an effort to justify behavior. Nixon's White House Counsel during
Watergate, John Dean, emphasized the limits on perception involved
in rationalization through the title of his book: *Blind Ambition*.

We saw that Martin Siegel thought of his gain as a "consulting
fee." And we have already seen how Enron's Jeff Skilling decided
that it would be "better not to know exactly how Mr Fastow . . . was
achieving his desired goal." Fastow, it has been suggested, displayed
a tendency that psychologists David Messick and Max Bazerman
describe in terms similar to those of Saul Gellerman: "There is a
tendency to reduce the set of possible consequences or outcomes to
make the decision manageable. In extreme cases, all but one aspect
of a decision will be suppressed, and the choice will be made solely
on the basis of the one privileged feature."[23]

As to NASA's culture, the CAIB Report Synopsis of Chapter 6
"begins with a review of the history of foam strikes on the Orbiter
to determine how Space Shuttle Program managers *rationalized* the
danger from repeated strikes on the Orbiter's Thermal Protection
System" [emphasis added]. In the Chapter 6 *Summary*, the Board
wrote: "[Space Shuttle Program] management techniques unknowingly imposed barriers that kept at bay both engineering concerns
and dissenting views, and ultimately helped create 'blind spots' that
prevented them from seeing the danger the foam strike posed."[24]

Thus, the second symptom of the hazard we are identifying – in
addition to McCoy's *fixation* – comes from Gellerman's account of
rationalization.

The Third Symptom

Psychoanalyst and anthropologist Michael Maccoby offers a third "window" in his insightful but disturbing book *The Gamesman*. In a *Fortune* article that predated his book, Maccoby described "careerism" as an emotionally self-destructive affliction of many successful executives:

> Obsessed with winning, the gamesman views all of his actions in terms of whether they will help him succeed in his career. The individual's sense of identity, integrity, and self-determination is lost as he treats himself as an object whose worth is determined by its fluctuating market value. Careerism demands (emotional) detachment.[25]

Maccoby believed that such emotional detachment was corrosive to integrity – that it led to disintegration of character because it did not allow for a proper balance between what he referred to as traits of the "head" (e.g., initiative, cooperativeness, flexibility, coolness under stress) in contrast to traits of the "heart" (e.g., honesty, friendliness, compassion, generosity, idealism). The problem, in his view, was that while managers need to *integrate* qualities of the heart with qualities of the head – modern corporations (and other institutions) often systematically selected against this kind of wholeness. Most executives writing to *Fortune* magazine in 1977, after the initial publication of these ideas, confirmed Maccoby's diagnosis.[26]

Maccoby identified a central psychological risk of business life. But when we look closely at the traits of "head" and "heart" to which he paid attention in his study, I think we can see that his *psychological* observation harbors an *ethical* observation. For it is the moral integrity as well as the mental health of business professionals that is behind the scenes in Maccoby's study.[27]

Integrity (as the word implies) is a kind of wholeness or balance that refuses to truncate or close off the qualities of the heart – that refuses to anesthetize our humanity in the face of what can sometimes be strong temptations to do so. Maccoby saw integrity as demanding balance and participation by the whole person in decisions and actions. Poet David Whyte seems to have had a similar insight when he wrote that "To preserve our deeper desires amid the pressures of the modern corporation is to preserve our souls for the greater life we had in mind when we first took the job."[28] Our discussions of

Martin Siegel, Andrew Fastow, and NASA suggest that, for a time anyway, they all lost their integrity.

Another "window" on what seems to be the same symptom comes from an old-but-classic article written 35 years ago by philosopher John Ladd entitled "Morality and the Ideal of Rationality in Formal Organizations." In the late 1970s, this article, which had been written years earlier, began to attract the attention of scholars in business ethics. Ladd described corporations (and "formal organizations" generally) as institutions in which:

> the interests and needs of the individuals concerned, as individuals, must be considered only insofar as they establish limiting operating conditions. Organizational rationality dictates that these interests and needs must not be considered in their own right or on their own merits. If we think of an organization as a machine, it is easy to see why we cannot reasonably expect it to have any moral obligations to people or for them to have any to it.[29]

If someone expects corporations "to conform to the principles of morality," Ladd wrote, "he is simply committing a logical mistake."

> [Such organizations] are like machines, and it would be a (logical) mistake to expect a machine to comply with the principles of morality. By the same token, an official or agent of a formal organization is simply violating the basic rules of organizational activity if he allows his moral scruples rather than the objectives of the organization to determine his decision.

As Maccoby saw a "dis-integration" of corporate executives through the lens of psychoanalysis, Ladd suggested a "dis-integration" through the lenses of philosophy and organization theory.

Ladd may have gone too far by implying that *amorality* in business was a matter of *necessity* rather than a matter of observation. But his lament should not be overlooked. While the comparison of organizations to machines may be too strong in most cases, it serves as a useful warning about the worst case.

Ladd drew largely from the landmark works of Herbert Simon and Chester Barnard. These authors saw decision-making as anchored in a set of institutional goals. The organization's "rationality" was defined in terms of the effective and efficient achievement of these goals, period. Simon had written that "decisions in private management, like decisions in public management, must take as their ethical

24

premises the objectives that have been set for the organization." Ladd concluded from this that ethics could not really function in the business organization. It was simply out of place:

> [F]or logical reasons it is improper to expect organizational conduct to conform to the ordinary principles of morality. We cannot and must not expect formal organizations, or their representatives acting in their official capacities, to be honest, courageous, considerate, sympathetic, or to have any kind of moral integrity . . . Actions that are wrong by ordinary moral standards are not so for organizations; indeed, they may often be required. Secrecy, espionage and deception do not make organizational action wrong; rather they are right, proper, and indeed, *rational*, if they serve the objectives of the organization.[30]

Ladd went on to describe the consequence for the *individual* decision-maker as an ethical double standard: "moral schizophrenia." Business executives, he argued, must possess goal-driven mindsets at work while marching to the beat of a different drum in their private lives. Maccoby's "traits of the head" seem to correspond to Ladd's account of the dominant logic of the organization, while "traits of the heart" correspond to the more conventional ethical awareness that we expect of one another outside of the work environment. Both authors (pessimistically) postulate a suspension of ethical reasoning and ethical character traits in business life. Both "detachment" and "schizophrenia" point to fragmentation, loss of consistency and wholeness.

Martin Siegel appeared to suffer from Maccoby's sense of detachment or Ladd's sense of schizophrenia. He was described by one friend as having disdained the fast-paced world of Manhattan society: "He was not a social climber. He didn't globe-trot. His main interest was his children." And yet in his business dealings he was driven by a different mindset. Andrew Fastow also exhibited something of a dual *persona* according to those around him:

> [Enron colleagues] say that during angry bouts, he was known to leave profanity-laced messages on the voice mail of colleagues. He could also be charming and generous, former colleagues said. He would reward employees with vacation travel when they met goals, for example, and defended them in Enron's competitive culture.[31]

Apparently Fastow viewed his business behavior (as Ladd might suggest) as a kind of "game" whose logic was very different from "real life" – a game with characters out of the movies: "Mr. Fastow became adept at creating complex partnerships to finance new projects. He worked on a series of partnerships – including one called Joint Energy Development Investment Inc. and known by its acronym, Jedi, one of several partnerships named for 'Star Wars' characters."[32]

As to NASA, both the *Challenger* disaster and the *Columbia* disaster were viewed as emerging from the same culture. The CAIB described the decision-making during the flight of the *Columbia* as both *separated* (walled off from concerned engineers) and *detached*:

> A tile expert told managers during frequent consultations that strike damage was only a maintenance-level concern and that on-orbit imaging of potential wing damage was not necessary. Mission management welcomed this opinion and sought no others. This constant reinforcement of managers' pre-existing beliefs added another block to *the wall between decision-makers and concerned engineers*. Another factor that enabled Mission *management's detachment from the concerns of their own engineers* is rooted in the culture of NASA itself. . . . When asked by investigators why they were not more vocal about their concerns, Debris Assessment Team members opined that by raising contrary points of view about Shuttle mission safety, they would be singled out for possible ridicule by their peers and managers.[33]

Maccoby and Ladd would no doubt see in this commentary an organizational analogue to detachment and a kind of group "schizophrenia" in decision-making. The logic of organizational rationality, Ladd might say, was ultimately amoral.[34]

Three Symptoms – Teleopathy

I believe that the phenomena highlighted by McCoy, Gellerman, Maccoby and Ladd fit together into a *pattern* or syndrome:

- *fixation* or *singleness of purpose under stress* (McCoy leaving the sadhu); leading to
- *rationalization* (Gellerman's account of unethical business behavior); leading to
- *detachment* (Ladd's "moral schizophrenia" and ultimately Maccoby's "suppressing traits of the heart").

These symptoms cohere in striking ways. Each is discernible in the stories of Martin Siegel, Andrew Fastow, and the NASA disasters.

Siegel and Fastow were both *driven by singleness of purpose* under what was for them both personal ambition and personal stress.[35] (We might note also that both had "mentors" that reinforced their drives.) Siegel and Fastow both *rationalized* their behavior, each engaging in selective perception about context and consequences. And *detachment* allowed both of them to repeat their activities over prolonged periods of time.

NASA's singleness of purpose was equally clear. In connection with the *Challenger*, one observer even speculated that the purpose included political timing, since the President's State of the Union Message was to mention the "teacher in space."[36] With *Columbia*, the fixation seems to have been on the schedule for the International Space Station.

The stresses led to rationalizations. NASA, once described as "an enlightened alliance between science and democratic tradition," appeared to have selective perception in the face of safety warnings.[37] "In briefing after briefing, interview after interview, NASA remained in denial. In the agency's eyes, 'there were no safety-of-flight issues,' and no safety compromises in the long history of debris strikes on the thermal protection system."[38]

Dennis Mileti, professor of sociology and director of Colorado State University's Hazards Assessments Laboratory at Fort Collins spoke in general terms about the NASA disaster in 1986: "In the face of uncertainty, people's preferences take over. The risk is denied, discounted, and the chance is taken. . . . This is not unique. It's just like any of us getting on an airplane – we all know that airplanes crash, but in our hearts we don't believe that the one we get on will crash."[39]

As to detachment, one NASA observer remarked about the organization that "conflicting goals, roles, and expectations produced an almost schizoid character." The CAIB Report spoke of the "cultural fence" that "impairs open communications between mission managers and working engineers."

Several NASA observers noted (in 1986 and in 2003) that despite official stringent safety standards, "the agency was more concerned with meeting deadlines than with safety issues." If this is true, then one might describe the NASA culture as having detached emotionally from operating concerns with safety.

The language may vary, but the kinship among these symptoms is undeniable. They point to a syndrome for which a label would be convenient, not only to facilitate our thinking about *individuals* in the corporate environment but also about *corporate cultures* in their environment.

Teleopathy

teleopathy, *n.*, the unbalanced pursuit of purpose in either individuals or organizations. This mindset or condition is a key stimulus to which ethics is a practical response. The principal symptoms of teleopathy are fixation, rationalization, and detachment.[40]

We can see through our various "windows" an all-too-frequent modern malaise. It is not a sickness that appears in medical or psychiatric manuals. Nor does it appear in the manuals of twentieth-century moral philosophy. Nor again is it part of most discussions in the literature of management studies or business administration.

Its symptoms include, as noted, (a) *fixation* on tangible goals or purposes without moderation, (b) a tendency to *rationalize* or even deny responsibilities and realities that might impede the accomplishment of those goals or purposes, (c) a general separation of the ethics of business goals from the ethics of everyday life, leading to emotional *detachment* regarding the full human implications of pursuing these goals. This detachment can be seen as the result of fixation and rationalization over time.

In 1986, I referred to this malaise as *teleopathy*, combining Greek roots for "goal" and "disease."[41] If there were manuals for character disorders in ethics as there are for physical and emotional disorders in medicine, I submit that teleopathy would be as central in its manual as heart disease and depression are, respectively, in theirs. Indeed, in Maccoby's language, the metaphor of "heart disease" may be particularly appropriate.[42]

Teleopathy, as I use the term, is a habit of character that values certain limited objectives as supremely action-guiding, to the relative exclusion not only of larger ends, but also of moral considerations about means, obligations, and duties. It is *the unbalanced pursuit of goals or purposes by an individual or an organized group.*

In its most extreme form, teleopathy involves a suspension of ethical awareness as a practical force in the decision-making process. It substitutes for the call of conscience the call of very different decision criteria: winning the game, achieving the objective, following the rules laid down by some goal-oriented framework independent of ethical reflection.

This *unbalanced pursuit of purpose* can take different forms. It can be rooted in the desires, goals, or objectives of a decision-maker, apart from any role that the decision-maker plays in an organization or in society (as when an individual or group seeks wealth, power, status, or survival). Or it can manifest itself indirectly in the form of loyalty to the requirements of a role or function such as "bread-winner," "doctor," or "employer." In such cases, the purposes involved are implied in the background – supporting a family, healing the sick, keeping a company going. But they are purposes nonetheless, and can be pursued with or without balance.

Teleopathy is not a theory; it is a *condition*. It is a condition that affects perception, reasoning, and action – the way an agent *sees* (or does not see) the world and the way an agent *responds* to what he or she sees in deciding what to do. Jon Krakauer, in his widely read book *Into Thin Air: A Personal Account of the Mt. Everest Disaster*, writes about "summit fever" in a way that clearly suggests teleopathy:

> Mountaineering tends to draw men and women not easily deflected from their goals. By this late stage in the expedition we had all been subjected to levels of misery and peril that would have sent more balanced individuals packing for home long ago. To get this far one had to have an uncommonly obdurate personality.
>
> Unfortunately, the sort of individual who is programmed to ignore personal distress and keep pushing for the top is frequently pro-grammed to disregard signs of grave and imminent danger as well. This forms the nub of a dilemma that every Everest climber eventually comes up against: in order to succeed you must be exceedingly driven, but if you're too driven you're likely to die. Above 26,000 feet, moreover, the line between appropriate zeal and reckless summit fever becomes grievously thin. Thus the slopes of Everest are littered with corpses.[43]

When teleopathy governs decision-making, the selection of goals and the means chosen to pursue them tends to be myopic. The natural and social environments tend to be seen as resources or playing fields. Responsiveness to the voices of those whose stake is high but whose power is low tends to be muted.

I believe that teleopathy – both in individuals and in organized groups – is fundamental to our concerns about "business ethics." Teleopathy does not always take the form of unethical behavior. But in the vicinity of most unethical behavior, we are likely to find teleopathy in one or another of its forms. It is the principal hazard to which the call for conscience is addressed.

Conclusion: A Response to the Stimulus Problem?

Our reflections on four tragic cases of decision-making have led us to a common pattern. This common pattern is of special interest because it can manifest itself not only in the lives of individuals but also – and not coincidentally – in the cultures of organizations. We have clarified its indicators or symptoms and given it a name, *teleopathy*. Moreover, teleopathy is not just a hazard for both individuals and organizations; its presence in one is probably encouraged or discouraged by its presence in the other. It is catchy, this disease, not only *within* levels of analysis but *between* them.

The challenge that this presents to management is to reduce or eliminate teleopathy as a source of unethical behavior in business. If teleopathy is an "occupational hazard" in business life, responsible management must address it – it becomes part of the *agenda*. As with other occupational hazards – like toxic substances in the workplace or sexual harassment – teleopathy must be identified and mitigated. If it is not, we can expect more tragic scandals and further erosion of our society's confidence in the business system.

The indications of teleopathy (goal fixation, rationalization, and detachment) warn us of decision-making that has lost perspective and balance. The distortion of judgment that teleopathy represents (often in the name of laudable traits like loyalty, dedication, enthusiasm, and drive) amounts to a kind of Faustian bargain. The unbalanced pursuit of a goal transforms the goal into a kind of idol. Teleopathy amounts to a secularized form of idolatry.

What started as the *choice* of a goal on the part of a decision-maker ends up as the enslavement of a decision-maker by a goal. Paradoxically, the unbalanced pursuit of purpose leads to behavior not unlike that of an addict. And just as paradoxically, the management response must search for a certain moderation at the heart of competition.

There were signs that Martin Siegel wanted out before his career came tumbling down around him. In Andrew Fastow's case, we can only speculate. There were signs that NASA was hesitating the night before the fatal decision to launch the *Challenger*, and there were missed opportunities to identify and solve the damage to *Columbia*. But teleopathy called the tune nonetheless. And on a smaller, less dramatic scale, it can call the tune in any of us if we are not as concerned about balance as we are about purpose. I am convinced that ethical problems in business exhibit this fundamental pattern again and again.

If there is to be a managerial response, therefore, as well as an educational response, we need to understand the nature of the balancing that is called for. To this task we turn in Chapter 2.

2

Mindsets and Culture

Corporate governance is really a *state of mind*. Whether it be pre-Sarbanes, during Sarbanes, or post-Sarbanes, the fact of the matter is, *without the right state of mind*, what we're creating are just more hurdles for people who are committed to gaming the system to jump over. We're not fixing the system.

(Stephen Cooper, interim Chief Executive Officer and Chief Restructuring Officer of Enron)[1]

Can a corporation, like an individual, have a "state of mind"? And if so, how can we describe, influence, and even transform corporate "states of mind" when circumstances seem to call for such responses? In this chapter, we shall take up these questions in connection with *teleopathy*, and in the next chapter, with the phenomenon of *conscience*.

Before pursuing a systematic response to the teleopathy problem, as we will in subsequent chapters, we should be clear about what it is *not*. Almost every human endeavor – individual or collective – can be seen as involving an intense pursuit of goals. Occupational health and safety was no more on the minds of the pharaohs as they sent conquered slaves out to build the pyramids than it was on the minds of the "robber barons" who built the railroads.

It would be impossible to get anything done at all if decision-makers worried obsessively about the minutest ramifications of every goal or purpose. To "de-cide," after all, is literally to *cut through* the potentially endless considerations that might precede a proposed objective and to *act*. We are limited in how far we can *see* and how long we can *wait* in making decisions.

32

Ethical companies must face such limitations, along with others, such as limited resources and limited abilities to dissociate themselves from commerce with others (including not only companies but governments) whose practices they may find repugnant. Companies, like individuals, must live in an imperfect and often unjust world that is less than hospitable to the best intentions. They must sometimes struggle with the organizational analogue of theologian Reinhold Niebuhr's portrait of "moral man in immoral society."

Teleopathy is not simply goal-directed behavior. Neither is it to be confused with determination, perseverance, courage, tenacity, hard work, or strong motivation toward cooperative goals. These are *virtues*, not *vices*. Indeed, the vitality of business life depends on these virtues. Free enterprise in the US and around the globe can boast reasonably that these virtues are its strongest credentials.

In the words of Irving Kristol, "two cheers for capitalism!" Perhaps the third cheer is missing because we recognize that, without vigilance, highly motivated, goal-directed behavior can be corrupted. And it is precisely this lack of vigilance that transforms healthy goal-directed behavior into the malignancy of teleopathy. Parents can overstate and "over exemplify" the importance of careers to their children. Supervisors can overemphasize the importance of loyalty, dedication, and "getting the job done." The unstated message – "whatever it takes" – *can* be powerful and corrosive.

We are a pragmatic, no-nonsense people. So we might interpret stopping to think and to feel as weakness or indecision. We are a nation of specialists and "professionals," each identified with a function or goal. We take pride in the division of labor that calls for specialization, experts, innovation, and efficiency. We are often better at evaluating means to ends than we are at evaluating ends themselves, which is why *effectiveness* is so important to us.

The difference between goal-directed intensity and teleopathy is best understood as a difference between frames of reference for judgment – what I shall refer to in this chapter as *mindsets*.

The Structure of a Mindset

cul·ture –*n.* the behaviors and beliefs characteristic of a particular social, ethnic, or age group (e.g., *the youth culture; the drug culture*). In *Anthropology*, the sum total of ways of living built up by a group of human beings and transmitted from one generation to another.[2]

33

I have referred to teleopathy as a frame of reference, a pathological "state of mind" or *mindset* without being very precise about the meaning of such phrases. And since ultimately I will be arguing that a very different mindset is essential for an individual or for an organization to avoid teleopathy, it will behoove us to explore this concept further.

What is it that individuals and corporations have in common (if anything), so that we can meaningfully attribute "teleopathy" to both?[3] In popular literature, individuals are typically said to have "personalities" or "characters," while organizations and even whole societies are said to have "cultures." Functionally however, ideas like "character" and "culture" exhibit some similarities. The underlying phenomenon that permits this comparison is what I shall call a "state of mind" or, more simply, a "mindset."

The dictionary definition of a "mindset" is simply "beliefs and attitudes which govern someone's behavior and outlook." I would like to develop and elaborate upon this definition, beginning with sociologist Philip Selznick's account of personal *character*:

> The idea of "character" as used by personality analysts is not altogether clear, but its usefulness is scarcely in doubt. There seems to be general agreement on four attributes. First, character is a *historical* product. Second, character is in some sense an *integrated* product, as is suggested by the term "character structure." Third, character is *functional*, in the sense that it is no mere accidental accretion of responsive patterns. Fourth, character is *dynamic* in that it generates new strivings, new needs and problems.[4]

What Selznick refers to as *character*, others seem to have called by different names, particularly in reference to organizations. Psychoanalyst Michael Maccoby, whose work we discussed in Chapter 1, refers to an organization as a *psychostructure* and social researcher Daniel Yankelovich has spoken of institutions manifesting *psychocultures*. George Lodge, drawing upon Thomas Kuhn's work on paradigms, speaks of *ideologies* that govern the application of basic values to management practice. A celebrated book by Robert Bellah uses as its title a phrase from Alexis de Tocqueville, "*Habits of the Heart*," to signify the basic character-forming mores or values of a person, a group, or even a whole society.

The idea of a *mindset* is intended to echo all of these constructs, at least insofar as they include habits and practices that are

34

action-guiding and not simply *thought*-guiding. What these constructs have in common is a person's or a group's practical orientation, including not only general values like competence, achievement, and satisfaction, but also more concrete work-related attitudes.[5] *Mindsets carry thoughts and values into action*, and this fact makes them particularly important in the guidance of persons and organizations. It also makes them difficult phenomena to study.

As we shall see, the idea of a *mindset* can be employed in two principal ways:

1 The first is as a *diagnostic* or *descriptive* tool. We can classify mindsets attributed to individuals and organizations with an eye toward a better empirical understanding of their structure and evolution in contemporary business life. The methods and resources of psychology (in the case of individuals) and the social sciences (in the case of organizations and larger groups) are appropriate for these purposes. One might set out to describe the mindset of General Motors at a given point in time or developmentally, over a period of time. Several decades ago, John DeLorean did this in his book *On a Clear Day You Can See General Motors.*[6]

2 A second use of the mindset idea draws more upon the resources of ethics since it is *prescriptive.* Here there are two principal strategies:
   * One strategy – mindset *critique* – is to take the descriptive and developmental attributions of the first approach and to assess them for their ethical strengths and weaknesses. Moral soundness (rooted in an empirical, diagnostic understanding), is the principal concern. In the DeLorean book about General Motors, it was clear that the mindset attributed to GM was not only being *described* – it was being criticized strongly on moral and other grounds.
   * Another strategy – *idealization* – involves neither description nor critique, strictly speaking. It is instead used to characterize a way of thinking (values and beliefs) that *would be* appropriate if certain ideal conditions obtained, even though such conditions might not currently obtain. St. Augustine suggested that if one loved perfectly, one could "do what one willed" without reference to rules and commandments. He was saying that – hypothetically – a mindset anchored in perfect love could be free of rule-based thinking. Few, if any,

human beings love perfectly, of course, so few if any could/ should actually adopt such a mindset.[7] John Rawls, in his classic *A Theory of Justice*, explains early on that he is offering an "ideal" or "strict compliance" theory, not one in which responses to injustice are the primary objectives.[8] Rawls acknowledges that "the problems of partial compliance theory are the pressing and urgent matters . . . the things that we are faced with in everyday life," but he maintains that "the reason for beginning with ideal theory is that it provides . . . the only basis for the systematic grasp of these more pressing problems."[9]

Both of these general approaches to mindsets – descriptive and prescriptive – will be adopted in this and subsequent chapters.

In *Chapter 1*, we spoke of teleopathy as a condition that can afflict individuals, and through them, organizations. Conversely, it can afflict organizations, and through them, individuals. By describing teleopathy as a mindset, we are suggesting that fixation, rationalization, and detachment cohere in a pattern that carries thoughts into action, both for individuals and for organizations.

Personal and Organizational Mindsets

A "decision-maker" is any entity capable of perceiving, understanding, valuing, deciding, and acting – including ordinary persons, small groups, organizations, and networks of organizations. In general, the ideas of *decision-maker* and *mindset* go together. They make sense where the notions of mind, purpose, strategy, values, competence, self-preservation, and conscience make sense – ultimately, where the concept of management makes sense. Decision-makers are similar to "players" in the framework of game theory. As one game theorist put it:

> The word "player," does not have quite the meaning one would expect. A player need not be one person; he may be a team, a corporation, a nation. It is useful to regard any group of individuals who have identical interests with respect to the game as a single player.[10]

Indeed game theory is an example of a wider category that we might call "mindset theory." In game theory, certain success factors having to do with winning are given reign as overarching values. The logic of *mindsets* is more embracing than, although it includes, the logic of games.[11] So mindsets involve *decision-making* – they are *bridges* between reflection and behavior, between thinking and doing.

If mindsets were *purely* behavioral, they would be easy to identify and describe. How a person or an organization *acted* would be the whole story. Questions would not arise about what might have been meant or intended or envisioned: the process *behind* the action. But fortunately or unfortunately, mindsets – like individual or corporate strategies – often lie enough *behind* overt behavior (verbal and non-verbal) to require some detective work in getting at them.

On the other hand, if mindsets were *purely cognitive*, their connection with decisions and actions would be weak. Detection would become pure guesswork, since any kind of behavior might be compatible with the mindset orientations we might consider. The relevance of mindsets to practical affairs would be minimal.

The point is that mindsets are *neither* purely behavioral *nor* purely cognitive. They involve elements of both. Recall the two elements in the dictionary definition: "*beliefs* and *attitudes* which *govern* someone's behavior and outlook." This "governance structure" means that we can be mistaken about the mindset behind a given action and about the action that follows from a given mindset in a specific situation. This can be perplexing, especially in the ethical domain.

The perplexity stems from the fact that decisions, actions, behavior (as indicated in Figure 2.1) are the result of *two* inputs, not one. As Aristotle argued two millennia ago, wisdom (*phronesis*) consists in the use of the "practical syllogism," an argument whose conclusion was an *action*, needed *two* types of premises to be valid.[12] One of the premises needed to express a "value" (or attitude or prescription or other *action-guiding* element), while the other premise needed to express a "fact" or a belief based on experience, testimony, or science. My decision to confront an intruder in my home, for example, could be justified by (a) my *value* of family responsibility together with (b) my belief that there is in *fact* an intruder whose intentions put my family at risk.

Without knowing both my values and my factual beliefs, however, an observer might not be able to understand my behavior. If I did truly value my family but did *not* really believe there was an intruder, the observer might misconstrue inaction on my part as *not caring*. For not caring about my family, together with a belief that there *was* a dangerous intruder, might lead to the inaction. The critical

37

"Anatomy of a Mindset"

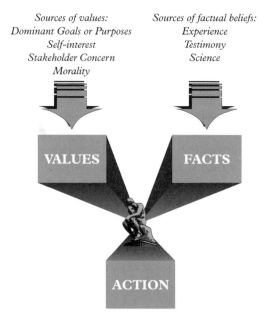

Figure 2.1 Action proceeding from values and factual beliefs

diagnostic element in this case is the *belief*. On the other hand, if I *did* believe there was a dangerous intruder and did *not* value my family, an observer might conclude mistakenly that my protective action was evidence for my familial caring – even that it was heroic. The truth might be that I cared only about *myself, not about my family*. This is why the attributions of mindsets to individuals or groups of individuals can be difficult. Mindsets are not always easy to discern because of what might be called their dual constitution.

The Mindset of Adam Smith

There is a parallel between this personal example (responding to an intruder) and the classic debate over the moral credentials of capitalism. Some argue that it is essential – morally – for individuals and organizations to embrace *other-regarding* principles (beyond self-interest) in the value composition of their mindsets. Opponents, quoting Adam Smith's *Wealth of Nations*, insist that: "It is not from the benevolence of the butcher, the brewer, or the baker, that we expect our dinner, but from their regard to their own interest. We address ourselves, not to their humanity but to their self-love, and never talk to them of our own necessities but of their advantages."[13]

How is it that an appeal to the *humanity* of the merchants is not part of our mindset expectation, according to Smith? The answer seems to lie in his beliefs about the dynamics of an ideal economic system. A January 2005 *Economist* article summarizes Smith's perspective:

> Smith did not worship selfishness. He regarded benevolence as admirable, as a great virtue, and he saw the instinct for sympathy towards one's fellow man as the foundation on which civilised conduct is built (he wrote another book about this: "The Theory of Moral Sentiments"). But his greatest economic insight – and indeed the greatest single insight yielded by the discipline of economics – *was that benevolence was not in fact necessary to advance the public interest, so long as people were free to engage with each other in voluntary economic interaction.* That is fortunate, he pointed out, since benevolence is often in short supply. Self-interest, on the other hand, is not.[14]

Conservative economists like Milton Friedman often point out that if one holds certain *beliefs* about the competitive system, the appeal to *humanity* as a value in the capitalistic mindset becomes unnecessary. Friedman would agree with the editors of *The Economist* just quoted:

> If self-interest, guided as though by an invisible hand, inadvertently serves the public good, then it is easy to see why society can prosper even if people are not always driven by benevolence. It is because Smith was right about self-interest and the public interest that communism failed and capitalism worked.[15]

What, then, are the beliefs that seem to relieve capitalists of their need for humanity? Essentially, they are idealized beliefs about the workings of the marketplace: full competition, voluntary and informed transactions, no externalities. To the extent, however, that ideal competitive market conditions do not obtain – i.e., to the extent that the beliefs in the capitalistic mindset about the presence of these conditions are only partially true in the real world, supplementary *values* appear to be needed. The supplementary values could – and probably do – include the "humanity" that was originally thought to be unnecessary, or perhaps a passion for *systemic change* that would make the appeal to "humanity" less necessary. Either way, there is a need for humanity in the capitalistic mindset: directly as a value or indirectly as a driver of systemic change that obviates such direct appeal.

Using our mindset vocabulary, we can ask of both Adam Smith and Milton Friedman three questions:

1   What is their *ideal* mindset, i.e., the mindset containing both their ideal factual circumstances and their ideal values?
2   What is the correct description of their *actual* mindset, i.e., the mindset containing both their beliefs about actual circumstances and their convictions about values to be embraced in those circumstances?
3   What prescriptive critique (if any) might we make of their *actual* mindset?

Putting the matter in this way, we notice that Smith and Friedman have views about an *ideal* world and the lack of *necessity* in that world for specifically ethical motives on the part of individuals and organizations. But since the real world is *not* ideal (a modest assumption), the need for specifically ethical motives may be critical. A person's real values and real beliefs are what support their real-world decision-making. Their views about an ideal world may have no direct bearing on their real-world decision-making, except perhaps in the way John Rawls mentioned in the passage quoted earlier: "the reason for beginning with ideal theory is that it provides . . . the only basis for the systematic grasp of the real-world decision making challenges that face business leaders."[16]

Cynics about morality like to argue that actions which *seem* to be ethically motivated may *really* stem from less-noble motives, such as power or greed. Non-skeptics sometimes want to convince us that ethical orientations that seem to dictate one kind of action may, depending on their accompanying beliefs, point in a number of directions. What we must remember is that *mindsets, because they are action-oriented but a step removed from overt behavior,* can be studied only indirectly and can be disclosed only contextually. This fact does not defeat – but it does complicate – research efforts. It means that "jumping to conclusions" about individual or corporate ethical values is a trap to be avoided.[17]

Personal and Organizational Teleopathy

The teleopathic frame of reference (*mindset*) is, as we have seen, single-minded. It is dominated by the need to achieve the goal in question and fearful of "giving up" or sacrificing the goal. Teleopathy is risk-averse at a very deep level, so much so that it refuses to even *look* at the goal from points of view that might threaten allegiance. The "values" box in the mindset structure is dominated by a goal or purpose and is devoid of competing values. The teleopathic decision-maker *gives over* his or her (or its) judgment to the goal, while in the case of more balanced intensity or determination, judgment is *retained*.

Psychiatrist M. Scott Peck, in his well-known book *The Road Less Traveled*, described the need for discipline in order to solve the problems that life presents to all of us. He identified four "elements" of discipline: delaying gratification, accepting responsibility or ownership for problems that are genuinely ours, dedication to truth by being willing to revise our "maps" of reality, and a fourth element that he called "balancing." Here is Peck's autobiographical anecdote to explain the fourth element:

> Mature mental health demands an extraordinary capacity to flexibly strike and continually restrike a delicate balance between conflicting needs, goals, duties, responsibilities, directives, etc. The essence of this discipline of balancing is "giving up." I remember first being taught this one summer morning in my ninth year. I had recently
> · learned to ride a bike and was joyously exploring the dimensions of my new skill. About a mile from our house the road went down a steep hill and turned sharply at the bottom. Coasting down the hill on my bike that morning I felt my gathering speed to be ecstatic. To give up this ecstasy by the application of brakes seemed an absurd self-punishment. So I resolved to simultaneously retain my speed and negotiate the corner at the bottom. My ecstasy ended seconds later when I was propelled a dozen feet off the road into the woods. I was badly scratched and bleeding and the front wheel of my new bike was twisted beyond use from its impact against a tree. I had lost my balance.[18]

Teleopathy is a condition that lacks the kind of discipline that Peck described. Avoiding fixation (by delaying gratification), refusal to rationalize (being dedicated to truth in matters of factual belief), and keeping head and heart together (balancing) – each counters one of the symptoms of teleopathy.

Neither Martin Siegel nor Andrew Fastow as individuals, nor NASA as an organization, exercised the kind of flexibility that Peck described as balancing. They seemed incapable of "giving up" on courses of judgment and action that led to much more than scratches and broken bicycle wheels. They appear to have been influenced by the fear of expanding their decision-making frames of reference to include not only needs and specific goals at hand, but also potentially conflicting "duties, responsibilities, and directions" regarding both their own futures and the futures of other parties.

The *disciplined* decision-maker, then, can be intense and purposeful. The absence of teleopathy is *not* the absence of dedication, commitment, and enterprise. Quite the contrary. The pursuit of goals and purposes is not the problem. The *unbalanced* and *undisciplined* pursuit of goals and purposes is the problem. Loss of balance comes from *truncating* the values in a decision-maker's frame of reference or mindset. Peck, Ladd and Maccoby all communicate the same basic message.

The maintenance of multiple values in decision-making makes it possible to "surrender," "give up," or at least *weigh* certain values differently from others – and it leads to better balance. This does not mean loss of commitment or dedication, but it *does* mean a strong-hearted ability to subject commitment and dedication to genuine scrutiny.[19]

Since most of us regard perseverance and determination as important *virtues*, we may become disoriented at the suggestion that they can harbor a great vice. Yet pursuing goals without balance can detach both individuals and organizations from their wholeness or integrity, with rationalization that bypasses human needs standing naked (like the sadhu) before them. Since teleopathy can masquerade as tough-minded virtue, managers run the risk of encouraging unethical behavior in their subordinates and in themselves. Let us now attempt to understand teleopathy as it manifests itself in the mindsets of individuals and organizations (see Figure 2.2).

In Chapter 1, I introduced the "principle of moral projection" to mark the ethical analogy between individuals and organizations. Bureaucratic organizations, of course, are *designed* to have a "mind" of their own, independent of those who hold offices in them. It is this feature of organizations that enables them to maintain themselves

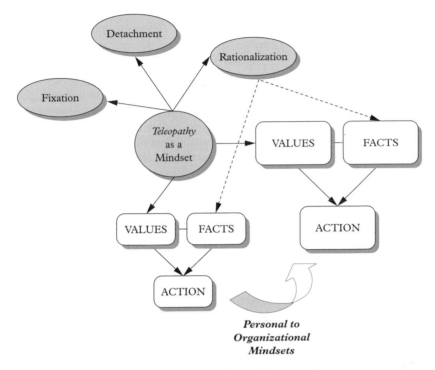

Figure 2.2 Individuals and organizations: Mindsets interact

over time, despite the regular entry and exit of individuals. Both the language of the law and our ordinary language recognize this simple but profound fact by referring to corporations in personal terms – as agents, entities with purposes ("missions") and strategies, bearers of rights and responsibilities, and subjects of attributes like "competence," "reliability," "efficiency," "aggressiveness" and "innovativeness." Lynn Paine refers to this transfer of attribution as the "moralization" of the corporation: "Through this process . . . companies have come to be regarded, at least implicitly, as moral actors in their own right. As such, they are presumed to have not only technical functions, such as producing goods or generating profits, but also moral attributes, such as responsibilities, aims, values, and commitments."[20]

Exploring this analogy need not entail careless anthropomorphism. The study of business has been profoundly enriched by exploring the parallels between individual psychology and the attributes of organizations. Lawrence and Dyer make the point persuasively in their classic *Renewing American Industry*:

> In talking about organizations as learning systems we do not mean to suggest that they have human properties. Organizations do not think, do not learn in a literal sense. Only people do. It is true, however, that members of an organization can not only learn as individuals but can transmit their learning to others, can codify it and embody it in the standard procedures of the organization. In this limited sense, the organization can be said to learn. When certain organizational arrangements are in place, an organization will foster the learning of its members and take the follow-up steps that convert that learning into standard practice. Then it is functioning as a learning system, generating innovations.[21]

What we often fail to notice is that if institutions can share the *non*moral mindset characteristics of their human architects (such as innovativeness and efficiency), they can also share their moral mindset characteristics. Business ethics as a discipline takes its departure from this simple truth. As Harvard's Lynn Paine put it in 2003:

> A company, as a moral actor in society, has commitments, values, and responsibilities, such as duties to its lenders or contractual obligations to its customers, that are distinct from those of its individual members. These corporate responsibilities survive even when a company's individual members and agents change. At the same time, a company's members and agents all have personal commitments and responsibilities outside of work as well as personal values that they need not share with one another or with their corporate employer. Failure to observe this distinction is a theme running through some of the most frequently heard criticisms of the corporate turn to values.[22]

There can be character flaws like teleopathy in each of us as individuals and in our institutions without the presence of hurtful intentions or hateful prejudices. Sometimes the explanations of such flaws are much more familiar: insecurity, inattention, tunnel vision, lack of courage. We call these *character flaws* because they have the potential to transform responsible decisions into irresponsible ones. They involve ethics because the freedom and well-being of our fellow human beings (and ourselves) are put at risk by their absence from the decision-making process.

44

Mindset Similarity and Mindset Interaction

We can now see that the connections between the mindsets of individuals and those of organizations are more than analogical. Mindsets may not only bear *structural similarities* to one another, they may actually *influence* one another causally. Individuals and organizations are not only comparable, taken in isolation as decision-making entities; they can and do interact. And the mindsets of individuals within organizations can be mutually reinforcing in crucial ways.

For this reason, we must add to the *Moral Projection Principle* mentioned in Chapter 1 another principle that encapsulates the *causal* accommodation that takes place between individuals and organizations. It can be formulated as follows:

> *Moral Accommodation Principle.* Given the phenomena of mutual selection and commitment in the relationship between participants and their organizations, it is reasonable to expect *over time* a convergence between the mindsets of individuals and the mindsets of their organizations.

Thus while teleopathy may be a problem for the individual in the social setting of the modern business organization, it can also become a self-reinforcing problem when it infects (like a virus) an organization's culture. Through the career progressions (or regressions) of those who shape companies and their cultures, teleopathy may be not only personalized but institutionalized. In turn, the reward system in such a culture may encourage more individuals to lose their balance in a (literally) vicious cycle. McCoy remarked about the sadhu incident: "Because corporations and their members are interdependent, for the corporation to be strong the members need to share *a preconceived notion* of what is correct behavior, a 'business ethic' and think of it as a positive force, not a constraint."[23]

Such a "preconceived notion" provides institutional support or resistance to what at the level of the individual we recognize as teleopathy. Martin Siegel could not have survived for long in a Wall Street firm that was inhospitable to his goal-driven values. Andrew Fastow could only flourish in the kind of culture that Enron provided (and that he in turn reinforced). Nor could NASA have survived for long without both promoting and weeding out individuals according to their "fit" with its culture. An interesting illustration of this

45

last point comes from a July 22, 2003 interview of NASA mission operations representative Phil Engelauf by William Harwood of CBS News:

> [Engelauf addressed] "the agency's long history of foam shedding and how senior managers slowly grew to accept what sociologist Diane Vaughn calls the "normalization of deviance."
>
> "We've had incidences of foam coming off the tank throughout the history of the program and the same management processes that I think got us comfortable that [these were] not really safety-of-flight issues have been allowed to continue, rightly or wrongly," Engelauf said. "I don't think you can point to individuals today and say that person got comfortable with it, because we've sort of inherited this from the time when Linda [Ham, Chairman of NASA's Mission Management Team at the time of the *Columbia* disaster] and I were back as front room flight controllers and there was a completely different set of people managing the program."[24]

Perhaps without intending to, Mr Engelauf attested to the persistence of beliefs and attitudes in an organizational culture over time that can influence individuals' judgments in tragic ways.

Reaching Beyond Teleopathy – a "Stakeholder" Mindset?

If we think of *teleopathy* as a hazardous business mindset with unbalanced values, then it should not surprise us to discover that there have been efforts for nearly a half-century to find a more balanced alternative. The phrase that has become entrenched in the literature is "stakeholder" thinking in contrast to pure "stockholder" thinking. And while I have reservations about the ultimate adequacy of stakeholder accounts of business ethics – indeed I find them paradoxical – it seems clear that the normative direction of these accounts is *away* from the symptoms of *teleopathy* (fixation, rationalization, and detachment) and *toward* a more ethically comprehensive mindset.[25]

Some very thoughtful observers of business believe that the decades since World War II have marked a significant shift away from the conventional business mindset. Peters and Waterman compare it to a scientific revolution:

What exactly do we mean by the fall of the rational model? We really are talking about what Thomas Kuhn, in his landmark book *The Structure of Scientific Revolutions*, calls a paradigm shift. . . . We are urging something of this kind in business. The old rationality is, in our opinion, a direct descendant of Frederick Taylor's school of scientific management and has ceased to be a useful discipline.[26]

The suggestion is that a shift is underway from the "rational" business paradigm to a new paradigm is significant.[27] In the language we have been using in this chapter, it may mean a change in the values, if not the factual beliefs, that constitute the business mindset.

Other observers, such as Harvard's George C. Lodge, have argued that the shift in business ideology or mindset has gone from individualistic values to communitarian values, from exclusively self-interested competition to a kind of community-oriented cooperation.[28] This view is sometimes put in terms of an expansion of corporate "stakeholders" from the traditional shareholder-owner constituency to such constituencies as employees, suppliers, consumers, and the general public.

We can return to Lawrence and Dyer for another perspective on the modern corporate mindset. In *Renewing American Industry*, these authors present as their ideal for organizational management what they call *readaptation*. Related to the concept of strategy, *readaptation* emphasizes the dynamic character of an organization's self-definition and goal-setting. In their words:

We define *organizational adaptation* as the process by which an organization and its environment reach and maintain an equilibrium ensuring the survival of the system as a whole. Readaptation is a form of organizational adaptation in which the organization and its relevant environment interact and evolve toward exchanges that are more acceptable to the *internal and external stakeholders* as evidenced by continuing high levels of innovation, efficiency, and member involvement. . . . *Readaptation* is a normative concept. We assume that innovation, efficiency, and member involvement are socially desirable, since in the long run each is necessary to the well-being of institutions and their members and, we believe, society at large.[29] (Emphasis added.)

According to this definition, *readaptation* is more than survival or competitive success, value elements of the conventional business mindset. Since it emphasizes *mutually acceptable exchanges* between an organization and the stakeholders in its environment, readaptation seems to call for a more socially responsible business culture. This becomes clear when Lawrence and Dyer connect readaptation with Kenneth Andrews' concept of corporate strategy:

> [Strategy is] the pattern of decisions in a company that determines and reveals its objectives, purposes, or goals, produces the principal policies and plans for achieving those goals, and defines the range of business the company is to pursue, the kind of economic and human organization it is or intends to be and the nature of the economic and noneconomic contribution it intends to make to its shareholders, employees, customers, and communities.[30]

What is striking about this definition of strategy, in contrast to that of Michael Porter and others, discussed in Chapter 3, is the inclusion of *moral* values among the very criteria for strategic "success." Some kind of stakeholder model is part of the concept of strategy presented by Andrews as well as the concept of *readaptation* presented by Lawrence and Dyer.

In the past decade, influential business authors like Stephen Covey, Peter Drucker, Jim Collins, David Messick, Max Bazerman, and Charles Handy have written on this broad stakeholder theme.[31] Handy calls for an expansion of the conventional business mindset beyond the single-minded pursuit of profits.[32]

From Peters and Waterman, through Lodge, Lawrence, Dyer, and Andrews, to Handy and numerous other business writers, we see the introduction and affirmation of stakeholders as key factors in corporate mindsets. We also see an emerging acceptance of the idea of *corporate conscience*, the subject to which we will turn in Chapter 3.

On the other hand, there are critics of this developing social consensus, typified by the extensive treatment of "Corporate Social Responsibility" (CSR) in the January 22, 2005 issue of *The Economist*:

> The one thing that all the nostrums of CSR have in common is that they are based on a faulty – and dangerously faulty – analysis of the capitalist system they are intended to redeem. Admittedly, CSR is now so well entrenched and amply funded that to complain about it may be pointless. We are concerned that it may even be a socially irresponsible use of scarce newsprint. *Nonetheless, if businessmen had a clearer understanding of the CSR mindset and its defects, they would be better at their jobs and everybody else would be more prosperous.*[33] (Emphasis added.)

48

The writers of *The Economist* seem to be suggesting that there are erroneous *beliefs* in the mindset structure of CSR advocates, leading them to ask of corporations social priorities (*values*) that are ultimately dysfunctional.

In the next chapter, we will examine the idea of an ethically healthy frame of reference (or *mindset*) for individuals and corporations. Balance will be built into the decision-making process by invoking *multiple* perspectives on the contemplated decision, perspectives that take into account the achievement of the goal, the special obligations of the decision-maker, the rights of affected parties, the consequences for other individuals and groups. This is compatible with tremendous profit-oriented intensity, both in the balancing process that leads to decision and in the implementation of the decision.[34] But the mindset I will call "corporate conscience" is neither fixated, nor rationalizing, nor detached.

3

Conscience as a Mindset: Personal and Organizational

conscience, *n.*, inner awareness of right and wrong, good and evil. Persons said to "have a conscience" manifest three characteristics: 1) they evaluate actions, motives, and states of character to determine if these are appropriate from a moral point of view; 2) they experience feelings such as guilt or satisfaction that are consistent with moral judgments that they have made; 3) they are disposed to act on the basis of their moral perceptions.[1]

We saw in Chapter 1 that *teleopathy*, or *the unbalanced pursuit of purpose* (with its symptoms of fixation, rationalization, and detachment) is an occupational hazard to which business ethics must respond, both on the level of the individual and on the level of the organization. In Chapter 2, I introduced the idea of a *mindset* in conjunction with teleopathy, as an initial approach to understanding both its personal and its cultural dimensions. Now we turn to the concept of *conscience* (again both personal and cultural) to understand its role in helping *avoid* the hazard.

The definition of *conscience* – conventionally thought of as a faculty possessed by individual human beings with some degree of maturity – makes explicit reference to *awareness*. This awareness manifests itself by evaluating "actions, motives, and states of character . . . from a moral point of view." But what is "the moral point of view"? And can we rely on it as a *shared* perspective guiding action by *shared* values? If so, then conscience may be able to provide a countervailing influence to teleopathy.

Let us look at the phenomenon of conscience first in its most natural setting, namely, the decision-making lives of individual persons. Then, in order to make the application of conscience to *organizations* clearer, it will be helpful – as it was with teleopathy in Chapter 2 – to think of conscience as a "mindset." Later, I will explore some of the complexities of corporate conscience as a guide to decision making.

Conscience in the Individual

Conscience as thoughtfulness

In a series of *New Yorker* articles that appeared in 1977, political theorist and philosopher Hannah Arendt wrote about the "banality of evil," the utter *thoughtlessness* of wrongdoing, in contrast to our often dramatic preconceptions. The context of Arendt's remarks was her recollection of the mindset of Adolf Eichmann during his trial in Jerusalem in the early 1960s:

> The question that imposed itself was, could the activity of thinking as such, the habit of examining whatever happens to come to pass or to attract attention, regardless of the results and the specific content of the activity, could this activity be among the conditions that make men abstain from evildoing, or even actually "condition" them against it? The very word "conscience," at any rate, points in that direction, insofar as it means "to know with and by myself," a kind of knowledge that is actualized in every thinking process.[2]

Arendt's idea – that evil resides in a kind of *thoughtlessness* – was rooted in her conviction that *thinking* (awareness) is the key not only to our relationship with ourselves but also to our relationships with others. She helps us to understand the meaning of psychological and moral integrity. She also offered us a clue to the meaning of conscience in decision-making. Conscience refuses to anesthetize our humanity in the face of what can sometimes be strong temptations to do so, as when people's lives are affected by our decisions in adverse ways. To quote Arendt again:

> Clichés, stock phrases, adherence to conventional, standardized codes of expression and conduct have the socially recognized function of protecting us against reality; that is, against the claim on our thinking attention which all events and facts make by virtue of their existence.[3]

51

I shall return to this theme, since it suggests the power of candid recognition of facts as a pathway to sound moral judgment.

Conscience as awareness

Anthony DeMello, a Jesuit priest-psychologist who was raised in India as a Buddhist until his teen years, tells a story about an eager young disciple who went to the master and said, "Could you give me a word of wisdom? Could you tell me something that would guide me through my days?" Since it was the master's day of silence, he picked up a pad and wrote on it. He wrote, "Awareness." When the disciple saw it, he said, "This is too brief. Can you expand on it a bit?" So the master took back the pad and wrote, "Awareness, awareness, awareness." The disciple said, "Yes, but what does it mean?" The master took back the pad and wrote, "Awareness, awareness, awareness means – awareness."[4]

The point of DeMello's story, and the source of its humor, is that we sometimes look for complex solutions when much simpler ones are available. But *simple* does not necessarily mean *easy*. DeMello would have agreed wholeheartedly with philosopher Hannah Arendt's observation that "A life without thinking is quite possible – but it is not fully alive. Unthinking men are like sleepwalkers."[5]

Conscience as moral insight

To understand "the moral point of view" as the departure point for conscience, let us turn to Harvard philosopher Josiah Royce. Royce, who wrote at the end of the nineteenth century and was a friend of William James, believed that all of ethics was grounded in something he called the *moral insight* (a gateway to what philosophers today call the "moral point of view"). Royce described the *moral insight* in his book *The Religious Aspect of Philosophy*:

> The moral insight is *the realization of one's neighbor,* in the full sense of the word realization; the resolution to treat him unselfishly. But this resolution expresses and belongs to the moment of insight. Passion may cloud the insight after no very long time. It is as impossible for us to avoid the illusion of selfishness in our daily lives, as to escape seeing through the illusion at the moment of insight. We see the reality of our neighbor, that is, we determine to treat him as we do ourselves. But then we go back to daily action, and we feel the heat of hereditary passions, and *we straightway forget what we have seen.* Our

52

neighbor becomes obscured. He is once more a foreign power. He is unreal. We are again deluded and selfish. This conflict goes on and will go on as long as we live after the manner of men. Moments of insight, with their accompanying resolutions; long stretches of delusion and selfishness: That is our life.[6]

The moral insight (as described by Royce) lies at the foundation of the "Golden Rule," the oldest and most widely shared ethical precept known to us (see Table 3.1). The moral insight is about reciprocity between self-love and love of "one's neighbor" (or more generally, one's "stakeholders"). Understanding and appreciating the moral insight is the essence of conscience for the individual – and, we shall see, for the organization as well.

From Royce and the many formulations of the Golden Rule in Table 3.1, we can see that conscience is *not* simply a matter of altruism or selflessness. In fact, it *presupposes* a high level of concern for self: "as you would have your neighbor do to *you*." The challenge of conscience, in the end, is not the *suppression* of self-interest, but the *coordination* of self-interest alongside respect for others.

The First and Second Polarities of Conscience

The field of ethics is about understanding the full implications of the moral insight as described by Royce and formulated in the *Golden Rule*. The first thing to be noticed is that conscience involves a fundamental polarity – the *self* and the *other* ("my neighbor") – but let us look a little more closely.

Included in the insight that would have each of us "realize" our neighbor, there must also be some idea of *how to respond to such a charge*. If there were only one "neighbor" in my life, the task would be simplified considerably. But of course, this is not the usual ethical situation. The usual situation involves many "neighbors" – and decisions among options that respond to these neighbors (persons and groups) in different ways. This is where the initial polarity ("a self realizing a neighbor") must be supplemented by a second polarity, *two approaches to or strategies for* "realization" – universal identification and impartial generalization.

Universal identification

On the one hand, I can approach the charge to realize my neighbor by *identifying* with my neighbor. That is, I imagine that my neighbor

Table 3.1 The Golden Rule: The oldest ethical proposition of distinctly universal character

Religion		Golden Rule
Confucianism	6th century BC	What you don't want done to yourself, don't do to others.
Buddhism	5th century BC	Hurt not others with that which pains thyself.
Jainism	5th century BC	In happiness and suffering, in joy and grief, we should regard all creatures as we regard our own self, and should therefore refrain from inflicting upon others such injury as would appear undesirable to us if inflicted upon ourselves.
Zoroastrianism	5th century BC	Do not do unto others all that which is not well for oneself.
Classical Greeks [Plato]	4th century BC	May I do to others as I would that they should do unto me.
Hinduism [Mahabharata]	3rd century BC	Do naught to others which if done to thee would cause thee pain.
Judaism [Rabbi Hillel]	1st century BC	What is hateful to yourself, don't do to your fellow man.
Christianity [Jesus]	1st century AD	Whatsoever ye would that men should do to you, do ye even so to them.
Sikhism	16th century AD	Treat others as thou wouldst be treated thyself.

Source: Will Durant, *The Story of Philosophy*[7]

and I are united as one, and I decide what to do as a "we" rather than an "I." As I would with my own family and friends, I "invite my neighbor in" to my decision-making life, giving my neighbor representation as part of my will. The key to "realization" here is the respect for the will of my neighbor by joining that will to my own, making us – in effect – *joint authors* of the norms guiding our lives. Since my neighbor is as real as I am, my neighbor is as entitled as I am to participate in the "legislation" that morality represents. It is not the *consequences* of this legislation that account for its authority, but its *genesis* in the wills of the authors.

Immanuel Kant seems to have had something like this in mind when he spoke of the *Categorical Imperative* of ethics. Kant first insisted that "Nothing could possibly be conceived in the world or out of it that can be called good without qualification except a good will." He then described the "good will" as "Acting so that one harmonizes one's will universally with all rational beings." This approach to *realizing* my neighbor emphasizes human freedom and equality, treating each human person with a special dignity. Kant also formulated his *Categorical Imperative* doctrine this way: "Act so as to treat humanity, whether in your own person or in others, always as an end, and never merely as a means."[8]

Alexis de Tocqueville, in his widely-read *Democracy in America* (1840), may have had this core idea in mind when he spoke of *associations* in the United States:

> Americans of all ages, all conditions, and all dispositions constantly form *associations*. They have not only commercial and manufacturing companies, in which all take part, *but associations of a thousand other kinds* – religious, moral, serious, futile, general or restricted, enormous or diminutive.

De Tocqueville then added:

> Feelings and opinions are recruited, *the heart is enlarged*, and the human mind is developed only by *the reciprocal influence of men upon each other*. I have shown that these influences are almost null in democratic countries; they must therefore be artificially created, and this can only be accomplished by associations.[9]

De Tocqueville's observations suggest external and social manifestations of the internal impulse of identification to which I have been referring. From sublime associations that further art, religion, and health to more mundane associations that promote hobbies, games, and sports, voluntary identification with our "neighbors" is the trait that draws his attention.

If we think of human beings as both rational/spiritual and emotional/material beings, two aspects of our lives stand out as deserving moral attention *from* our neighbors (and deserving our attention *toward* our neighbors as well): our freedom (self-determination) and our well being (happiness). This first approach to realizing my neighbor through *identification* or *association* emphasizes the importance of freedom or self-determination – by placing myself and my neighbor alongside one another in determining how best to guide our conduct. The second approach or strategy emphasizes human well being or happiness.[10]

Impartial generalization

I can engage the imperative to *realize* my neighbor in another way – not by *identifying* with my neighbor, but by *not* identifying with *myself*. That is, instead of "inviting my neighbor in" to my decision-making life, I can try to assume the position of a detached external observer of *both* myself *and* my neighbor, seeking to maximize the well being of all concerned. I will refer to this approach as *generalization*, contrasting it with *identification*. In the words of Jeremy Bentham, "each should count for one, none for more than one." Some have called this the pursuit of "the greatest good of the greatest number," signaling that while decisions from this point of view may not reflect my *personal* greatest good (or yours); they will represent the "best for the most." The rules or moral precepts that stem from this approach do not derive their authority from their *genesis* (in contrast to universal identification discussed above), but from their *consequences for those affected*. Impartial generalization in the political realm underwrites the logic of democracy. It reaches toward community by abstracting from the wills and identifications of persons in an effort to accommodate the widest possible differences.

Historically, these two ways of responding to the moral insight or the Golden Rule (universal identification and impartial generalization) have led to very different ethical frameworks, but all of these frameworks share a desire to take seriously the proposition that my neighbor is as *real* as I am.[11] Universal identification tends to emphasize the importance of *duty, obligations*, and *rights of liberty*, while impartial generalization tends to emphasize the satisfaction of *interests* and on some interpretations, *rights of equality* (John Rawls). Both support the importance of *virtues* as habits or dispositions to act in accordance with morality.

These broad approaches to the moral insight accord to "my neighbor" personal dignity and consideration as part of a social

56

whole. Personal dignity is affirmed in the reluctance of universal identification to countenance sacrificing innocent lives, even in the face of group pressure. In US law, the presumption of innocence until guilt is proven illustrates how profoundly this dignity is valued. We would prefer to see a guilty party set free than to see an innocent party punished. Another manifestation of the value of dignity in American culture is the protection of religious freedom from state intervention.[12]

In addition to personal dignity, the importance of the *social whole* is emphasized by our conviction that representative democracy is to be preferred to monarchy or oligarchy or any other form of government. It is not that democracy is *flawless* as a political paradigm; it is that it represents a presumption in favor of the common good over the goods of various elites.

Seventeenth-century philosopher Jean Jacques Rousseau framed the challenge of the moral insight this way as he reflected on the terms of a "social contract": "The problem is to find a form of association which will defend and protect with the whole common force the person and goods of each associate, and *in which each, while uniting himself with all, may still obey himself alone, and remain as free as before.*"[13] Rousseau understood the conundrum associated with: (1) *each* neighbor being respected as a free human being while at the same time; (2) *all* are defended and protected as a united group. In twentieth-century philosophy, Thomas Nagel has been influential in his reflections on this issue:

> We are faced with a choice. For the purposes of ethics, should we identify with the detached, impersonal will that chooses total outcomes, and act on reasons that are determined accordingly? Or is this a denial of what we are really doing and an avoidance of the full range of reasons that apply to creatures like us? This is a true philosophical dilemma; it arises out of our nature, which includes different points of view on the world. When we ask ourselves how to live, the complexity of what we are makes a unified answer difficult. I believe the human duality of perspectives is too deep for us reasonably to hope to overcome it. A fully agent-neutral morality is not a plausible human goal.[14]

Nagel was convinced that the interior view ("partiality writ large") is different from the exterior view ("impartiality"). And he did not believe that either view could trump the other:

It is an important question in moral thought, how much impartiality we should try for. You are a particular person, but you are also able to recognize that you're just one person among many others, and no more important than they are, when looked at from the outside. How much should that point of view influence you? You *do* matter somewhat from outside – otherwise you wouldn't think other people had any reason to care about what they did to *you*. But you don't matter *as much* from the outside as you matter to yourself, from the inside – since from the outside you don't matter any more than anybody else.[15]

Nagel makes his point by contrasting the special attention we accord to ourselves "from the inside" and the impartial attention we accord to ourselves "from the outside." But Nagel's special attention "from the inside" can be extended (through *identification*) to our neighbor in much the way that it is extended to our intimate friends and family – partiality writ larger and larger.

A third polarity – ideal to real

It may be tempting to ask at this point: What is the difference? After all, don't *identification* and *generalization* arrive at the same destination, even though they take different approaches? In an *ideal* world, it may be true that identification and generalization lead to the same place. After all, they both *depart* from the same place, namely, the moral insight, the "realization of one's neighbor."

In our non-ideal world, however, we frequently find that *identifying* with the wills of others is much easier when we can assume a degree of cultural common ground with them. Family members, members of the same local community, religious tradition, ethnic group or nation – these are the "neighbors" with whom *identification* poses the least severe challenges. Those within our familiar culture who are aberrant or hostile (e.g., criminals) or those outside our familiar culture (e.g., from other "civilizations" as Samuel Huntington puts it[16]) may strain our capacities to identify.

Generalization and *impartiality* put less strain on our capacities in such contexts. But *generalization* carries its own challenges. The "greatest *good* of the greatest number" has to have some practical measure of "goodness" – and the most common approach is to allow the *preferences* of all parties to provide that measure. When these preferences are fanatical or repugnant, however, such as preferences anchored in prejudice against certain racial groups, we see how *impartiality* might lead to injustice.

The biggest moral challenge presented to most people by the events of September 11, 2001 was the idea of *identifying with* or even *counting* (impartially) the fanatical desires of the terrorist hijackers in our assessment of the World Trade Center tragedy. Our shock was fed by the failure of our moral imagination and our inability to view the matter impartially.[17] The use of the word "evil" in this context signals a breakdown of our idealistic moral aspirations. The living out of these ideals in the *real world* – a world that (sadly) harbors not only love but hate – adds another dimension to our understanding of conscience.

Our capacities for *universal identification* and our capacities for *impartial generalization* are limited in the non-ideal world, a world in which empathy is limited, interested factions collide, fidelity to traditions is passionate, and yet respect must still be shown to humankind. Expanding our identifications and embracing impartialities when possible is the work of the moral life. Recognizing our *limitations* in these arenas is also the work of the moral life. There may be some with whom we may never be able to identify. And there may be some whose professed "good" we cannot count among the greatest number. In such cases, *self-defense* may be the only realistic moral response. Neither partiality nor impartiality resides comfortably in the real world. In the end both are aspirations of limited human hearts and minds (See Figure 3.1).

Summary of the three polarities

Often we remark about our human tendencies toward self-centeredness in the face of others who need our respect. We also note the ethnocentric human proclivity to contrast "we" with "they." But the problems implied in these observations can be overcome in two ways: (1) by *realizing* our neighbor and breaking through Royce's "illusion of selfishness" (the *first* polarity), and then (2) by extending the "we" until there is no more "they," or by impartially regarding all of us, "we" included, third-personally as a "they." These are the two ideal approaches to the moral insight and the Golden Rule that constitute a *second* polarity. In addition to these two polarities (between the self and the other, and between partiality and impartiality) a *third* polarity emerges when we ask ourselves *how* we realize our neighbor *in practice*.

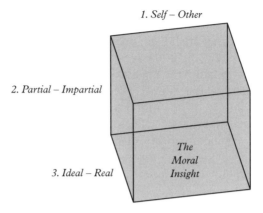

1. Self – Other

2. Partial – Impartial

3. Ideal – Real

The Moral Insight

Figure 3.1   Three polarities of moral insight

In order to act on the "resolution" that the moral insight calls forth from us, we need to have some idea – not just that there *is* a neighbor out there – but that my life and the lives of my neighbors must somehow be *harmonized* in a world of conflict and limited enlightenment. At the core of the moral insight, the insight which gives rise to what we call *conscience*, there is the "self–other" polarity, the "partial–impartial" polarity, and the "ideal–real" polarity as we seek alignment among the wills and interests of our fellow human beings. I have tried to depict the "three polarities" involved in the moral insight – self–other, partial–impartial, and ideal–real – in the three-dimensional Figure 3.2.

Moments in the unfolding of the moral insight

Royce speaks of the "illusion of selfishness" from which we are rescued by moral insight and to which we nevertheless regularly *return*: "Moments of insight, with their accompanying resolutions; long stretches of delusion and selfishness." The first stage in what we might call the "unfolding" of the moral insight, then, is our (apparently natural) self-centeredness. The second stage is the "realization" of our neighbor, which carries with it a "resolution to treat him unselfishly." But the third stage, often brought on by the resistance of the real world to the living out of our ideals, is that we "straightway forget what we have seen." And then we repeat the process: "That is our life."[18] (See Figure 3.3.)

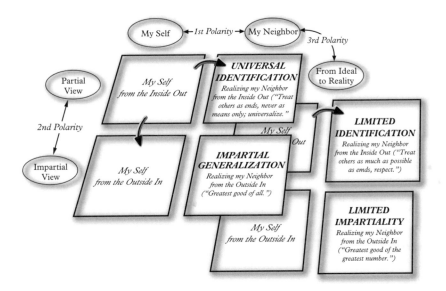

Figure 3.2 Three polarities at the core of conscience

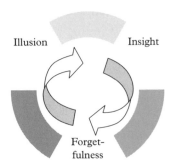

Figure 3.3 Illusion, insight, forgetfulness

What can often make it difficult to follow conscience is the fact that it asks us to care about both self and other, to be both *partial* and *impartial* at the same time, and to be idealistic and realistic at the same time – to *remember*. These are the three "polarities at the core" of conscience.

Bowen McCoy in "The Parable of the Sadhu," asks "What are the practical limits of moral imagination and vision? Is there a collective or institutional ethic beyond the ethics of the individual?"[19]

Perhaps one of the key functions of a *corporate* conscience and the culture surrounding it is to help with the problem of *individuals'* forgetting – even though it is possible for organizations to forget as well.

A friend of mine once "reminded" me (when, frankly, I needed it). His words were: "You're *special*, but you're *no damn different!*" Painful as it was for me to hear such a message, it expressed the very essence of the "triple dedication" that the moral point of view asks of us. We must *realize* our neighbor, *embrace* both our partialities and our impartialities, and do so in our real world *behavior*, not just aspirationally. The moral insight at the heart of conscience is more than a mere *intellectual* insight; it is profoundly *practical*. In order for it to guide our choices and our behavior, it must be as anchored in our will (our affective life) as it is in our belief system (our cognitive life).

Joining Royce's account of the *moral insight* with Arendt's reflections on *thoughtfulness* and DeMello's on *awareness*, we can appreciate the essence of conscience as *an active, engaged, perspective on decision-making that realizes the significance of others*. We might say that conscience resists our all-too-human tendency to forget who and where we are among others – resists the thoughtless complacency that accompanies such forgetting.[20]

Human nature and conscience

On July 9, 2002, in the wake of many corporate scandals after Enron, President George W. Bush said to a large Wall Street audience, "There's no capitalism without conscience; there is no wealth without character." But some might be concerned that conscience – understood as moral insight and ethical awareness – is somehow too private, too subjective (and so too unstable) to serve as a foundation for judgment, especially for individuals living in a pluralistic society. After all, we have no guarantees that the moral insight is anchored in truth, in our shared world. Might it not be just a subjective emotion that some share and some do not? Might the appeal to conscience ultimately be an appeal to a kind of moral anarchy? This is an important challenge. If such "postmodern" skepticism is warranted, business ethics as a field could be a waste of effort, leading to an ethical "Tower of Babel." If the skepticism is not warranted, the way is open for a rich dialogue about conscience not only for individuals, but for organizations.

Skepticism and relativism in ethics are not new. Neither is the substitution of a tough-minded "might-makes-right" attitude for the moral point of view. Conscience has been thought by some to be motivationally fragile and interpersonally disputatious. One has only to think of Thucydides' description of the Athenians at Melos or of Machiavelli's advice to the Prince to appreciate that amoral self-assertion is as "premodern" as it is "postmodern." History shows us nothing if it does not show us that violence and (eventually) tyranny are frequently preferred alternatives to moral dialogue among human beings.[21]

Must recognition of the importance of emotion in ethical thought, however – recognition of the presence of "heart" in addition to "head" in moral dialogue – lead to a rejection of the idea of *shared* values? Despite the many ethical tensions that we witness both locally and globally, *the very persistence of debate* suggests that the parties to the debate are reaching out to a *shared* moral consciousness. Both emotion and reason are present in the moral insight, and this fact makes universal consensus extraordinarily difficult.[22] But civilization has always involved the quest for ethical common ground.[23]

The most obvious place to look for this common ground is in what philosophers have called *human nature*. Our humanity is presumably the one "thing" we have in common across the ages and across cultures, lifestyles, social and political arrangements. The norms and laws and customs of human communities are diverse and varied. But the fact that they are *human* communities is a constant. It is this simple observation that has for millennia supported the idea of a *natural law*, prior to and superseding any of the human-made laws and norms that may be divergent. From Aristotle to Aquinas, and from Thomas Jefferson to the trials at Nuremburg to Martin Luther King's *Letter from Birmingham Jail*, the "laws of nature and nature's God" have been cited as the ultimate source of moral authority, and the final appeal in the face of tyranny and injustice.[24]

In the modern era, biological science has sometimes pushed hard against the notion of a natural law that represents a higher calling for human beings. Followers of the Darwinian paradigm often suggest that (a) there is no higher power or higher law, and (b) the only "natural law" is the law of survival through random variation and natural selection. Nature is real, but "nature is red in tooth and claw." This paradigm is anything but uncontroversial, solely on scientific grounds – never mind on the basis of its moral implications.

The origins of life and the origins of species are not easily explainable using Darwinian premises. And the information and communication sciences of the twentieth century offer new evidence for design in a universe that some have claimed to be the product of mere chance.[25]

The significance of discussions of natural law for an account of conscience is hard to overstate, for without some kind of anchor in human nature, appeals to conscience can lose their traction. If conscience is interpreted as – at best – an emotion that may have survival value, it is unlikely that it will sustain the principles to which human beings have appealed over the centuries: principles such as caring for the weak, social justice, natural rights, fiduciary duty, and the pursuit of the common good. If it is rooted in an awareness of a *natural* law, however, the idea of conscience can function as a source of moral reasoning with some hope of moral progress – and ultimate moral consensus. The authority of conscience lies in an order not *decided upon* by each person, even if it is ultimately *interpreted by* each person. In the words of John Paul II:

> Conscience is not an independent and exclusive capacity to decide what is good and what is evil. Rather there is profoundly imprinted upon it a principle of obedience vis-à-vis the objective norm which establishes and conditions the correspondence of its decisions with the commands and prohibitions which are at the basis of human behavior.[26]

There need not be an "either/or" between emotion and reason. We seek for ourselves and for our children a purpose, a community, a tradition, and a set of virtues. We seek to discern in our (shared) human nature a platform for non-arbitrarily resolving competing ethical loyalties. Perhaps the "postmodern" fear is that in adding *reason* to the emotional aspects of conscience, we run the risk of having to sacrifice freedom or autonomy. But on this point, we would do well to consider the wisdom in philosopher Richard Norman's observation that:

> [t]he sacrificing of one's own interests need not be a sacrificing of oneself to something *external*. My commitment to my friends or my children, to a person whom I love or a social movement in which I believe, may be a part of my own deepest being, so that when I devote myself to them, my overriding experience is not that of *sacrificing* myself but of *fulfilling* myself.[27]

Norman suggests that for each of us, our own "deepest being" reaches for the same moral insight – and ultimately the same basis for conscience. Ethical inquiry, at any rate, is rooted in the presumption of a *shared moral consciousness*, which we can approach in a disciplined way rather than fleeing it as if it were fragile and fragmentary.[28]

"Awareness, awareness, awareness," wrote DeMello. Instead of *looking away* at the first sign of moral disagreement or of ethical imperatives that seem economically and legally expensive, conscience encourages us to *look more closely*. Often, looking more closely leads to more agreement than disagreement about, for example, appropriate workplace safety or product safety practices, marketing strategies, sales incentives, financial reporting. *The best response to the postmodern assertion of moral fragmentation is simply to look more closely.* Of course, looking more closely at the economic and legal consequences of *not* following shared ethical values frequently reveals new arguments by surfacing unanticipated economic costs and legal exposure.[29] To quote again from George W. Bush's *Wall Street* speech in July 2002:

> Tougher laws and stricter requirements will help – it will help. Yet, ultimately, the ethics of American business depend on the *conscience* of America's business leaders. We need men and women of character, who know the difference between ambition and destructive greed, between justified risk and irresponsibility, between enterprise and fraud.[30]

Conscience and Organizations: The Polarities Revisited

Conscience, as we know, emerges over time. The "polarities at the core" of conscience are not something that typically afflicts infants and small children. But in due course, it becomes a coordination challenge for us as adults, and a leadership challenge in organizations. Philip Selznick's observations about institutional character draw upon an analogy between individual personality and organizational development:

> The study of institutions is in some ways comparable to the clinical study of personality. It requires a genetic and developmental approach, an emphasis on historical origins and growth stages. There is a need to see the enterprise as a whole and to see how it is transformed as new ways of dealing with a changing environment evolve.[31]

This comparison suggests that a leader's choice among orientations for his or her company is more than a matter of taste. It is a matter of heeding certain natural tendencies in the very process of organizational growth. These tendencies may well be similar to those that guide the moral development of individuals. The depth of a company's *cultural* commitment to ethical values in the pursuit of economic values – its integration of partiality with impartiality – may be a mark of *corporate* moral development. And a society's attention to this development could come to be, if it is not already, a measure of its satisfaction with business.

One of the most famous students of moral development in this century was the Swiss psychologist Jean Piaget. His observations of the mindsets of children are clinically rich. Piaget spoke of an initial stage of *egocentrism* in which the child guides its decisions primarily out of a concern to satisfy its own desires and interests. This stage was followed, he believed, by a second stage called "moral realism" (*heteronomy*). At this stage external forces in the child's environment (for example, game rules, peer pressure, and parental norms) are given full sway as restraints on self-interest. But only in the third stage (*autonomy*), did Piaget see the emergence of genuine conscience:

> For conduct to be characterized as moral there must be something more than an outward agreement between its content and that of the commonly accepted rules: it is also requisite that the mind should itself be capable of appreciating the value of the rules that are proposed to it.[32]

The third stage required, according to Piaget, inner direction born not of egocentrism, but of mutual respect; and cooperativeness born not of submission, but of a sense of reciprocity.[33] At the third stage, the individual sees others as deserving of consideration in their own right, whatever the rules may be. And at the third stage, the individual must confront the "polarities at the core" discussed earlier in this chapter.

Rationality and respect

If we understand *mindsets* and *decision-makers* as described in Chapter 2, we can see that actions, choices, and policies are the result of both value-inputs and factual beliefs. What a person or an organization values and believes about the world (physically, politically,

66

economically) are the factors that govern action. Understanding the case of Dow Corning Corporation's response to the breast implant controversy, for example, is impossible without understanding the *beliefs* of the company's scientists that silicone gel is biologically inert and incapable of causing autoimmune disease. Conclusions about whether the company *cared about its consumers* need to consider this factor.[34]

Let us now focus on the values side of the mindset anatomy introduced in Chapter 2 (the upper left-hand box in Figure 2.1). The first polarity pointed to two general governing values – one *partial*, the other *impartial*. These values govern the concrete goals and purposes of both personal and corporate behavior. In what follows, I will refer to these governing values as *rationality* and *respect*.[35]

Rationality organizes the criteria by which a person or a group defines success (for example, profitability, efficiency, competitive advantage). Michael Porter analyzes the main ingredients of corporate rationality in his book, *Competitive Advantage*. In his words:

> Competition is at the core of the success or failure of firms. Competition determines the appropriateness of a firm's activities that can contribute to its performance, such as innovation, a cohesive culture, or good implementation. Competitive strategy is the search for a favorable competitive position in an industry, the fundamental arena in which competition occurs. Competitive strategy aims to establish a profitable and sustainable position against the forces that determine industry competition.[36]

Rationality may include attention to others, of course, as it does in marketing strategy and labor negotiations. But this attention is usually instrumental or secondary to the objectives and interests of the decision-maker. It is not independently accorded to those on the receiving end. (Philanthropic decisions may or may not be an exception.)

Respect refers to a principle that takes others' goals, needs, and interests into account not instrumentally, but as deserving consideration in their own right. *Respect*, according to some, is essential for there to be a moral or ethical dimension to personal and organizational mindsets. But I suggest that *rationality* is just as essential. Respect calls for impartiality (Royce's "*realization* of one's neighbor") while rationality emphasizes partiality (treating one's neighbor "*as oneself*") in the decision-making process. The *Golden Rule* is a merger or *combination* of rationality and respect. And as we have seen,

67

Josiah Royce's description of the "moral insight" sees it as an awakening of respect from the rib of rationality. The same could be said of Hannah Arendt's and Anthony DeMello's reflections on *thoughtfulness* and *awareness*. In its ideal form, respect guides behavior as universal identification or impartial generalization (or both), permitting us to explore the attribution of conscience to *organizational* cultures through the core values of rationality and respect.[37]

Attention to rationality and respect in moral philosophy has a long and distinguished history. One of the themes of Plato's *Republic* was the relationship between self-interest and concern for others as reflected in the question "Is justice profitable?" In the nineteenth century, British philosopher Henry Sidgwick described the central problem of ethics in terms of what he called prudence and rational benevolence:

> Even if a man admits the self-evidence of the principle of Rational Benevolence, he may still hold that *his own happiness* is an end which it is irrational for him to sacrifice to any other; and that therefore a *harmony* between the maxim of Prudence and the maxim of Rational Benevolence must be somehow demonstrated, if morality is to be made completely rational.[38]

Contemporary discussions of these two action-guiding principles have been numerous, but perhaps most sharply focused around the *Prisoners' Dilemma* in game theory. These discussions, reminiscent of Plato and Sidgwick, ask how self-interested rationality – either on the part of individuals or on the part of organized groups – can be joined with a concern for social welfare or justice without self-defeating results stemming from mistrust and competitive pressure.[39] Economist Francis Fukuyama pursues a similar theme in his book *Trust: The Social Virtues and the Creation of Prosperity*:

> [P]eople who do not *trust* one another will end up cooperating only under a system of formal rules and regulations, which have to be negotiated, agreed to, litigated, and enforced, sometimes by coercive means. This legal apparatus, serving as a substitute for trust, entails what economists call "transaction costs." Widespread distrust in a society, in other words, imposes a kind of tax on all forms of economic activity, a tax that high-trust societies do not have to pay.[40]

Like Sidgwick, and like many game theorists, Fukuyama sees the establishment of a convergence between rationality and respect (trust) as essential not just for individuals but for organizations.

Corporate moral development: A typology

There are parallels between Piaget's three stages of moral development and the ways rationality and respect can figure in the mindsets of organizations.[41] *Egocentrism* corresponds to pure economic rationality (with concern for others as a merely instrumental value). *Heteronomy* seems to come in two forms that echo the ways in which respect might be thought to be part of the business system: market forces and legal constraints. *Autonomy* or moral maturity suggests an integration of respect with rationality in an organization's policies and decision-making. It does not rely solely on market or legal signals for guidance. It is only at this last stage that Piaget would describe the mindset as a fully moral one.[42] Yet even at this stage, there are several avenues for moral reasoning, not just one. Let us reflect on the organizational analogues to Piaget's categories.

Type 1 thinking: Conscience as a guide to self-interest

We can imagine someone holding that his basic value is to look out for himself in a rational way, and that one way of doing so is to be respectful of other persons most of the time. I will refer to this as *Type 1* thinking. Organizational cultures might reflect a similar mindset. The belief would be that treating stakeholders well, like honesty, is usually "the best policy."

Type 1 thinking is present wherever ethical norms are followed solely with an eye to the rational self-interest of the decision-maker as the overriding value. This need not mean *ignoring* others in the ordinary sense of that phrase. Some interpretations of "issues management," "public relations," and "cause-related marketing." for example, seem to fit the Type 1 pattern because of the ultimately self-interested principles behind them, even though they may appear on the surface to involve independent concern for others.

Type 2 thinking: Conscience as a systemic constraint

This type of thinking incorporates ethical norms not through the logic of self-interest but through systemic constraints on the choice of business goals. There are two distinct subtypes. The first looks primarily to *market* forces as surrogates for morality (Type 2a); the second, to *political* and *legal* forces (Type 2b):

- The invisible hand pattern (Type 2a): Some accord importance to ethical norms in business decision-making, but quickly add that they are already built into the competitive system. This makes special management attention to ethics redundant. It is what we shall call, remembering Adam Smith, the "invisible hand" pattern. Nobel laureate Milton Friedman often seems to endorse this way of thinking. The suggestion is that whatever ethical values the business system needs are already programmed in, making supplementary efforts unnecessary, even morally suspect.
- The visible hand pattern (Type 2b): This type of thinking relies on non-economic forces outside the organization to secure the value of, say, environmental protection without direct managerial involvement (a more "visible" than "invisible" hand). Understanding moral judgment in this way places responsibility for ethics outside the manager's principal (economic) concerns. We might say that Type 2b leaders acknowledge authority, but not accountability, when it comes to ethical values.

Type 3 thinking: Conscience as an authoritative guide

According to this type of thinking, securing respect for others by the invisible hand – and even by more visible hands external to the marketplace, such as government, labor, and the media – is insufficient. Corporate self-interest is not ignored, and neither are competition and the law, but respect for the rights and concerns of affected parties (stakeholders) is given independent force in the leader's operating consciousness. Type 3 thinking rejects surrogates for conscience in the form of systemic constraints. Managerial accountability for ethics goes hand in hand with recognition of its authority.

Reflecting on this typology, we can see that only Type 3 thinking captures the full meaning of both individual and corporate *conscience*. For only Type 3 embraces respect *unconditionally*. The others do so *conditionally*: in the case of Type 1, subject to self-interest; and in the case of Types 2a and 2b, subject to social structures or systems (the market and the law), which themselves require ethical vigilance both in principle and in operation.

As we saw earlier, worries about ethical relativism in connection with the moral point of view are natural and deserve patient attention from both philosophers and managers. This is especially true in the context of multinational business operations. But these concerns

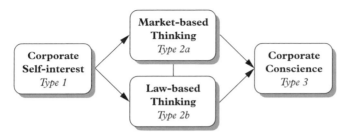

Figure 3.4 Moral development and mindset typology

are not insurmountable. The moral point of view is not a monolith, but it is a practical perspective that takes all human beings seriously. In the words of philosopher Mary Midgley: "Moral judgment is not a luxury, not a perverse indulgence of the self-righteous. It is a necessity. . . . Morally as well as physically, there is only one world, and we all have to live in it."[43] As we shall see in the upcoming section on Type 3 organizations, it was this spirit that lay behind the development of the Caux Round Table *Principles for Business* as a transcultural set of ethical norms.

In summary, there are four principal ways in which ethical norms can be acknowledged in the business mindset. Each involves *espousing* values like honesty, concern for others, fidelity to contracts, and so forth. But each connects these values to business decision-making using a different logic. Only Type 3 thinking mirrors the polarities at the core of conscience in the individual, Piaget's third stage of moral development (understood organizationally). It is in the realm of Type 3 thinking that we can expect to find *corporate conscience* (see Figure 3.4).

The typology and stakeholders

It is important to observe that *all four* of the patterns in the typology described above can recognize the conventional notion of *stakeholders* or constituencies in the business environment: consumers, employees, suppliers, communities, competitors, and of course, shareholders. The differences among the avenues lie in the *kind* of attention that each gives to these stakeholders. Type 1 thinking can give attention to stakeholders as factors that might affect self-interest, i.e., that might affect one's achievement of one's goals. Type 2a thinking can regard stakeholders as so many market forces within which companies must operate for profit. Concern for each is seen as built into the market system. Type 2b thinking can regard stakeholders as non-market checks on market reasoning: sociopolitical limits on the exercise of economic rationality. Only Type 3 thinking views stakeholders apart from their instrumental, economic, or political clout. It refuses to see them merely as what philosopher John Ladd once called "limiting operating conditions" on management attention.

We should note here that the notion of a "stakeholder" (originally a play on the word "stockholder") is not, by itself, at the core of business ethics. An examination of the four types of thinking suggests that, while all four can accommodate the stakeholder idea, only one type (Type 3) embraces the moral point of view as an authoritative guide.

If there is a new openness since the scandals of 2002 among business leaders and the general public to the idea of independent moral judgment guiding business conduct – and there is evidence for this in courts, boardrooms, academic studies, and public opinion research – then we need to improve our understanding of the full implications of making Type 3 thinking part of the very definition of corporate governance and leadership.

Type 3 Organizations

The implications of applying Piaget's account to organizations are similar to those for applying it to individuals: (1) that growth consists in a fuller acknowledgment of the reality and dignity of others and (2) that external or environmental constraints, while they may be necessary guides, are not morally sufficient. Indeed, just as Piaget saw the moral development of the child as a kind of liberation, so we might suggest that the moral development of the corporation is a kind of liberation. To quote Piaget once more:

> The unique contribution of cooperation to the development of the moral consciousness is precisely that it implies the distinction between what is and what ought to be, between effective obedience and an ideal independent of any real command. If unilateral respect and social constraint were alone at work, moral good would be given once and for all under the imperfect and often grotesque forms assigned to it by the duties and regulations of existing society.[44]

The evolution of respect from purely instrumental status (for example, public relations) through the status of an environmental constraint (for example, legal or regulatory requirements) to being a direct management concern is driven by a series of value-laden decisions at significant moments in an organization's history. Such decisions either reinforce or reorient the prevailing pattern of policy formulation and implementation. They either impede or contribute to what Selznick called character formation:

> [T]he process of "character formation" seems worth exploring for the insights it may yield to students of institutionalization and critical decision-making. When we have seen the connection between these two phenomena we shall be in a better position to analyze the nature and tasks of institutional leadership.[45]

This process of organizational character formation leads to a shared understanding of what counts as *success* in a given corporate setting.

We expect corporate mindsets to include respect-oriented values, as with individuals. We usually view extreme cases of *indifference* to others (on the part of organizations *or* individuals) as reprehensible if not pathological (*teleopathy*). Nevertheless, there is much variation in the authority and the salience of respect-oriented values among corporate cultures. Indeed, there are significant barriers and tough challenges facing leaders who would integrate respect with rationality in the mindsets of their companies.

Corporate rationality: Messick and Bazerman

In "Ethical Leadership and the Psychology of Decision-Making," David Messick and Max Bazerman suggest that rational decision-making is a goal to strive for.[46] By increasing our awareness of the biases we encounter in making decisions, we can increase our level of *rationality* and improve the quality of our decisions. We can also increase our level of *respect* by correcting for distortions in our beliefs or "theories" about the world, about other people, and about ourselves.

Our theories about the world can suffer from "selective perception" by:

- ignoring low-probability events, when they should not be ignored;
- limiting the search for stakeholders, focusing only on the powerful;

- ignoring or discounting the possibility that the public will "find out;"
- discounting the future by concentrating on *immediate* consequences; and
- undervaluing *collective* outcomes, focusing on individuals only.

Our theories about the world can suffer in other ways as well. Our judgments of *risk* can be distorted by strong desires for certain outcomes, leading us to frame the risks and their trade-offs and uncertainties carelessly. In addition to our judgments of risk, our perception of *causes* can get distorted as we think about why things do or do not happen:

> There is a tendency to reduce the set of possible consequences or outcomes to make the decision manageable. In extreme cases, all but one aspect of a decision will be suppressed, and the choice will be made solely on the basis of the one privileged feature.[47]

Our "theories about others" can be ethnocentric ("Unusual is less good.") or can rely on stereotypes ("us versus them"). Finally, "theories about ourselves" can distort our rationality through illusions of our own superiority:

> [People] tend to view themselves positively and think that their judgments are better than others. In addition, people tend to have the illusion of control, that outcomes and circumstances are more under their control than is actually the case. And finally, people tend to be overconfident about what they know. Studies have shown that when people feel they are 100% certain, they are actually only right 80% of the time.[48]

According to Messick and Bazerman, the beliefs about matters of fact that inform our mindsets (upper right-hand box in Figure 2.1) are often distorted by certain psychological tendencies. Sometimes these distortions come from failures of rationality-related values (for example, ignoring low probability events, discounting the future, overconfidence) and sometimes they come from failures of respect-related values (for example, selective perception of consequences to others, ethnocentrism, illusions of superiority). The main point is that leaders of organizations need to examine how they process information and "facts," because frequently values and attitudes lead to flawed decisions. Prejudices can cloud impartiality as we look at certain facts, and this represents an *indirect* value contribution (not a psychologically positive contribution) to the quality of decision-making in organizational cultures.[49]

Wall Street Journal columnist, Holman W. Jenkins, Jr. applied the Messick and Bazerman framework to the collapse of Enron and specifically to distorted judgments on the part of Jeff Skilling and Andrew Fastow.[50] Writes Jenkins in direct reference to the Messick and Bazerman article:

> Their clinical point of view, on first glance, will infuriate those who believe moral condemnation is the end of analysis: "Unethical business decisions may stem not from the traditionally assumed trade-off between ethics and profits . . . but from psychological tendencies that foster poor decision making."

Awareness by leaders of the ways in which distortion can enter into conscience, undermining either rationality or respect, is an important preventative. Again we see how *awareness* can add quality to ethical decision-making. Messick and Bazerman suggest that improving awareness in this arena comes from more careful assessments of consequences and risks, attention to potential biases in relation to certain stakeholders, and in general, avoidance of self-deception in judgments about the world, other parties, and oneself. In Chapters 5, 6, and 7, we will discuss in some detail ways in which companies can systematically enhance such awareness.

We must think *critically* about the "theories" we hold and evaluate their potential influence on the process by which we make decisions. These theories represent *voices* identifying barriers to rationality (and respect) in our ethical decision-making processes. Compensating for predictable biases can aid us as we attempt to obtain the insight of *the moral point of view* using these theories and the four avenues of ethical analysis to be described in the next section. Figure 3.5 links mindset typology and corporate conscience.

Corporate respect: Varieties of Type 3 management

Historically, the "respect" half of the "rationality and respect" structure of conscience has been parsed in many ways. And while a comprehensive review of these ways is beyond the scope of this chapter, we have already explored their ultimate source in the "moral insight" and the polarities with which it is associated. What I referred to

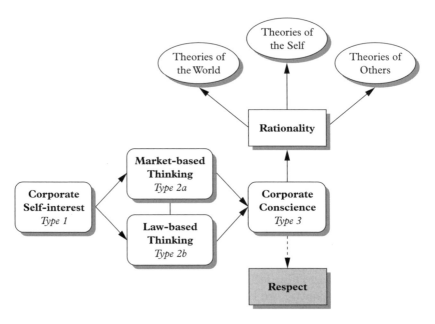

Figure 3.5 Mindset typology and corporate conscience: Theories of world, self and others (rationality)

earlier as *universal identification* and *impartial generalization* can be seen as the fountainheads of most accounts of normative ethics. From these two broad strategies for acting on the moral insight, we can discern four recurrent normative patterns or "avenues" of ethical analysis. The four avenues – interest-based, rights-based, duty-based, and virtue-based – can be thought of as tactical interpretations of the universality and impartiality that the moral point of view calls for in decision-making. Some philosophers see them as *competing* interpretations, while others see them as *complementary*.

Interest-based avenues

One of the most influential avenues of normative ethical analysis, at least in the modern period, is what we can call *interest-based*. The fundamental idea behind interest-based analysis is that the moral assessment of actions and policies depend solely on their consequences, and that the only consequences that really matter are the interests of the parties affected (usually human beings). *On this view, ethics is all about harms and benefits to identifiable parties.* Moral

76

common sense is governed by *a single dominant objective*: maximizing net expectable utility (happiness, satisfaction, well-being, pleasure). Critical thinking, on this view, amounts to testing our ethical instincts and rules of thumb against the yardstick of social costs and benefits.

There is variation among interest-based analysts, depending on the relevant beneficiary class. For some (called *egoists*) the class is the actor alone – the short- and long-term interests of the self. For others, it is some favored group – Greeks or Englishmen or Americans – where others are either ignored or discounted in the ethical calculation of interests. Sociologists call the latter phenomenon *ethnocentrism*. The most widely accepted variation of interest-based thinking (called *utilitarianism*) enlarges the universe of moral consideration to include all human beings, if not all sentient (feeling) beings. The justification for this approach is attributed to the *impartiality* that the moral insight demands. Jeremy Bentham and John Stuart Mill in the nineteenth century are the best-known formulators and defenders of utilitarianism.

There are, of course, debates over different aspects of interest-based thinking:

- How does one *measure* utility or interest satisfaction? Does economics provide a metric using monetary value?
- For *whom* does one measure it (self, group, humankind, beyond)? How do we factor in the interests of the aged and the unborn? Do animals count?
- What about the *tyranny of the majority* in the calculation? Are some interests just wrong even if the majority might be in favor?

In business administration, interest-based reasoning often manifests itself as a commitment to the social value of market forces, competitive decision-making, and (sometimes) regulation in the public interest. *Interest-based thinking* represents a "democratization" values.[51]

Illustrations of interest-based avenues

Recent controversies in human resource management (company owned life insurance, employee assistance programs) raise questions about the interests of companies in the lives of key (and not-so-key) employees. Often the removal of structural conflicts of interest (Sarbanes-Oxley) between the auditing function and consulting are justified as maximizing interests in accurate financial reporting.

Arguments for "Environmental Impact Statements" in connection with major private (or public) capital expenditures for roads, buildings, power plants, etc. represent the application of "cost–benefit analysis" (maximizing benefits, minimizing costs). The debate over using the Arctic National Wildlife Refuge (ANWR) for US domestic oil production is a cost–benefit debate that runs up against not only human interests, but the interests of other species. If the interests of the many can be served by the sacrifices of a few, interest-based reasoning is often invoked.

Rights-based avenues

A second important avenue is what we may call *rights-based* analysis. The central idea here is that moral common sense is to be governed *not* by maximizing interest satisfaction, but by equalizing rights protection. And the relevant rights are of two broad kinds: rights to fair distribution of opportunities and wealth (Rawls' *contractarianism*), and rights to basic freedoms or liberties (Nozick's *libertarianism*). Social justice as "fairness" is often explained as a condition that obtains when all individuals are accorded equal respect and equal voice in social arrangements. Basic liberties are often explained in terms of individuals' opportunities for self-development, work's rewards, and freedoms including religion and speech.

Rights can be viewed as interests that we believe are *not* subject to majoritarian adjudication (as in Jefferson's insistence on the *Bill of Rights*). They are "trumps" in debates with utilitarians over "the greatest good for the greatest number." Ultimately, rights-based thinking is anchored in the moral insight by appeal to either the fountainhead strategies of *universal identification* or *impartial generalization*.

Problems and questions regarding this avenue include:

- Is there a trade-off between equality and liberty when it comes to rights?
- Does *rights-based thinking* lead to *tyrannies of minorities* that are as bad as tyrannies of majorities?
- Is this type of thinking excessively focused on individuals and their entitlements without sufficient attention to larger communities and the *responsibilities* of individuals to such larger wholes?

In business administration, *rights-based* reasoning is evident in concerns about stakeholder rights (consumers, employees, suppliers) as well as stockholder (property) rights.

Illustrations of rights-based avenues

Debates about diversity in the workforce (gender, race) often are rooted in rights-based thinking. The *Reell Precision Manufacturing* case series is about the rights of employees not to be discriminated against on the basis of religion.[52] The *Joe Camel's Mom* case series is about the rights of the citizenry against cigarette advertising to minors.[53] As we move into suits against McDonald's for promoting obesity, some think that the limits of rights-based thinking are being reached. Instead, they claim, individuals have to take responsibility for their own choices and they do not have a rights-claim against corporations. The "buyer beware" marketing culture of the first half of the twentieth century seems to have been displaced by a "seller beware" marketing culture in the second half.

Internationally, rights claims come up against *interest-based thinking* in connection with tariff justifications and other WHO issues. The European Union's policies on employee rights to privacy have caused no small amount of interest-frustration on the part of US-based companies with many employees in Europe. It should also be mentioned that recent debates over giving up certain civil rights or liberties in the name of the greatest good (security against terrorism) illustrate the power of both avenues of ethical analysis.

Duty-based avenues

The third avenue, duty-based thinking, is perhaps the least unified and well-defined of the four avenues. Its governing ethical idea is *duty* or *responsibility* not so much to other *individuals* as to *communities* of individuals.[54] Critical thinking depends ultimately on individuals conforming to the legitimate norms of a healthy community. Ethics is not finally about interests and rights according to the duty-based thinker, since those are too individualistic. Ethics is about playing one's role as a member of a larger whole, either a web of relationships (like the family) or a community (Amitai Etzioni's *communitarianism*). The epitome of this line of thinking was expressed in President John F. Kennedy's inaugural: "Ask not what your country can do for you, ask what you can do for your country." In the nineteenth century, duty-based thinking was defended eloquently by British philosopher F. X. Bradley in his famous essay "My Station and Its Duties." In relation to the moral insight, discussed earlier, duty-based thinking is most often anchored in what we called *universal identification*.

Problems and questions regarding this avenue include:

- a concern that an individual might get swallowed up in a kind of collective (under the communitarian banner); and
- puzzles surrounding the "weighing" of potentially conflicting duties, e.g., duties stemming from different relationships (e.g., family) and communities (workplace) to which decision-makers may belong.

In business administration, *duty-based thinking* appears in appeals to principles like the fiduciary duties and obligations of Boards of Directors; invocations of "public trust" in connection with calls for more independence in the accounting profession; and in calls for corporate community involvement.

Illustrations of duty-based avenues

Recent debates over the "patriotism" of corporations that move their headquarters offshore to avoid taxes indicate that *duty-based thinking* is alive and well in US society. (*CALPERS* came close to eliminating such companies from its portfolio; and the US Congress came close to changing the law on this subject.) Controversies surrounding "socially responsible investing" (SRI), both in the US and in the European Union invoke obligations and responsibilities (*duty-based*) of investors (institutional and individual) to contribute to the common good and avoid supporting socially destructive enterprises (e.g., cigarette companies).

A recent case series entitled *US Citizen Bank* revolves around the question of whether banks marketing credit to potentially vulnerable populations (immigrants, senior citizens, students who are new to credit) have a special *duty* that they might not have in relation to the rest of their customers, whatever the bank's interests might be.[55]

In general, ethical challenges over "divided loyalties" involve *duty-based thinking*, e.g., work/family; employer/client; company/community; department/college/university.

Virtue-based avenues

In virtue-based thinking, decisions are subjected to scrutiny not on the basis of their consequences for individuals' interests or rights, or for their conformity with duties of fidelity. The focus here is on developing and reinforcing certain habits of the heart, character traits, and, in the case of organizations, cultures. (The focus is also on *avoiding* certain habits, vices, and cultures that could corrupt the decision-maker.) The traditional list of basic (or "cardinal") virtues includes prudence, temperance, courage, and justice. Theologians add faith, hope, and love to this list.[56] "Love, and do what you will," said Augustine, indicating that the virtue of love was ethically more basic and more directly practical than attempting to determine "the right thing to do" (in terms of interests, rights, duties). *Newsweek* magazine devoted an issue to the theme of virtue-based ethics in American culture. One of the articles observed that:

> [T]he cultivation of virtue makes individuals happy, wise, courageous, competent. The result is a good person, a responsible citizen and parent, a trusted leader, possibly even a saint. Without virtuous people, according to this tradition, society cannot function well. And without a virtuous society, individuals cannot realize either their own or the common good.[57]

There is an emphasis in virtue-based analysis on cultivating the traits and habits that *give rise* to actions and policies, on the belief that too often "the right thing to do" cannot be identified or described *in advance* using one of the other avenues. The justification of virtue-based thinking in terms of the moral insight invokes both *universal identification* and *impartial generalization* – which give rise to virtues like "compassion" and "fairness." In the Christian tradition, "love of God" is included as part of the moral insight and is manifested in the virtues of faith, hope, and love.

Problems or questions associated with the *virtue-based thinking* include:

- What are the central virtues and their relative priorities in a postmodern world in which moral consensus seems fragmented?
- Are there timeless character traits that are not culture-bound, so that we can recommend them to anyone, particularly those in leadership roles?

In business administration, the language of virtue is often heard in executive hiring situations as well as in management-development training. Some of the more popular management books in recent years have hinted at virtue-based thinking in their titles: *In Search of Excellence* (Peters and Waterman, 1982), *The Seven Habits of Highly Effective People* (Covey, 1989), *Good to Great* (Collins, 2001).

Illustrations of virtue-based avenues

The Columbia Accident Investigation Board report (August 28, 2003) insisted that "NASA's organizational *culture* and structure had as much to do with this accident as the external tank foam." So too, we might argue, with the cultures of Enron, Arthur Andersen, WorldCom, and Tyco.[58]

It is important to emphasize that these four "avenues" for ethical thinking give rise to what philosophers often call prima facie moral guidelines. That is, each "avenue" suggests ethical norms, but no one avenue, *by itself*, is ethically definitive. If three or all four avenues point collectively to a positive or a negative assessment for a given option, decision-makers may take this as *a strong case* for or against that option. (See Figure 3.6 combining rationality and respect in the corporate mindset.)

If and when avenues *conflict*, however, decision-makers must think through the nature of the conflict – asking whether they are prepared to affirm the positives and override the negatives in comparable cases. They are not encouraged to conclude in such cases that *moral insight* is unattainable – or that the *moral point of view* is subjective, arbitrary, or self-contradictory. A legitimate conclusion, instead, is that *moral insight* in this case is more elusive and must continue to be sought through further reflection and dialogue.

We might imagine the avenues as analogous to a *jury* of deliberative voices from which we seek a verdict – voices that are interest-based, rights-based, duty-based, and virtue-based. We hope that this jury will speak with unanimity and strong conviction. As with a more conventional jury in the context of judicial proceedings, we are dealing with ordinary human beings, not gods, but we look to them for dispassionate reflection with appropriate diversity in their approaches to ethical conclusions.[59] Most of us do not believe that a jury is immune from error and misjudgment – that what a jury says must, even if unanimous, be correct *just because the jury said so*. But most of us *do* believe that the jury system is the best of the systematic alternatives that we have for reaching a fair and just outcome. As the judgments of juries are our best approximations to *justice* in matters of *law* – the voices represented in the four avenues and the corrections for psychological biases are our best approximations to the *moral point of view* in matters of applied *ethics*.

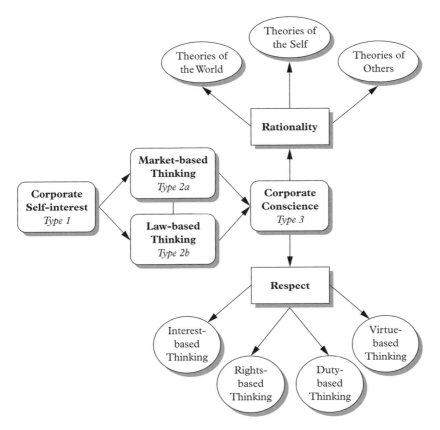

Figure 3.6 Mindset typology and corporate conscience: Theories of world, self and others (rationality) and four avenues of ethical analysis (respect)

Combining rationality and respect

In this chapter, I have introduced the idea of conscience as a mindset that provides an antidote to teleopathy, and we have seen how the inner structure of conscience (a) involves a developmental typology by analogy with Piaget, and (b) includes two core values at its most mature stage: rationality and respect. We saw that *rationality* often involves correcting for certain biases in our perception of the world in which we make decisions, in our thinking about other persons, and in our attitudes toward ourselves. And we have seen that *respect* includes four families ("avenues") of thinking anchored in interests, rights, duties, and virtues.

The task of searching out the insight provided by the *moral point of view* is no small task, partly because the voices involved may not always agree, but also because decision-makers may not recognize the potential biases involved with their "theories" about the world, others, and themselves. The success of the process depends on awareness of the different voices of the avenues and the psychological theories as we apply them to ethical situations. In addition, we must avoid "falling back" on other tempting ways of thinking, using *surrogates* for ethical reflection rather than the real thing – surrogates like personal self-interest, market competition, and existing law and regulation.[60] We must strive for quality, breadth, and honesty in our consideration of all of the avenues and potential biases we may encounter.

Conclusion

Corporations caught up in the worship of market competition and government regulation *as excuses for ethical indifference* must discover new policies and practices for humanizing their decision-making. Communism has demonstrated its economic and political weaknesses. It remains for modern capitalism in an age of globalization to demonstrate that it is capable of a more human demeanor and worthy of a significant level of *trust*. This sentiment is articulated well by Francis Fukuyama in his insightful book *Trust: The Social Virtues and the Creation of Prosperity*.[61] It also lies behind the wager that Harvard's Lynn Paine places on capitalism:

> What is the most likely future: a world in which companies are expected to behave as moral actors, or a return to the corporate amorality doctrine? . . . [A] future in which companies are expected to show a moral face to the world while at the same time fulfilling their functions as wealth creators, producers, and employers.[62]

The life of a corporation is similar in some ways to the life of an individual, and this may have a bearing on the way we think about the response of business to the "occupational hazard" identified in Chapter 1. *Teleopathy* bears some resemblance to the "pre-moral" stages of child development. The unbalanced pursuit of purpose is the most significant obstacle to adulthood – but also the most significant obstacle to a healthy organization and a healthy market economy. Corporations that are fixated on economic objectives without restraint – rationalizing a lack of concern for the well-being of many stakeholders (employees, customers, and local communities) – must become aware of this fact and find a collective conscience. They must put into place internal safeguards against blindness and detachment.

4

Challenges to the Very Idea

The difficulty for many CEOs is encapsulated in this kind of thinking: "I operate in a hypercompetitive global marketplace. My primary responsibility is to be profitable in order to serve my shareholders. I have to obey the local laws, for sure. I must also follow the laws imposed by the country in which I am head-quartered if they apply overseas. But if I go beyond that – if I pay wages or uphold environmental standards that are higher than legally required in a foreign country, and if that causes my company to be less competitive than my rivals and hence to be less profitable, am I doing the right thing?"

(Jeffrey Garten (2002))[1]

The proper business of business is business. No apology required.

The Economist (20 January 2005)

In Chapter 1, the occupational hazard of *teleopathy* was introduced and explained. Chapter 2 focused on the idea of a mindset as a vehicle for understanding teleopathy in the individual and in the organization. In Chapter 3, we explored the idea of conscience as a mindset that protects against the hazard, a mindset anchored in both rationality and respect. Conscience in corporate culture can be seen developmentally (as it can be seen in children) – Type 1 through Type 3 thinking. We saw that the contours of rationality are evolving in more communitarian directions according to a number of commentators, and as psychological distortions of rational judgment are identified, their avoidance goes a long way toward accommodating both self-interested *and* other-centered thinking. At the same time, the contours of *respect* are evident in stakeholder thinking that takes others' interests, rights, duties, and virtues seriously.

Philosophically, the stimulus (*teleopathy*) should be met with a response (*conscience*) in the life of the corporation just as much as in the life of the individual. But is the argument for conscience and its presence as a mindset in corporate culture really so straightforward? Unfortunately, there is resistance. And in this chapter, we shall look at various objections and replies – challenges to *the very idea* of corporate conscience.

Can Conscience Be Trusted?

Let us begin with an illustrative story from poet David Whyte's book *The Heart Aroused*. Whyte attributes the story to a friend of his named Joel Henning:

> The idea, issuing from the boardroom, was to offer tempting prizes and outlandish financial rewards to the one department in the company that could achieve the highest level of growth over the following financial year. Before long it became evident that one particular department had it completely sewn up, and Jim Harrison, the vice president in charge of that area, was the hero of the occasion. By the end of the following financial year his department had doubled its income; no one else came even close to the seductive figures appearing on his reports to the president. Harrison was sent back and forth across the country to give speeches and talks at all the company plants. The toast of the company, by the middle of the following year he had been disgraced and fired. The success of Jim Harrison was based on the neglect of every constituent part of the system except the one order programmed from above to improve profitability. *Rather than being educated into the broad needs of the business, he was manipulated to produce one result at all costs. In his turn he reflected back to upper management an almost Biblical parable of their own narrow vision.* To achieve this, his department had dropped all its education and training programs, stopped all new hiring, cut its research and development to the bone, and instilled the chill atmosphere of a police state onto the office floor. In the second year Harrison's department *lost* money at a greater rate than any other department. His people were leaving in droves despite the glittering prizes of the previous year, he had trained no one to replace them, and there were no new products appearing on the horizon for them to sell.[2]

This story illustrates what I have called the *unbalanced pursuit of purpose*. It indicates how business life, like political life, can frequently suffer from an atmosphere in which destructive behavior is actually incentivized or encouraged.[3] In the same spirit, we recall with chagrin from Chapter 1 the comment of former McKinsey Managing Director Ron Daniel: "[W]e look to hire people who are first, very smart; second, insecure and thus driven by their insecurity; and third, competitive."[4]

Whyte's story and the Ron Daniel quote embody our concerns on one side of a longstanding social dilemma: Americans are apprehensive about organizational tendencies to become fixated on goals while putting ethical considerations aside. This apprehension has been exacerbated in the wake of the corporate scandals of 2002, beginning with Enron and Arthur Andersen. The Sarbanes-Oxley Act is a powerful testimony to the intensity of that concern.[5]

Nevertheless, our attitudes toward the scandals are *conflicted* at a fairly deep level, revealing the "other half" of our dilemma. For we are *also* apprehensive about the most natural way to resolve these problems. *We are apprehensive about the very idea of "corporate conscience" – bringing ethics into the decision-making of organizations.* Let us explore this classic approach-avoidance conflict.

Distrust of Spirituality and Religion

In a June 1993 cover story in *Training* magazine entitled "The Search for Spirit in the Workplace," authors Chris Lee and Ron Zemke mentioned the baby-boom generation's quest for a spiritual home.[6] But what is particularly significant for purposes of understanding the dilemma to which I have been referring is the authors' acknowledgment that there is real *worry* about this emphasis on spirituality in the workplace. The skeptics seem to see the work–spirituality linkage either as a "fad" or as a dangerous and imperious intrusion, an invitation to inefficiency and lack of accountability in both private and public sector economic activity. Management guru Tom Peters (co-author of *In Search of Excellence*) lamented that "by getting overtly into the spiritual stuff, the pendulum is swinging too far." Peters apparently feared the loss of a safe secularity in the quest for ethical values in business. In Peters' less-than-eloquent phrasing: "When you cross the line between the secular and the spiritual you're edging up on something that bugs me."[7]

But the problem goes deeper. The *Reell Precision Manufacturing* (RPM) case series, in which a Minnesota company articulates its ethical convictions in explicitly Judeo-Christian terms, never fails to elicit suspicion from a substantial number of my students, both graduate and undergraduate. The students' first concern in the case discussion is about company leaders seeking to "impose their religious values" on employees.[8] It is interesting to observe, however, that when I ask students whether their apprehension about the RPM case is anchored in the Judeo-Christian language of the company's "Direction Statement" or in the ethical substance of that statement (abstracted from any faith-based source), their response is *equivocal*. The issue moves from "imposing religious values" to "imposing values" period, full stop. Arguments against the sacred or the spiritual often mask underlying arguments about moral substance of *any* kind, *including* the secular.[9]

Distrust of Secular Conscience as Well

Even if we do not cross the line that "bugs" Tom Peters, there are obstacles. For our postmodern culture identifies *almost any substantive moral commitment*, whether its foundation be faith or reason, as suspect.

Many arguments offered in legal and regulatory contexts[10] caution against too much "moral discretion" on the part of corporate leaders, presumably out of a concern that fiduciary responsibility might be threatened without significant boundaries on executive conscience. Even though most states in the US passed "constituency statutes" to protect corporate boards of directors that sought during the hostile takeovers of the 1980s to consider the interests of all stakeholders, not just the stockholders, the often-voiced counter-arguments were (and still are) that directors should stick to their knitting and tend to the *principal* stakeholders – the stockholders – those who put up the capital. Even long-time champions of corporate social responsibility like Christopher Stone have been cautious about encouraging the transformation of private sector corporations into public sector organizations.[11]

As indicated in the Introduction of this book, the second half of the dilemma about the Enrons and Andersens of the business world manifests itself in our reluctance to prescribe the most obvious cure for the problem of the first half, namely, the use of *moral* criteria to balance managerial (and political) decision-making.

Think of it. *We emphasize the importance of ethics in business and in politics, but are often reluctant to see chief executives and politicians take our advice!* For many in American society, it appears to be *essential, yet somehow both dangerous and illegitimate, to guide business decision-making by moral values.* It appears to be essential because the requirements of business life are often so intensely goal-directed that they blind both individuals and organizations to the ethical aspects of what they do. It appears to be dangerous and illegitimate because appeals by organizational leaders to ethical values, when they are not looked upon as questionably sincere, are often looked upon as outside either their zone of discretion or their competence.[12]

Even management guru Peter Drucker gives expression to this conundrum in one of his most widely read articles:

> In a society of organizations, each of the new institutions is concerned only with its own purpose and mission. It does not claim power over anything else. But it also does not assume responsibility for anything else. Who, then, is concerned with the common good?[13]

Rationality seems safe, but *respect* seems less safe. So much for the statement of our conflictedness. But if we now ask what we typically *do* in the face of that conflictedness, the answer turns on the simple fact that *nature* (including "organizational" nature) *abhors a moral vacuum.*

Our social reality seems to be that ethics is more easily *invoked* than *institutionalized.* Efforts to avoid the "occupational hazard" are muffled by worries about fanaticism and fiduciaries. The *very idea* of conscience in corporate culture presents more formidable challenges to ethically motivated managers than we may have anticipated.

Calls for integrity and responsibility in institutional life – usually in the wake of scandals like Enron and Andersen – seem to lose energy and effect on a regular basis. Like pebbles in a pond, their initial splash dissipates and seldom results in very much structural or cultural change. Business-as-usual (and politics-as-usual) is reinforced *by the system itself* in many ways.[14]

Is Corporate Conscience Really Necessary?

Objections to the very idea of corporate conscience come from several quarters, some from the left and some from the right in conventional political and ideological terms. Let us catalogue them under two broad headings: objections to the *necessity* of corporate conscience (in this section), and objections to the *legitimacy* of corporate conscience (in the next section).

Under the first heading, we find objections claiming that there are other forces at work in the environment of the modern corporation that serve as surrogates or substitutes, making it *unnecessary* to invoke the idea of corporate conscience. These objections appeal broadly either to (a) the market and competitive forces or (b) the law and regulatory forces.

The market-based objection

Market approval is often thought to be the most effective ethical influence on business. Measured by stock price, market share, or (in the entertainment industry) box office receipts and Nielsen ratings, market approval is the economic analogue to electoral approval in a democracy. Appeals to ethical considerations *beyond* the discipline of market forces are seen by some as unenlightened, economically unsophisticated. A special survey in a January 2005 issue of *The Economist* articulated this objection well:

> The premise that CSR [Corporate Social Responsibility] advocates never question is in fact wrong. It is an error to suppose that profit-seeking, as such, fails to advance the public good, and that special efforts to give something back to society are needed to redeem it.[15]

Criticizing the idea of "triple bottom line" economic, social, and environmental reporting, the *Economist* editors write: "The great virtue of the single bottom line is that it holds managers to account for something. The triple bottom line does not. It is not so much a license to operate as a license to obfuscate."[16] The editors go on, invoking the patron saint of market forces, Adam Smith (1732–90):

> Thus, the selfish pursuit of profit serves a social purpose. And this is putting it mildly. The standard of living people in the West enjoy today is due to little else but the selfish pursuit of profit. It is a point that Adam Smith emphasized in "The Wealth of Nations": "It is not from the benevolence of the butcher, the brewer, or the baker, that we expect our dinner, but from their regard to their own interest." This is not the fatal defect of capitalism, as CSR-advocates appear to believe; it is the very reason capitalism works.[17]

The basic idea here is straightforward. If markets are kept competitive – that is, if monopolies are prevented – the forces of business competition will generate the most efficient use of economic resources and ultimately the greatest social good. The role of the state, on this view, must be kept to a minimum. The state should serve as umpire of the competition, keeping it fair. It should perhaps also see to certain basic redistributions of wealth through progressive taxation. What it should *not* do is usurp the market's role in the economy. The implication for the corporation is that morality is not its business. The concept of corporate conscience is either out of place, or, what comes to the same thing, exhausted by the obligations of market competition.

Replying to the market-based objection

In responding to this objection, we should acknowledge an important truth that it contains, namely the ethical value of market forces in attracting resources to socially valued goods and services. Market-based economic systems are *not* value-neutral. They are respectful of freedom, enterprise, efficiency, innovation, and growth. The fact that most business leaders are, simply by being competitive, already making an important social contribution is an important fact. Similarly, it is an important fact that most individuals do what is necessary to grow and stay healthy, support themselves, and pursue happiness.

In an editorial entitled "Leaders: Bad Arguments against the Good Company?" that appeared online in *Ethical Corporation* just days after the *Economist* survey, the following response to the market-based objection appears:

> Nobel Prize winning economist Joseph Stiglitz proved that where the market lacks perfect information or perfect competition – in other words always – the pursuit of self-interest may indeed be in conflict with the interests of shareholders and others touched by the corporation's activities.
> *The Economist* acknowledges the real world problem of building "externalities" into the pricing mechanism. These public goods – including a clean environment, water for life, a stable climate, biodiversity, beautiful countryside – are often not priced at all into goods that consume those resources. The resource – often a resource without substitute – is consumed with impunity.[18]

In other words, the question is not whether market forces contribute value to society, but whether individual and organizational decision-making are sufficiently conscientious *simply by virtue of those forces*. It seems clear that the answer is *no*. Indeed, even the editors of *The Economist* seem to acknowledge this point, affirming that there *is* such a thing as business ethics and that "managers need to be clear about that."[19]

There are ethically responsible and ethically irresponsible ways to engage in market competition and this tells us that the market alone is not a sufficient substitute for conscience. Ethics is not about whether market competition is *valuable*; it is about whether conscience has a critical role to play *within* market competition.[20]

The law-based objection

The other "necessity objection" appeals to the law and regulatory forces as surrogates for corporate conscience. It comes from those who would prefer to see the state provide whatever "conscience" the corporation might need – through the courts, the legislature, and the regulatory process. Again, the editors of *The Economist* weigh in:

> The proper guardians of the public interest are governments, which are accountable to all citizens. It is the job of elected politicians to set goals for regulators, to deal with externalities, to mediate among different interests, to attend to the demands of social justice, to provide public goods and collect the taxes to pay for them, to establish collective priorities where that is necessary and appropriate, and to organize resources accordingly.[21]

The thought is that organizations, especially corporations, are essentially engines of profit, driven by special interests – and that the guidance of these entities for *moral* purposes must be external. Law and the political process, it would be added, are the appropriate sources for this external guidance. "Moralizing" the behavior of the corporation is best achieved not by modeling its decision-making processes on those of the responsible individual, but by using whatever legal sanctions are available to make wrongdoing unprofitable. Government regulation, not corporate self-regulation is the key to business ethics:

> All things considered, there is much to be said for leaving social and economic policy to governments. They, at least, are accountable to voters. Managers lack the time for such endeavors, or should do. Lately they have found it a struggle even to discharge their obligations to

shareholders, the people who are paying their wages. If they want to make the world a better place – a commendable aim, to be sure – let them concentrate for the time being on that.[22]

In the US, there is a multi-layered network of laws (e.g., The Foreign Corrupt Practices Act of 1977 and the Sarbanes-Oxley Act of 2002) and regulations, represented by agencies like the FDA, the FCC, the EPA and OSHA. In this domain, an organization's "conscientiousness" takes many forms, including complex reports, board level committees, external auditors, preliminary rulings, and paying the costs of lobbying, usually for industry protection. There are also international treaties and regional trade agreements (like NAFTA) that for some governments and corporations represent the highest moral authorities.

Replying to the law-based objection

This objection only partially resolves the problem pointed out in the response to the previous objection. That problem is the need for sound, responsible judgment in the exercise of market freedom. Laws and regulations usually bring a moderating influence to the decision-making processes of both individuals and organizations. But laws and regulations may be too little too late, or too much too late – and in any case, they are *themselves* the products of organizational decision-making.

The *Ethical Corporation* rejoinder has this to say about the law-based objection:

> Governments lack the political will to act against problems of social justice that transcend borders, even where those problems originate at least in part from within their borders. We lack the necessary global institutions to counteract this reluctance, and global businesses have the power to exploit it.[23]

Even *The Economist*'s editors – eloquent skeptics regarding CSR – quoted approvingly from Elaine Sternberg (philosopher, consultant, and former investment banker) in her book, *Just Business*[24] that there are two main things, "ordinary decency" and "distributive justice," that need to guide the pursuit of the goals of the firm. "Without these basic values, business would not be possible."[25]

A former colleague of mine at the Harvard Business School, Shoshana Zuboff, has spoken to this matter in terms of the rebuilding of society's trust:

[We] have to invent a thousand new ways to rebuild trust, because that's what will make us rich, both financially and in our quality of life. This means facing up to a problem that can't be fixed by regulation or legislation. *What's wrong is that nobody seems to know what's wrong anymore.*[26]

To acknowledge the importance of values like decency and justice in corporate decision-making is to appreciate the insufficiency of both market forces and legal constraints as surrogates or substitutes for conscience. Let us now consider the objections and replies associated with our second main category, what we have called *legitimacy* objections.

Is corporate conscience really legitimate?

Under the second of our two original broad headings, are objections claiming that even if the market and the law are, strictly speaking insufficient as surrogates for corporate conscience, it is *illegitimate* for corporations (and their leaders) to invoke the idea of corporate conscience. These objections appeal broadly to: (a) the property rights of *shareholders*; (b) the rights of *employees* to be free of moral coercion; and/or (c) the risks to *society* of a wasteful and even dangerous implementation of the very idea of corporate conscience.

The shareholder-based objection

Probably no objections to the legitimacy of corporate conscience are more frequently mounted than those based on the property rights of shareholders. The keystone here is the agency relationship between management and the providers of capital (the shareholders). The overriding fiduciary duty of managers and boards of directors to shareholders is said to trump any moral imperatives that might be defended in the name of corporate conscience. To quote again from the editors of *The Economist*:

The crucial point is that managers of public companies do not own the businesses they run. They are employed by the firms' owners to maximize the long-term value of the owners' assets. Putting those assets to any other use is cheating the owners, and that is unethical. If a manager believes that the business he is working for is causing harm to society at large, the right thing to do is not to work for that business in the first place. Nothing obliges someone who believes that the tobacco industry is evil to work in that industry. But if someone accepts a salary to manage a tobacco business in the interests of its owners, he has an obligation to those owners. To flout that obligation is unethical.[27]

Note that this objection does not claim – like the market-based objection – that market forces are simply sufficient *substitutes* for corporate conscience. It goes further to claim that it is *wrong* to try to institutionalize conscience beyond the fiduciary obligations of managers to shareholders. The only legitimate moral consideration is, in the end, a kind of *loyalty*.

British commentator Digby Anderson gives voice to this objection in an essay entitled "Good Companies Don't Have Missions" when he writes:

> Those outside a company are entitled to their views as to what they think its responsibilities are – including the stakeholder view. But it raises severe problems when this view is espoused or even toyed with by the Board. It threatens the clear and special responsibility to the shareholder. These extra moral liabilities are yet more obligations to be settled before the poor shareholder gets his share. Moreover, in stakeholder theory, they are to be imposed whether or not the shareholder agrees to them. Even if they could be shown to be moral obligations, they threaten the company's existing and special moral obligation to its shareholders. By making the Board responsible to plural persons and bodies they pose the problem: by what rule will the Board decide the priority of its plural and competing obligations?[28]

Anderson believes that mission statements that articulate lofty moral aims for corporations go beyond the limits set by both law and morality for corporate leaders. He and others would apply the same principle to corporate philanthropy, claiming that it usurps the prerogatives of shareholders to give to charity in their own names. Again, *The Economist* editors:

> Remember that corporate philanthropy is charity with other people's money – which is not philanthropy at all. When a company gives some of its profits away in a good cause, its managers are indulging their charitable instincts not at their own expense but at the expense of the firm's owners. That is a morally dubious transaction.[29]

96

Such critics argue that CEOs who would emulate Robin Hood can and should expect protests and lawsuits from their shareholders.[30]

Replying to the shareholder-based objection

Ethical Corporation challenged the above lines of argument head on: "It is unethical, argues *The Economist*, for directors to act against the profit interests of the owners to whom they owe a fiduciary duty. Is ethics that simple?"[31] Is it possible for us to *require* that the consciences of managers and directors be *silenced* in the name of an overarching fiduciary duty? If ethical obligations to shareholders conflict occasionally with ethical obligations to other stakeholders, "the ethical solution may well not fulfill the legal duty."

> Are company directors to be denied freedom of conscience? Go and work somewhere where your conscience is not offended, retorts *The Economist*. Yet no industry is free of ethical issues requiring a trade-off between the interests of shareholders and other stakeholders.[32]

My own response to this challenge is based on a principle that I once called the *Nemo Dat* principle.[33] We might think of this principle as a formal requirement of consistency in business ethics (and professional ethics generally):

> *Nemo Dat Principle*: Investors cannot expect of managers (more generally, principals cannot expect of their agents) behavior that would be inconsistent with the reasonable ethical expectations of the community.

While Digby Anderson may be right to remind us of the special relationship between shareholders and boards of directors, he is wrong to imply that shareholders are free to demand *anything* of their agents (management and the board). Investors are not morally immune in their relationships with those who do their bidding. *There is a moral proviso*. The responsibilities of management toward stakeholders are extensions of the obligations that *stockholders themselves* would be expected to honor in their own right.

Harvard Professor Lynn Paine reinforced this point eloquently in her 2003 book, *Value Shift*, when she compared the fiduciary relationship to the parental relationship:

> Becoming an agent for shareholders does not cancel out this general obligation [to refrain from injuring innocent third parties] any more

than, for example, becoming a parent does. Just because parents are obliged to protect and promote their children's interests, they are not therefore relieved of the usual duties of citizenship or permitted to wrong others.[34]

The point, Paine argues persuasively, is quite general, and it undermines what she refers to as "the fiduciary objection" – what I am calling the shareholder-based objection:

> This result follows from the basic logic of obligation. Except under exigent circumstances, an obligation to one party cannot normally be unilaterally extinguished by taking on an obligation to another. By the same token, general obligations to the community at large – to refrain from fraud, avoid injury, respect others' rights, obey the law – cannot be extinguished simply by taking on special obligations to particular individuals. In other words, if it is wrong to steal to enrich oneself, it does not become right to steal to enrich someone else.[35]

The conscientious corporation maintains its private economic mission, but in the context of fundamental moral obligations owed by any member of society to others affected by that member's actions. Recognizing such obligations does *not* thereby transform an institution into a public one. Private institutions, like private individuals, can be and are bound to respect moral obligations in the pursuit of private purposes. This conviction appears to underlie the argument against the sufficiency of law found in the response of *Ethical Corporation* to the *Economist* articles of January 2005:

> Given legal constructs of the company that deny the reality of business' place in society, such actions [based on stakeholder thinking] might be considered a form of civil disobedience to the injustice of a law-embedded ethic that considers important only the interests of one party to a social relation. . . . [But if] capitalism and ethics are in conflict, it is not its ethics that society will change.[36]

The *Nemo Dat* principle mentioned above is the primary warrant for this line of argument.

The employee-based objection

The second legitimacy objection points to the rights of employees to be free of moral coercion. The idea is that while it sounds laudable for business leaders to try to influence the value orientations of individuals within or outside the corporation – this is (at worst) impossible and (at best) imperious. That is, corporate conscience – because it involves the *culture* of the organization – involves a kind of *coercion* that is as questionable as the actions of the "company towns" of yesteryear. The issue is analogous to the challenge of civil liberties in a pluralistic society.

Replying to the employee-based objection

There are clearly boundaries on how organizations should implement shared values, respecting individual rights, but these rights are themselves limited within the "at-will" employment relationship.

The core of this objection seems to be that the articulation of corporate norms and their associated disciplines – what we will later call institutionalization – amounts automatically to a kind of coercion of the members of the group. But this is to forget the fact that members (and groups for that matter) have *choices* about participation. It is the element of choice in this arena that underlies the free market system in a democratic society. If we treat all forms of institutional mission and conscience as mindless "impositions of values," we are falling into a postmodernist trap that Clarence Walton, in his book, *Archons and Acolytes*, warned us against. We end up aligning ourselves with those who believe that "convictions are simply tentative holdings of insecure minds." But, Walton adds, "If you believe that what you believe is no better than what others believe, then you do not really believe."[37]

If ethical awareness cannot lead us in the direction of ethical wisdom, and if there is no way to tell the difference between ethical wisdom and ethical bankruptcy, then surely the *coerciveness* objection gains a foothold. We shall see in Part II of this book that managing shared values *without coercion* (which does not mean *without discipline*) is one of the central tasks of effective leadership.

The society-based objection

If the first legitimacy objection relates to *shareholders* and the second to *employees*, the third warns of risks to *society* of wasteful and even dangerous behavior in the name of corporate conscience. A warning of this kind was on the minds of *The Economist* editors: "Unwarranted, misguided or contradictory public demands on companies,

99

especially if these demands emerge in due course as government mandates, can affect decisions in such a way as to detach profitable business conduct from the public good."[38]

The alleged illegitimacy comes from misguidedness, not from bad intentions – but the results can be socially costly nonetheless. An uninformed *rhetoric* of corporate responsibility is wasteful when it is not harmful in other ways.

Replying to the society-based objection

In some ways, this objection is self-answering, because it is premised on ignorance of causes and effects, consequences and relationships of policies and patterns of behavior. Misguided conscience is not the objective in combating teleopathy. Enlightened and informed conscience is the objective – both personally and organizationally. Even the editors of *The Economist* seem to agree:

> Does this mean that managers need not concern themselves with ethics? Just the opposite. Managers should think much harder about business ethics than they appear to at present. It is lack of clarity about business ethics that gives rise to confusion over what managers' responsibilities are, and over where the limits of those responsibilities lie.[39]

And their otherwise adamant critics at *Ethical Corporation* join in this view, articulating in the process a version of what I have been calling the *moral projection* principle:

> The common thread running through these arguments is that being a corporation does not entitle a business to approach its social relations differently from any other element of society. The social responsibility of business is the same as that of everyone else. So what standard of behaviour does society expect? Moral philosophy yields a wealth of responses.[40]

Taking Stock

We began this chapter with the realization that there is a fairly deep ambivalence in our society over the very idea of corporate conscience. Teleopathy seems clearly to be a moral and social hazard that calls for a response. So we cast about for other solutions, *and what we often settle for are surrogates or counterfeits of conscience.*[41] Because we are skeptical about the necessity and the legitimacy of a *moral* response (like corporate conscience), we look to the market, law, and regulation instead.

The conventional surrogates seem to respond to worries about unethical business conduct *and* to worries about incompetence, fanaticism, and fiduciaries. They provide more-or-less "objective" and "reliable" standards (market value, legal compliance), accompanied by visible, public criteria (codes, rules, measurement systems, and sanctions). They supply us with a sense of discipline and orderliness in organizational life without the risks of runaway private mysticism and spirituality that so "bugged" Tom Peters. What more could we want? What more *should* we want? Isn't this the profile of the institutional habits of a postmodern society at the beginning of the twenty-first century?

But alas! When faced with the replies to the objections, and ultimately the *inadequacy* of the surrogates – both individually and collectively – we have little choice but to face our moral skepticism once again. We have little choice but to ask soberly with *Ethical Corporation*: "If not by virtue of markets . . . and if not necessarily with the intervention of government, what will drive corporations to conduct themselves as society expects?"[42] Indeed, Peter Drucker asks a similar question, with the implication that we must find an answer to it: "In a society of organizations, each of the new institutions is concerned only with its own purpose and mission. It does not claim *power* over anything else. But it also does not assume *responsibility* for anything else. Who, then, is concerned with the common good?"[43]

The "scare" involved in taking conscience seriously can be transcended in the face of the problems that go with failing to do so. This, at least, is a hypothesis worth testing.

Deja-vu in Modern Ethics

We have come to a point which may seem vaguely familiar to philosophers who may be reading this book. I ask other readers to be patient with a brief historical excursion that I believe is relevant to the current issue of conscience and its counterfeits in organizational ethics.

Early in twentieth-century ethical theory, a key debate centered on the definability of basic concepts like "the right" and "the good." So-called "naturalists" offered *definitions* of, or *substitutions* for, these terms aimed at putting normative ethics on a solid, usually empirical, foundation. Without translations of the basic predicates of ethics, naturalists argued, we would never be in a position to *verify* ethical claims about right and wrong, good and bad, virtue and vice. And without *verifiability*, we were left with nonsense or fanaticism or, at best, highly personal expressions of moral emotion.

On the opposite side of this now-classic debate were the "intuitionists," who, while they agreed that ethics had to avoid nonsense, fanaticism, and mere emotivism – insisted that the solution lay not in empirical definitions of "the right" and "the good." The solution lay instead in recognizing that these core ideas of ethics were *simple* and *indefinable* – and that moral answers were to be found more directly, more intuitively, than the naturalists thought. Indeed, one of the most powerful weapons in the arsenal of the intuitionists was the "Open Question Argument" made famous by British philosopher G. E. Moore.

Confronted with a naturalistic definition or translation of "good," such as "pleasurable" or "preference-satisfying," Moore would ask if the question "This is pleasurable (or preference-satisfying), but is it good?" *made any sense*. If it *did* make sense, then identifying "good" with "pleasurable" (or preference-satisfying) was mistaken. Intuitionists like Moore, H. A. Pritchard, and others were convinced that this line of argument extended far beyond the case at hand, revealing a basic flaw in the definitional program itself – what came to be called the "Naturalistic Fallacy." The question would *always* remain open because *no satisfactory substitute could ever be found for ethical intuition.*

Now, this old debate in ethical theory may seem quaint and irrelevant to the challenges of organizational ethics in our new millennium, but we should look more closely. For while applied ethics today is less preoccupied with the language of "indefinability" and "simple properties," it is *very much* preoccupied with how to translate ethical values into organizational operations.[44] The open question in today's context becomes: "This is permitted by market forces and the law, but is it good?"

Systems So Perfect . . .

T. S. Eliot once observed that humankind spends a great deal of time "dreaming of systems so perfect that no one will need to be good."[45] The power of this poetic phrase can be appreciated in connection with the objections and replies identified above. And it can serve as a useful warning when in Part II the objective is to operationalize conscience.

The "systems so perfect" are the *external* systems of the market, the law and regulatory machinery of government, the social infrastructure that supports constituency threats to executive decision-makers, and the *internal* organizational systems of rewards, incentives, and sanctions that guide the behavior of individual managers. But the "dreaming" in Eliot's phrase signals the limitations of such systems relative to the need for individuals and organizations to be *good*.

The central question in applied ethics in the twenty-first century is a practical analogue of the central challenge in ethical theory at the beginning of the twentieth century: *Can we identify a system or a process to guide organizational decision-making so that no one will need to be good?*[46] If we affirm the need for ethical categories to avoid teleopathy, and yet are conflicted by concerns of fanaticism, subjective judgments, and fiduciary responsibility, can we find suitable *systemic* substitutes for conscience – either outside the organization or inside? Can we dream up systems so perfect that they escape "open questions"? "Yes, this practice is warranted by the market, but is it good? Or yes, this policy is permitted by the law, but is it right?"

It is my conviction that the quest for "systems so perfect" in organizational ethics is doomed to failure because there are no such systems. And the reason lies in what we have already seen in Chapter 3 as the nature of conscience itself – a form of *thoughtfulness* (Arendt) or *awareness* (DeMello) that cannot be "outsourced" or "automated" as many organizational functions can be (like payroll services, employee assistance programs, and advertising campaigns).

Conscience as Systematic Awareness

So now we ask, is there a way to avoid the unbalanced pursuit of purpose on the one hand and moral fanaticism on the other – *without* relying solely on the "systems so perfect" that capitalism so often embraces "so that no one will need to be good"? My answer, here and throughout Part II of this book, is that we *can* try to build ethical awareness or conscience as a mindset into organizational cultures. As the editors of *Ethical Corporation* responded to the editors of *The Economist*:

That means embedding a culture that questions the firm's impacts on other members of society, striving to gain empathy with those stakeholder concerns through dialogue, then agreeing [upon] any necessary trade-offs between stakeholder interests, including those of shareholders.[47]

What drove us to surrogates was the worry that conscience was somehow too subjective – and so too unstable – to serve as a foundation for business judgment. But what if this worry is exaggerated? What if there really is something we could call a *shared moral consciousness*, which we can approach in a disciplined way rather than fleeing it as if it were fragile and fragmentary?[48] Peter Drucker answers the question he posed about "who is concerned with the common good?":

[We have] to think through how to balance two apparently contradictory requirements. Organizations must competently perform the one social function for the sake of which they exist – the school to teach, the hospital to cure the sick, and the business to produce goods, services, or the capital to provide for the risks of the future. They can do so only if they single-mindedly concentrate on their specialized mission. But there is also society's need for these organizations to take social responsibility – to work on the problems and challenges of the community. Together, these organizations *are* the community.[49]

What if, like a corporation's strategy, a corporation's conscience could be identified, articulated, symbolized, developed, adapted, celebrated, reinforced, and sustained by awareness at all levels and in all parts of the organization? If so, then our twenty-first-century challenge may be more a matter of making moral awareness *pervasive*, than of fleeing it as somehow *risky* or *dangerous*.

To be sure, ethical disagreements will occur among and between executives, employees, consumers, suppliers, and shareholders regarding corporate policies and their implementation. And allegations of fanaticism or incompetence or fiduciary failure *may sometimes be warranted*. The key point to remember for the sake of avoiding counterfeits is that such allegations are not self-justifying.

Conscientious Capitalism – Risking Fanaticism in Search of Good Judgment

The approach-avoidance conflict that Americans (and others) experience in the quest for conscientious capitalism is understandable, but needs to be transcended. Part II of this book is an effort to provide balanced and practical guidance along the path. "Nothing ventured, nothing gained" is an aphorism that applies well in this context. Invoking conscience – in both individuals and organizations – carries a risk by definition, because it means relying in the end on *judgment* rather than rules or compliance schemes. The alternative, however, is that we end up policing from the *outside in* values that can only be realized if they are lived from the *inside out*.

My youngest daughter, who is a national champion equestrian, shared with me the advice that her instructor gave her for riding a magnificent beast in a highly competitive arena: "You need to ride with *soft eyes* and *soft hands!*" This advice works as much in the realm of ethical corporate leadership as it does in the competitive horse ring. *Hard eyes* and *hard hands* are analogues to the unbalanced pursuit of purpose, what in this book has been called *teleopathy*. The fear that an appeal to conscience – far from being an antidote to teleopathy – could actually *replicate* it in certain ways, is not without foundation. *Soft eyes* and s*oft hands* involve vision and control that incorporate peripheral awareness while at the same time pursuing excellence with intensity, rationality with respect.

What are the key characteristics of a corporate culture that "builds in" both rationality and respect – *a conscientious mindset* – as described in this and the previous chapter? Based on my own experiences in the classroom as an educator and in corporate offices as a consultant, I suggest four principal manifestations of corporate ethical awareness: reflectiveness, humility, anticipation, and community involvement. These support the soft eyes and soft hands of ethical leadership. And while I will develop these ideas more concretely and at more length in Part II of this book, it will be useful to sketch them briefly here as previews of coming attractions.

Four Manifestations of Corporate Ethical Awareness

Reflectiveness

Reflectiveness is a cultural disposition to encourage periodic relief from the goal-directedness and busy-ness of everyday work life. In our individual lives, few of us would have trouble appreciating how important it is to create regular – daily, weekly, yearly – opportunities for silence, reflection, and meditation on the meaning of what we do. It is much easier to become fixated if we deny ourselves access to a larger understanding of our efforts. It is much easier to settle for counterfeits when we are impatient for results – operating out of a closed attitude of *demand* rather than a more open attitude of *request*.

Organizations, like people, can suffer from the condition of "activism," the misplaced devotion of never stopping to reflect on their missions. An organizational culture can be too busy or too focused to *think* – to be *aware of what it is doing*. An atmosphere of reflectiveness helps organizations insure their ethical integrity more than any preoccupation with rules, laws, and programs for policing wrongdoing.

This can take the form of daily, weekly, monthly, and/or annual periods of silence, thoughtfulness about the purpose and practices of the enterprise. Some companies actually construct special spaces (meditation rooms) and support annual retreats for executives aimed at rekindling their sense of corporate mission and values.[50] What is distinctive and powerful about this feature of an organizational culture is that it recognizes a need for *balance* in the pursuit of goals and objectives, and affords opportunities to cultivate that balance. *Soft eyes, soft hands.*

In an age of information overload and noise, of voice mail, email, and fewer people doing more work; in a culture of competitiveness and workaholism, it is relatively easy for corporations to evacuate whatever vestiges of silence and thoughtfulness there might be and to treat executive development more as "skills development" than as a chance to get in touch with the meaning of the enterprise.

Humility

Humility may seem an odd virtue to attribute to a corporate culture, so let me clarify. Companies that have the courage to articulate their core values and to communicate them clearly to insiders and outsiders are inviting the charge of *hypocrisy* on a regular basis. None of us is immune to observations of disconnection between aspiration and action ("talk" and "walk"), one definition of hypocrisy. Some corporate cultures manifest humility in the sense that they are willing to be self-critical about gaps between their articulated core values and practice. Several companies that I have worked with do regular exercises and listening audits designed to elicit from managers and other employees their perceptions of such gaps and their suggestions about repairing them.

Such companies can, without much hesitation, initiate newly hired employees into the culture and symbolize and celebrate their core values in memorable ways. Awareness of falling short, together with a commitment to improving on the shortfalls, is understood and taken seriously. Humility is also reinforced by corporate communication channels (newsletters, help lines with ombudspersons) and employee development efforts aimed at confirming and clarifying the ethical values of the company in specific contexts.

Jim Collins, in his celebrated article on "Level 5 Leadership" surprises many of his readers by identifying humility as a critical virtue for CEOs. A "Level 5" leader, says Collins, is:

> an individual who blends extreme personal humility with intense professional will. According to our five-year research study, executives who possess this paradoxical combination of traits are catalysts for the statistically rare event of transforming a good company into a great one.[51]

Collins goes on to point out the irony of this empirical observation in the face of conventional wisdom about leadership:

> The great irony is that the animus and personal ambition that often drives people to become a Level 4 leader stands at odds with the humility required to rise to Level 5. When you combine that irony with the fact that boards of directors frequently operate under the false belief that a larger-than-life, egocentric leader is required to make a company great, you can quickly see why Level 5 leaders rarely appear at the top of our institutions.[52]

It is much easier to rationalize wrongdoing when we deny ourselves access to honest and candid feedback from our peers on both our walk and our talk. We can help one another avoid the dangers of

107

groupthink and the conventional filters that we put on our perception of the environment. Self-deception (both of the personal variety and of the group variety) is not *impossible* in the presence of the discipline of dialogue, but it is more difficult. Organizations that institutionalize *awareness* by regularly setting aside instinctive preoccupations with the material efficiencies, attending to the spiritual and interpersonal dimensions of workplace culture are less vulnerable to counterfeits of conscience, less likely to settle for less in the constant pursuit of more.

Anticipation

If a corporation's ethical awareness is to sustain itself over time, then the leaders in the organization need to *anticipate* and avoid loss of awareness through attentive recruiting, promotions, and succession planning. If there is physical entropy in our world, a tendency toward loss of order and substance, we might expect corresponding "ethical entropy" in the realm of organizational values. Anticipating this phenomenon means providing for constant vigilance and renewal. Awareness is sustained by careful selection and orientation of both new hires and new leaders.

In addition, many companies, especially in the past three decades, have grown by acquisition, and the *cultural* implications of acquisitions can be profound, not only economically but ethically. A corporation contemplating a merger or an acquisition would be foolish to look solely at the compatibility of balance sheets and other economic synergies. Cultural compatibility – including especially shared ethical values – is at least as important in the life of the new organization, and awareness on this front is another form of anticipation.

Community involvement

A fourth characteristic of an ethically aware corporate culture is *community involvement*. The essence of this characteristic is engagement with the various communities in which the company does business – through avenues like philanthropy, in-kind contributions, and employee-release time. This characteristic of corporate culture is not simply "nice-to-have" in relation to the first three. It is an extension of ethical awareness, especially to those less advantaged in the company's relevant communities, to stakeholders who are least able to reciprocate, at least in the short term.

One of the key roles of service in the lives of each of us as individuals is to break us free from the bonds of self-centeredness and the detachment that can accompany it. And I use the term "bonds" quite deliberately, since there is a kind of *imprisonment* associated with being disconnected from family and community, and a paradoxical threat to one's own integrity in the process.[53] Corporate community involvement is an institutional manifestation of what for individuals is an acknowledgement of *connectedness* and some degree of *responsibility* for the well being of the surrounding social system.[54]

Organizations that practice community involvement not only by corporate financial contributions, but also by encouraging employees to contribute *pro bono* time and talent, are fostering an *awareness of vulnerable stakeholders* – those less able to demand the attention of corporate decision-making, though often every bit as influenced or affected by it. They are at the same time avoiding the habit of treating government as the sole vehicle of compassion, outsourcing our encounters with the less-advantaged.

Summary and Conclusion of Part I

This chapter has sought to explain and defend three propositions: (1) that our attitudes toward organizational conscience are *conflicted*; (2) that as a consequence we often *default* to various substitutes for conscience, reminiscent of the "naturalistic fallacy" in early twentieth-century ethical theory; and (3) that we would do better to foster a culture of *ethical awareness* in organizations.

Four key manifestations of such corporate ethical awareness are *reflectiveness, humility, anticipation*, and *community involvement*. While these characteristics may sound old-fashioned, they keep corporate conscience awake and alive without assuming "systems so perfect that no one will need to be good." Companies displaying these characteristics need be neither fanatical nor anti-fiduciary. They simply need to avoid the occupational hazards of fixation, rationalization, and self-centered detachment. In Part II, we will develop these ideas in more operational detail.

Part II

The Moral Agenda of Leadership

> Why were we so reluctant to try the lower path, the ambiguous trail? Perhaps because we did not have a leader who could reveal the greater purpose of the trip to us. For each of us the Sadhu lives. What is the nature of our responsibility if we consider ourselves to be ethical persons? Perhaps it is to change the values of the group so that it can, with all its resources, take the other road.
>
> (Bowen McCoy)[1]

My goal in Part I of this book has been to clarify the hazard to which business ethics is a response and to identify the idea of conscience in relation to corporate culture. As we saw, the more conventional value of organizational *rationality* often profoundly narrows the vision of corporate leaders. Adding *respect* to rationality balances a person's and an organization's pursuit of purpose, recognizing obligations to all stakeholders who are affected.

In the four chapters of Part II, my goal is to articulate the *practical* implications of the conceptual foundations laid in Part I. This goal can be accomplished best by framing it in terms of the responsibilities of corporate *leaders* as the "architects" of corporate conscience. Two important books on leadership, *Good to Great* by Jim Collins (2001) and *Authentic Leadership* by Bill George (2003), provide valuable insights into the responsibilities of ethical leadership, and I shall draw upon both of them throughout Part II.

Moral Agendas

Business leaders not only have an economic and a legal agenda, but a moral one as well. *Webster's Dictionary* defines an *agenda* as "a list, outline, or plan of things to be considered or done." A moral agenda, then, is an action-oriented set of considerations for guiding business behavior in an ethical manner. To say that management has a moral agenda means that it must approach business decisions with a view to their ethical implications (for example, harm, fairness, rights and duties, integrity), and not solely their economic and legal implications. Lynn Paine put it well:

> Whether by design or default, managers define and shape company values through virtually everything they do. At the same time, values implementation is something done by everyone in a company every day. If the aim is to build a company capable of meeting the new performance standard on a sustained basis, the approach must be comprehensive, management led, and oriented toward a moral center that recognizes both social and economic responsibilities."[2]

It is, of course, one thing to say that since ethics is on the agenda of those with whom a company interacts, the company had better pay attention; it is quite another to say that ethics is on the company's *own* agenda, part of the way that its management looks at the world. In both cases, attention is paid to ethics. But there is a difference in the *way* the attention is paid. In the first case, ethics is an environmental *constraint* that is only indirectly part of the decision-making process. In the second case, ethics is something that is brought *to* the environment. Making decisions that have ethical implications is not optional. What *is* optional is whether those ethical implications will be considered *outside* forces or made part of the *internal* decision process itself. It is the latter option that I believe management must undertake when I use the phrase "moral agenda."

Having a moral agenda does not necessarily mean *following through* on it, of course, any more than having children means caring for them. But to set aside such an agenda is to let forces other than conscious choice determine one's ethical values. As with individual moral character, a corporation's character takes shape by default when it is not given shape by design. It has become increasingly clear that, left unmanaged, the ethical aspects of corporate policy and practice take on a life of their own.

Three Imperatives for Corporate Leadership

There are three "practical imperatives" that anchor the moral agenda of leadership: orienting; institutionalizing; and sustaining shared values.

The first two involve placing moral considerations in a position of salience and authority alongside considerations of profitability and competitive strategy in the corporate mindset. The third imperative (sustenance) has to do with passing on the spirit of this effort in two directions: to future leaders of the organization and to the wider network of organizations and institutions that make up the social system as a whole. In Chapters 5, 6, and 7, I will clarify each of these imperatives and then identify some of the ways in which they can present operational challenges to practitioners.

In Chapter 5, I will focus on the meaning and practical implications of *orienting* the ethical values in a corporate culture. I will illustrate this process with several case studies as well as a commentary on current employee survey practices in one large company that I have come to know well. In Chapter 6, the focus will shift to *institutionalizing* the shared values that have been identified by the organization in the process of orientation. Finally, in Chapter 7, I will address an often-overlooked imperative – *sustaining* the shared ethical values that have been identified (Chapter 5) and institutionalized (Chapter 6). This last imperative falls as much to the board of directors as to the senior leadership of the organization, making it a governance issue.

All three of these imperatives – orienting, institutionalizing, and sustaining – were salient issues during the business scandals of 2002, including Enron, Arthur Andersen, WorldCom, Tyco, and others. Each has been disregarded, if not resisted. Some companies have simply failed to orient themselves, failed to come to a collective understanding of their shared values. Others have *articulated* an orientation, but have failed to implement or align their espoused values with operational norms and practices – institutionalization. And still others, "scandals-in-waiting" perhaps, have oriented and institutionalized ethical values, while failing to make provisions for *sustaining* those values over the long term. This is particularly important because it is the "long term" to which appeal is often made in arguments about the convergence of conscience and profitability. Failure to *sustain* shared ethical values, besides increasing long-term risk, can also mean failure to realize the subtle returns on investment that accrue to enlightened corporations.

Sustain

Orient

Institutionalize

The importance of educational support structures for the moral agenda of management is the theme of Chapter 8. There I describe the implications for conventional business *education* of the three imperatives of corporate leadership (orienting, institutionalizing, and sustaining shared values). But I also argue that there are two other "academies" that are essential to the achievement of the moral agenda of corporate leadership. We need the collaboration of *three* academies to address the challenges posed in Part I of this book.

5

Orienting Corporate Conscience

In Chapter 3, I suggested an organizational analogue to Piaget's third stage of moral development (*autonomy*). I called it "Type 3" thinking – the "hand of management" beyond the "invisible hand" of the market and the "visible hand" of government. This is the anchor for the idea of "corporate conscience" – but to make this idea useful to leaders, we need to cast it in "operational" terms. And the first step in making corporate conscience operational lies in *orienting* the values of the group.

Giving Direction to the Type 3 Organization: The Reell Precision Manufacturing Case

Reell Precision Manufacturing, Inc. (*aka* RPM) is a small-to-medium-sized company headquartered near St. Paul, Minnesota. The company was incorporated in 1970 as a producer of wrap-spring clutches for precision applications. Since then it has grown and diversified its product line, today employing about 250 people in the US and Europe.

Some years ago, I wrote a case study about Reell to document the efforts of senior management in 1992 to address disagreements over the content of the firm's Direction Statement. Specifically, the language in the Direction Statement made reference to "Judeo-Christian values" and to work as a form of cooperation with the "will of God." Most of the company's employees strongly agreed with the language of the Direction Statement, but a small minority felt that it did not represent their views and that it was potentially discriminatory in the work environment.

Reell was (and is) an unusual company, founded by three entre-preneurial ex-3M engineers who wanted to create a business that was friendly to faith-based values. In 1985, the founders established an Employee Stock Ownership Plan (ESOP) and by 1990, the em-ployees owned more than 30 percent of Reell stock. A commitment to full employment provided that, even when faced with a loss, the company would reduce all salaries on a percentage basis rather than implement any layoffs. There were other unusual policies: executive compensation did not exceed six times the lowest pay of five-year employees or ten times the pay of newcomers; vendors were paid within 30 days, even if it meant borrowing money to pay them; travel requirements were family-friendly; and contributions to charity were at an extraordinary 10 percent of pretax earnings.

Students and executives in discussion usually responded to the Reell case with a certain amount of consternation. On the one hand, the company "walked the talk" of its faith-based ethical idealism in ways that were truly remarkable. On the other hand, many expressed reservations about a perceived lack of inclusiveness in its Mission/Direction statement toward those outside the Judeo-Christian tradition.

Nevertheless, employee comments about working at Reell were almost uniformly positive. As Steve Wikstrom, at the time Reell's Vice President of Manufacturing, said:

> If you asked people around here "What's the worst thing that could happen?" going out of business would not be the number one response. I believe they would say, to abandon the "north" that we have defined on the compass. If we were to abandon that, I know the people I work with would say, "Pull the plug on it and walk away. It's not that important to us."[1]

Reell, despite its atypical culture, illustrates a number of aspects of the first leadership imperative – *orienting* corporate conscience.[2] The company was founded with a relatively clear (albeit eventually con-troversial) mission and direction. It periodically sought reaffirmation by the employees of this general orientation. And the magnitude of the company's commitment to this direction was evident in a list of policies and practices aimed at institutionalizing and sustaining the "north" that it had defined on the compass.

116

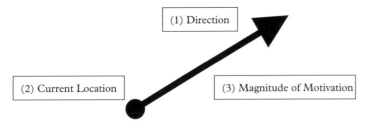

vector, n., a quantity possessing both magnitude and direction, represented by an arrow the direction of which indicates the direction of the quantity and the length of which is proportional to the magnitude.

Figure 5.1   Direction, location, motivation

In mathematics, "orientation" is explained using the idea of a *vector*, "a quantity possessing both magnitude and direction, represented by an arrow the direction of which indicates the direction of the quantity and the length of which is proportional to the magnitude."[3] The analogue of a "vector" for a company's ethical orientation would be: (1) the company's *direction* (the mission and values to which it aspires); (2) the company's current understanding of its *location* in relation to that direction; and (3) the magnitude of the company's *motivation* to get from "here" to "there" (see Figure 5.1). Let us examine each of these elements in turn.

The First Step of Orientation: Direction (Mission)

Charles Handy wrote in the *Harvard Business Review* ("What's a Business For?") that:

We cannot escape the fundamental question, Whom and what is a business for? The answer once seemed clear, but no longer. The terms of business have changed. Ownership has been replaced by investment, and a company's assets are increasingly found in its people, not in its buildings and machinery. In light of this transformation, we need to rethink our assumptions about the purpose of business.[4]

Handy continues:

117

The purpose of a business, in other words, is not to make a profit, full stop. It is to make a profit so that the business can do something more or better. That "something" becomes the real justification for the business. Owners know this. Investors needn't care.[5]

Without an understanding of the "something" which profit enables the business to do "more of" or to do better, *orienting* the corporate conscience is impossible. Reflecting on his time as CEO of Medtronic, Inc., Bill George wrote:

> The most frequent reason companies get into trouble is trying to grow without a well-understood mission. Without clarity over purpose, it is difficult if not impossible for your customers, your employees, and your shareholders to know what your company stands for and where it is going. Internal decision makers have no framework for making decisions.[6]

In Medtronic's case, the mission was articulated well over 40 years ago, when the company was in need of clarity for both its employees and its outside providers of capital. The six-part mission statement (see below) has survived the test of time. When the company summarizes its mission in abbreviated form, it is the first item in the list that receives the emphasis and that almost all employees can quote on the spot if asked: "*To contribute to human welfare by the application of biomedical engineering [to] alleviate pain, restore health, and extend life.*" This is Handy's "something" – the real justification for the business. It is, for Bill George "what the company stands for and *where it is going.*"

New employees of Medtronic attend a "mission-medallion" ceremony in which the founder, Earl Bakken, or the CEO presents each person with a medallion on which these words are embossed. The company's logo (see Figure 5.2) depicts the message symbolically with a "rising figure" being restored to full health.

The remaining five items in the list indicate the shared values of the company: *focused growth*; *unsurpassed quality*; *fair profit*; *the personal worth of employees*; and *good citizenship in its communities*. These are aspirations of the company as it pursues its mission.

The Medtronic Mission

1   To contribute to human welfare by the application of biomedical engineering [to] alleviate pain, restore health, and extend life;

Figure 5.2 Medtronic logo. Reproduced by permission of Medtronic, Inc.

2 To direct our growth where we display maximum strength and ability, avoiding areas where we cannot make unique and worthy contributions;

3 To strive without reserve for the greatest possible reliability and quality in our products;

4 To make a fair profit on current operations to meet our obligations, sustain our growth, and reach our goals;

5 To recognize the personal worth of employees, providing personal satisfaction, security, advancement opportunity, and a share in the company's success;

6 To maintain good citizenship as a company.

There are numerous examples of companies like Reell and Medtronic that have a shared sense of direction, Handy's "something" that explains "what they are for" beyond generating profits.

Sometimes the *direction* of the company is expressed in terms of a set of value priorities, as with Reell: responsibilities to various participants in the enterprise, whatever its product or service might be. The point is framed in terms of "the way business is done here" more than "what business we are in." At other times, the direction of the company is framed very much in terms of "what business we are in" – its overarching mission – as with Medtronic. A company's mission is analogous to a "calling" or a "vocation" in the life of an individual. Frequently, the company's direction has *both* of these components – value priorities and overarching mission – touchstones to explain, in Handy's terms, "what it is for" and to provide moral guidance when *dis-orientation* occurs.

Jim Collins and Jerry Porras, in their book *Built to Last*, tell a number of stories about such companies.[7] Three in particular deserve mention in this context: Merck Pharmaceuticals, Johnson & Johnson, and Hewlett-Packard. A fourth story from other sources, about Cummins, Inc., reinforces the lessons learned about the importance of corporate *direction*.

Merck Pharmaceuticals

Handy's insight (about there having to be a "something" that is the "real justification" of a business) was, and continues to be, borne out in the story of Merck. Like Medtronic, Merck placed its business activities in a larger human context:

> In 1935 (decades before "values statements" became popular), George Merck II articulated those ideals when he said, "[We] are workers in an industry who are genuinely inspired by the ideals of advancement of medical science, and of service to humanity." In 1991 – fifty-six years and three full generations of leadership later – Merck's chief executive P. Roy Vagelos sang the same idealistic tune: "Above all, let's remember that our business success means victory against disease and help to humankind."[8]

Collins and Porras refer to this mindset as "pragmatic idealism" and refuse to see it as a luxury for successful companies. To the contrary, they found that "high ideals – a core ideology – often existed in the visionary companies not just when they were successful, but also when they were struggling just to survive."[9]

Should we be surprised by these findings? Not at all. For the company that is truly oriented by conscience inevitably sees its reason for being in terms of its human contribution. Profitability is valued, of course, *but as a condition and a consequence of that contribution*, not as an end in itself. When we speak of a company's "direction," then, we are speaking of its "goods" and "services" in ways that admit of critique from a *moral* point of view, not just an *economic* point of view.

Johnson & Johnson

Like Merck, Johnson & Johnson has a long history of clarity about its direction, once referred to over a century ago as "aiding the progress of the art of healing."[10] In 1943, Robert W. Johnson, Jr., codified the J&J mindset and value priorities in what he referred to as "Our Credo," a document that stood the test of time and arguably served the company four decades later in one of its most traumatic moments as it responded to the *Tylenol* crisis. In the early 1980s, Jim Burke (who spent much of his time as CEO communicating the credo throughout the company) described the relationship between the credo and profits:

All of our management is geared to profit on a day-to-day basis. That's part of the business of being in business. But too often, in this and other businesses, people are inclined to think, "We'd better do this because if we don't it's going to show up on the figures over the short term." This document [the Credo] allows them to say, "Wait a minute. I don't *have* to do that. The management has told me that they're . . . interested in me operating under this set of principles, so I won't."[11]

Collins and Porras contrast the J&J direction and sense of mission with that of Bristol-Myers:

At Bristol-Myers, we found a much less ideologically guided company than at Johnson & Johnson. Whereas J&J formalized and published its credo in the early 1940s and had a clear sense of its ideology dating back to the early 1900s, we found no evidence whatsoever that Bristol-Myers had anything analogous to the credo until 1987, when it published the "Bristol-Myers Pledge" (which looks suspiciously like a paraphrased version of the J&J Credo).[12]

Clearly, not all companies have a clear sense of direction and/or Handy's "something beyond profit" as a moral compass.

Hewlett-Packard – Value priorities and cultural change

Other companies, well-known for their enlightenment, seem to have suffered cultural setbacks in this arena. Hewlett-Packard is one such company. When a company loses sight of its direction – or, recalling our discussion of McCoy's "Parable of the Sadhu" – *forgets the purpose of the trip*, serious negative consequences become likely.

Like Medtronic, Hewlett-Packard was started in a garage over 60 years ago. William Hewlett and David Packard "were visionaries in creating a corporate culture and management style – the HP Way – that could keep pace with the ever-accelerating evolution of the electronics industry."[13] Creative innovation in electronic technology was a passion at HP, and its contribution "was ultimately social, not solitary, and as much organizational as technological."[14]

In a 1960 speech to his management team, David Packard anticipated Charles Handy by over four decades, asking *why a company exists in the first place*:

121

I think many people assume, wrongly, that a company exists simply to make money. While this is an important result of a company's existence, we have to go deeper and find the real reasons for our being. As we investigate this, we inevitably come to the conclusion that a group of people get together and exist as an institution that we call a company so they are able to accomplish something collectively that they could not accomplish separately – they make a contribution to society, a phrase which sounds trite but is fundamental.

Packard then continued:

You can look around [in the general business world] and still see people who are interested in money and nothing else, but the underlying drives come largely from a desire to do something else – to make a product – to give a service – generally to do something which is of value. So with that in mind, let us discuss why the Hewlett-Packard Company exists.[15]

With the hiring of Carly Fiorina as CEO in 1999, however, and the merger with Compaq in 2002, commitment to the "HP Way" became "lip service" according to one *Business Week* observer.[16] Stanford Emeritus Professor (and co-author of *Built to Last*) Jerry Porras said in 2003: "I think the 'HP Way' is headed for oblivion."[17] Cultural change can be refreshing in a company, but it can also be destructive of values that orient a company and motivate its best employees. When the constant reinforcement of a company's mission and value priorities are replaced by largely rhetorical gestures, "dis-orientation" occurs, confidence and clarity diminish, and passion about Handy's special "something" loses intensity:

Unfortunately, Fiorina's efforts tore at less tangible but nonetheless important employee morale. Rather than believing they were at a special enterprise, many HP employees came to think of their jobs as just the source of a paycheck. They lost faith in the outfit because they sensed that HP had adopted a new view of them.[18]

Fiorina was forced to step down as CEO in February 2005, due (in the opinion of many) to a cultural lack of fit. The optimistic view was that "the 'HP Way' isn't dead. It's dormant – and waiting for the right executive. . . . The HP Way was never the problem. But it may be part of the answer."[19]

Hewlett-Packard announced a restructuring in July 2005, "in what would likely be the biggest action so far by new Chief Executive Officer Mark Hurd," *The Wall Street Journal* reported.

Mr. Hurd, who joined H-P in late March following the ouster of Carly Fiorina, has said he plans to make significant cost cuts at the Palo Alto, Calif., technology company. . . . The company has indicated a restructuring . . . could bring $100 million in headcount-related savings . . . H-P has stumbled in recent years against rivals Dell and IBM. Mr. Hurd, who was recruited from NCR Corp., has been charged with reigniting growth.[20]

A company without a shared sense of direction has no "compass" when crucial decisions (strategic or otherwise) confront it. Without the value priorities that such a compass affords, the leaders of the company default to goals and objectives that are externally imposed by financial markets, for example, or by government regulators. This is what we referred to in earlier chapters as a Type 2 company.

Cummins Engine – Convictions confront continued existence

If Hewlett-Packard risked cultural assets in the face of urgent business challenges, Cummins, Inc. seems to have used its cultural assets to *overcome* such challenges. Cummins, Inc. has long been recognized for its proactive engagement of a range of stakeholder groups. Since 1919, the Columbus, Indiana-based company has designed, manufactured, and distributed diesel engines. It has successfully maintained a strong presence in the highly cyclical heavy-duty on-highway truck market, while developing new applications for diesel technology and new product lines (e.g., electric power generators, filtration and emission systems, turbochargers, etc.).

Diesel production is capital-intensive. A diesel engine company must consistently provide investors with superior returns if it is to attract the capital it needs to fund future investments. Nevertheless, *capital* was never seen by Cummins' founders as the primary reason for the firm's existence. The *mission* or *purpose* of the company was clearly distinguished from its financial stability:

> This economic reality suggests that shareholders' interests would assume a place of privilege in the company's deliberations. Yet a unique feature of Cummins' history is that the *first* stakeholder acknowledged by the company, the community, is commonly the *last* one recognized by other corporations.

In response to a 1939 memo from Cummins' senior managers, which requested a clear statement of the firm's purpose, W.G. Irwin

123

clearly linked his family's financial support of the company to a purpose beyond mere profits. *"Had it not been for our desire to have a place to develop the young men around Columbus,"* W.G. wrote, *"we should not have taken the risks we did."*[21]

Throughout its history, Cummins has demonstrated a strong commitment to Columbus and southern Indiana. The company has provided employment for generations of Columbus residents, either directly or indirectly. Its willingness to pay the design fees for new public buildings helped to transform this small Hoosier town into a showcase of contemporary architecture. Furthermore, the company has resisted hostile takeover attempts in part to protect the community's interests.[22] But since the early 1980s, Cummins has faced a changing set of economic realities, including ferocious competition from overseas. T. Dean Maines, a former Cummins executive and a keen observer of the company's culture, recently wrote:

> Had Cummins not taken its 1984 pricing action [reducing the cost of its products by a full one-third], it would have permanently surrendered market share to its [Japanese] competitors – an outcome that would have resulted in a much smaller company with more limited capabilities, one unlikely to retain its independence. Had Cummins not invested in new products, it simply would have gone out of existence. By as early as 1990, nearly 40% of the company's sales were from products that did not exist prior to the 1979 product expansion.[23]

Confronted by globalization, stiff price competition, and increasingly stringent restrictions on diesel emissions promulgated by the EPA, the company had to confront its core values, walking a fine line between local dedication and global survival:

> In Columbus, a tightly knit community of about 39,000, the story of globalization is not a tale of "Benedict Arnold CEOs" or macroeconomic theory. It's the story of how an intimate relationship between company and town can clash with the relentless march of technology in a world with shrinking borders.[24]

All this being said, Tim Solso, Cummins Chairman and CEO since 2000, has had to make excruciating decisions to address the challenges facing the company, including a decision to close the Columbus Engine Plant in favor of a newer, more efficient factory in Jamestown, New York. "It was awful," he said. "That plant had been here 80 years and I had lived here 30 years. There were all kinds of questions about Cummins' commitment to Columbus and Tim Solso's commitment on a personal basis. But that was a decision that saved the company $20 million a year. It had to be made."[25]

What does a company do when it realizes that its very survival depends upon shifts in production and technology that could lead it away from the very community it viewed as its primary stakeholder? Some companies might respond with: "Times change and some priorities just can't be honored. The shareholders must come first." Cummins responded differently, with a two-part strategy.

The first part of the strategy was to reduce the dependence of the Columbus, Indiana community on Cummins, helping to bring in employers that could take up the slack if Cummins had to reduce its workforce.

In the mid-1980s, when the nation's manufacturing employment began to decline, executives from Cummins and Arvin [Industries] helped form the Columbus Economic Development Board. Its mission: to find other employment sources. And find them it did. . . . Over the years, the new companies have invested $2 billion in the local economy. More important, they have gradually added 10,000 jobs to offset the losses from other companies. That has held the county's unemployment rate to around 4 percent, below state and national levels.[26]

The second part of the strategy was to re-frame the core value of *community support* to include the new global realities of its industry – looking to communities in India, China, and Brazil – as part of this commitment. In the words of CEO Solso:

An employee in India is just as important as an employee in New York, as an employee in China, as an employee in Brazil. That's a maturation for this company. If you believe that if you don't take these actions you won't survive, then you take them. But you take them with as much dignity and respect as possible for the workforce and communities where you operate.[27]

Re-framing and enlivening a company's mission and shared values are not simple matters. Fortunate are the companies (like Reell, Medtronic, Merck, J&J, and Cummins) that have clear, substantial, and agreed upon direction or mission statements. For arriving at or revising such statements can be a complex task, involving "top down" and "bottom up" dialogues within an organization, considerations

125

of company tradition and history, and external expectations from the market and the law, domestically and internationally. Value orientation must ultimately receive support from the employee base of the company, of course, and one way to encourage such support is to involve the rank and file either in the formulation or the regular reaffirmation of the mission and value manifestos. A company's *direction*, newly articulated or inherited from predecessors, provides the platform for an authentic "we" when the leader speaks for the organization as a whole.[28]

Mission skeptics

As we saw in Chapter 4, not everyone embraces the significance of a company's direction or mission statement as central to the orientation of conscience. Or perhaps it would be more accurate to say that some prefer to orient corporate conscience far more narrowly than others. British commentator Digby Anderson articulated this perspective some years ago in an essay entitled "Good Companies Don't Have Missions." Anderson claimed that his ideal "mission statement" would read as follows:

> Our company is there to make money for its shareholders. They own it. They risk their money in it. It will only make money if it pleases customers more than its rivals and keeps its workforce happy enough to attract a good and loyal one. However when actions which benefit the customer or employee diverge from those which benefit the shareholder, our duties are unequivocally to the shareholder.[29]

Despite his cynicism about most corporate mission statements, Anderson nevertheless believed that there was a *moral* imperative at issue and that leaders needed to orient their companies in the direction of that imperative. Bill George, of course, disagreed even on the terms that Anderson laid out:

> Some executives mistakenly believe serving all stakeholders results in trade-offs and compromises shareholder value. As the examples of J&J, Merck, and Target amply demonstrate, the opposite is the case. In serving all the company's stakeholders, the company's sustained success makes shareholders the ultimate beneficiaries.[30]

Unlike Bill George, Anderson failed to appreciate the ethical obligations of the corporation to the full range of its stakeholders, but he

126

did appear to understand the moral agenda of a more reactionary capitalism. Reminiscent of Martin Luther King, Jr., the editor of *Ethical Corporation* (quoted earlier) counters in dramatic terms:

> Given legal constructs of the company that deny the reality of business' place in society, [missions] might be considered a form of civil disobedience to the injustice of a law-embedded ethic that considers important only the interests of one party to a social relation. . . . If capitalism and ethics are in conflict, it is not its ethics that society will change.[31]

Clarity about a company's direction or mission, then, is the first step of orientation.

The Second Step of Orientation: Location (Inventory)

The second operational step for leaders is to *identify* and where needed, *adjust* their organizations' current value profile. This calls for a kind of "values inventory." Leaders must listen to and understand their organizations in ways that reach its moral strengths and weaknesses.[32]

There is inevitably a gap between what Harvard professor Chris Argyris calls "espoused values" and "values-in-action." Just as the values of individuals are not always transparent to their "owners," so too for organizations. We do not always see ourselves as others see us – a cause for caution in both us *and* others.

Earlier I pointed out how the attribution of mindset characteristics involved uncertainty because mindsets are neither purely behavioral nor purely cognitive.[33] Since they involve both beliefs and attitudes, we can easily be mistaken about the mindset behind a given action or about the action that follows from a given mindset in a specific situation. And if *we ourselves* can be mistaken, so can others who observe our "values-in-action" over time. Nevertheless, the difficulties involved in this kind of self-awareness should not be taken as a reason to avoid the attempt. "Know thyself" is a prescription that may be difficult, but it is not impossible. What is needed is a "sounding" or listening process sophisticated enough to get behind the natural cautions, defenses, and espoused values of all concerned.

The objective is *to discern the dominant ethical values of the company* – large or small. This is essentially a descriptive – not a prescriptive – task. Unlike small companies, large divisionalized or diversified firms will no doubt have some business units with distinct underlying cultures. This will be true whether the company grew by internal diversification or by acquisition. There may also be differences stemming from international business operations in contrast to domestic operations.

Employee surveys and questionnaires provide an initial scan and (over time) some trend data. More qualitative, clinical methods may also be needed to identify "deeper data" – the moral victories, defeats, and dilemmas that operating managers experience as they do their work and pursue their careers in the organization.[34]

Listening to *outside* stakeholders can also be useful in this process: suppliers, customers, regulators, neighbors, creditors, shareholders. Exit interviews with departing employees can also provide helpful insight into company values. We need to remember that the idea of a "stakeholder" is not just the idea of someone who is *affected by* the decision-making of the organization. Stakeholders also *possess valuable information about the organization* – sometimes more objective information than is available inside. Organizations have a "stake" in listening to their stakeholders, in much the same way that executives have a stake in listening to those around them in 360° performance evaluations. Important by-products of employee survey efforts, it should be noted, could be correlations between these findings and financial performance indicators, customer satisfaction indicators, and reputation measurements.

Poet David Whyte, in his book *The Heart Aroused: Poetry and the Preservation of the Soul in Corporate America,* shares an old Native American elder's poem about the importance of listening. It was told to children in the Pacific Northwest where ventures into towering redwood forests could lead to disorientation. It suggests that *organizational* orientation might also have a lot to do with a kind of listening.

Lost[35]

Stand still. The trees ahead and bushes beside you
Are not lost. Wherever you are is called Here,
And you must treat it as a powerful stranger,
Must ask permission to know it and be known.

128

The forest breathes. Listen. It answers,
I have made this place around you,
If you leave it you may come back again, saying Here.
No two trees are the same to Raven.
No two branches are the same to Wren.
If what a tree or a bush does is lost on you,
You are surely lost. Stand still. The forest knows
Where you are. You must let it find you.

The result of such sounding efforts will be an inventory of attributions, issues, responses, and concerns that serve as a preliminary map for leadership initiatives. Is this a Type 3 organization? If not, why not? Leaders can ask how and where policies and practices could be changed to improve ethical awareness and behavior, to move from the "here" of survey reports to the "there" of mission and value statements.

An illustration of employee sounding – Medtronic's "Global Voices" survey

"Global Voices" is the name of a comprehensive 70-question survey that has been administered at Medtronic to all employees biennially since 1994. The survey originated from a felt need to coordinate and centralize multiple survey efforts that used to go on as the company was expanding in the early 1990s.[36] The idea was to make survey efforts more efficient and to enhance response rates in the process. Thus the first versions of *Global Voices* were fairly cumbrous and disparate (about 150 questions). Over the years, more thought has gone into the content of the survey, streamlining it and incorporating insights from the Baldrige organizational model.

According to Paul Erdahl, Vice President for Executive and Leadership Development at Medtronic, whose office administers the survey, "Global Voices is the most comprehensive and complete internal measure of how the organization is doing." It is sent out in several different languages, and provides an anonymous evaluation of the corporation through the eyes of over 30,000 employees worldwide with an 80 percent response rate, far beyond normal survey expectations.[37] Erdahl adds that the survey "is also a communication vehicle – sending messages implicitly to the employees about what variables are important to measure and to improve upon." Table 5.1 shows an overview of the survey.

129

Table 5.1 Medtronic Global Voices Worldwide Employee Survey:
15 Question Categories and Examples

Category	Sample question
1 Mission and strategic alignment	Medtronic's mission is consistent with my personal values.
2 Community	My organization demonstrates concern for the environment and the community in which I work.
3 Senior management	Senior management is honest and ethical in its business practices.
4 Customer focus	My organization places a higher priority on customer/client satisfaction than on achieving short-term business goals.
5 Measurement	We regularly use customer/client feedback to improve our work processes.
6 Operating effectiveness	Where I work, day-to-day decisions demonstrate that quality and improvement are top priorities.
7 Working conditions	I am satisfied with the safety and health conditions of my work environment.
8 Immediate manager/supervisor	My immediate manager/supervisor treats employees fairly.
9 Collaborative environment	The people I work with cooperate to get the job done.
10 Valuing employees	My organization allows me sufficient flexibility to balance work and family commitments.
11 Employee involvement	I am satisfied with my involvement in decisions that affect me.
12 Employee development	I am satisfied with the career development opportunities in my organization.
13 Company and job satisfaction	I am proud to tell people I work for Medtronic.
14 Supplemental questions	[Provided by the leaders of the business units.]
15 Demographics	[Functional area, position, length of service, gender, age group, race (US only), etc.]

Questions to be answered using the following range: strongly agree; agree; neither agree nor disagree; disagree; strongly disagree.

Two questions arise in the wake of thoughtful survey tools such as Medtronic's Global Voices: (1) What happens to the results of the survey after each administration of it? And (2) To what extent does the company survey other stakeholders besides employees to aid in orienting the values of the company? To (2), Erdahl answers that at the moment, there are no other stakeholder surveys of comparable comprehensiveness. He notes, however, that the clients and customers of the many Medtronic businesses would be difficult to survey except *by business unit*, since they often do not overlap. To (1), the response is that a detailed report is presented to and discussed with the Executive Committee and the Board of Directors after each biannual administration of the survey. The results are then shared with the business units, including the data on the special questions each unit was invited to include in the survey.

At the moment, there are no *Global Voices Action Plans* required of the business unit leaders, although this idea has come up and has been tested.[38] Some efforts have been made to develop trend data from year to year and to correlate *Global Voices* data by business unit with financial results in those units. An interesting conundrum in this connection is: Which variable leads? Are employee attitudes positive because financial and market performance are high – or is performance high because employee attitudes are positive? Research on this question continues and is far from unanimous.[39]

Bill George points to the Global Voices survey as one of the achievements of his tenure as CEO of Medtronic. And he highlights the four specific responses seen in Table 5.2 in the year 2000 results that indicate the "orientation" of the company in relation to its stated mission.

Table 5.2 Top rated questions from the year 2000 employee survey*[40]

Comment	Percentage favorable
1. My work supports the Medtronic mission.	92
2. I really understand Medtronic's mission.	90
3. Medtronic's mission is consistent with my values.	84
4. I am proud to work for Medtronic.	84

*18,000 respondents worldwide (80% return)

Soundings by third parties

It should be mentioned that soundings of the kind used by Medtronic need not be undertaken by companies solely as in-house activities. Soundings can be outsourced to third parties. For example, the *Center for Ethical Business Cultures* (CEBC) at the University of St. Thomas in Minnesota has partnered with Gantz Wiley Research in developing a set of survey tools called the *Integrity Measurement Program*.™ The CEBC Integrity Survey™ is a 28-question stand-alone employee survey tool used to obtain an in-depth assessment of an organization's ethical environment. The CEBC Integrity QuickCheck™, a subset of the CEBC Integrity Survey, is a five-question instrument which can be used as a stand-alone assessment or added to an existing employee survey. This program is aimed at helping organizations understand their ethical environments more systematically.[41] CEBC also licenses the *Self-Assessment and Improvement Process* (SAIP™), described later in this chapter and in Chapter 6, for use with companies in its geographical region.

The Third Step of Orientation: Motivation (Priority)

We saw at the beginning of this chapter that there were three important steps involved in "orienting" corporate conscience. The first step consists in identifying the "there" to which the company would go, its mission and shared values. The second step consists in clarifying the "here" from which the group must depart in order to get "there." The third step in orienting corporate conscience has to do with the *importance* attached to the process itself (the "magnitude" of the vector that represents orientation).

Years ago, Professor John Hennessy, recently retired from his role as Provost at the University of Vermont, wrote a classic (and disguised) case entitled "Viking Air Compressor, Inc." In the case, a young man named George Ames, upon receiving an MBA from the Tuck School, was hired by Viking to be its director of public affairs. As his first assignment, Ames was made executive secretary to Viking's newly formed Board Committee on Corporate Responsibility, with the task of drafting policy guidelines for possible approaches to the issue of corporate responsibility. Largely without supervision or substantive contact with others in Viking, Ames spent the summer preparing recommendations for the committee to present at Viking's September board meeting.

In early September, Ames met with John Larson, Viking's chairman of the board and chief executive officer, and presented four very specific recommendations. Larson bluntly countered the recommendations, pointing out their incompatibility with principles and operations in place at Viking. Ames was told by Larson that he had gotten the assignment "all backwards" and had revealed himself to be a "woolly-minded theoretician." Larson indicated that the subject would not be presented to the board until some indefinite point in the future.

The reality of the Viking situation – and perhaps the reality of many other company situations in the wake of Enron and Sarbanes-Oxley – was that *motivation* for corporate conscience emanated from the board, not from senior management (especially not the CEO). This fact led to serious confusion when young Mr. Ames assumed otherwise in his new position at Viking. But quite apart from the communication problems and the career progression issues faced by Mr. Ames, he had to confront a lukewarm corporate interest at Viking in getting from "here" to "there." Here are two further examples.

In a large manufacturing company that I once studied, the importance attached to "sounding out" employees was minimal and the resulting ethical communications to employees from senior management were regarded as Sunday school sermons. Little contact was made with the organizational mindset in its operational reality, i.e., where the employees had to make business choices. The leader wanted vaguely to "orient" corporate conscience, to be sure, but he never really located it to begin with. "Getting there from here" was wishful thinking *both* because "here" was a mystery *and* because the motivation just wasn't present. Orienting corporate conscience was not a priority.

In another company, a multinational service firm, the commitment to a sounding was much more in evidence. In an initial workshop session with office managers from around the world, strengths were identified in certain client relationships; policies were identified that enabled managers to avoid conflicts of interest; practices were highlighted that ensured more attention to the accuracy of company reports. Weaknesses were acknowledged in specific personnel practices that seemed unfair and discriminatory.

The CEO did not stop there, however. Plans were laid to focus the sounding at lower levels and horizontally by type of service rather than just geographical location. The board of directors then intended to articulate a statement of values and to take steps toward institutionalizing and sustaining the strengths and eliminating or reducing the weaknesses that were meaningful to managers and staff throughout the company. The motivation to guide the company toward identifiable shared values was strong – a high priority.

We have discussed the Medtronic mission under the first step of orientation and the Medtronic Global Voices survey under the second step. Former CEO Bill George was convinced that "The best path to long-term growth in shareholder value comes from having a well articulated mission that inspires employee commitment."[42] Bill George, Jim Collins, and other reflective observers remind us that *orienting* an organization is not just a matter of *clarity* about where the organization is and where leaders want it to go – it is also a matter of how *passionately* they want to go there.

Stop, Look, Listen, and Lead

There are a number of puzzles associated with the idea of a "sounding" process. One lies in the challenge of getting a relatively objective profile of the values-in-action of the company. Opinion surveys can be helpful, but they need to be supported by other data that measure the behavioral dimension. The point is to describe accurately a "here" for any initiative to move to "there" (which is the very meaning of "to orient"). If our vector is defined by two points, the origin and the terminus, the puzzles about the origin come first. But there are puzzles about the terminus as well.

Who gets to decide where "there" is for an enterprise, large or small, when it comes to ethical values? The answer to this question might seem obvious, as it did to one senior executive I had in a seminar some years ago. I had asked about the orientation of his organization in relation to the typology laid out in Chapter 3 (where Type 1 was driven by self-interest, Type 2 was by compliance, and Type 3 by corporate conscience). Impatiently, he insisted that in his organization, subordinates knew well that Type 3 was the only way other than the "highway" – and he enforced this mindset vigorously. There was silence at first. Then his peers began to smile, as eventually did he. For the contradiction was apparent: "I *demand* a

Type 3 organization, in effect fostering in my subordinates a Type 2 (compliance-oriented) mindset!"

In the cases of Reell and Medtronic, it was the *founders* who initially decided where "there" was, but it has been critical to the success of both organizations (one small and one large) that there are regular opportunities for reappropriation by the employees of the mission and core values. *The orientation of a company is a dynamic leadership imperative, not a static fact of its history.* The literature on leadership is replete with observations about the importance of gaining "buy in" and "ownership" of goals and objectives. Leaders who are ineffective on this front are not followed, except perhaps out of fear. And fear, while a powerful motivator is unreliable in situations where it cannot be enforced. Machiavelli said "It is better for the Prince to be feared than loved," but the challenge of corporate ethical leadership is to make the *mission*, not the person of the CEO, the key to orientation.

Those who think of the "orientation" of a company's values as a matter of senior leaders simply deciding what they want those values to be, and issuing a kind of "decree," miss the subtlety of the orienting imperative. They ignore the motivational component of their leadership.[43] The magic happens when leaders can say "*I* speak for *us*," when they can use the first person *plural* ("we") with authenticity. This does not mean that corporations are democracies, although some, especially in Europe, attempt to approximate this political model. But it does mean that in order to speak of the values or the conscience of an organization *as a whole*, it is necessary to remind everyone regularly of "the purpose of the trip." As Charles Handy says:

> This is a moral issue. . . . To mistake the means for the end is to be turned in on oneself, which Saint Augustine called one of the greatest sins. Deep down, the suspicions about capitalism are rooted in a feeling that its instruments, the corporations, are immoral in that they have no purpose other than themselves.[44]

In discussions of Bowen McCoy's "Parable of the Sadhu," mentioned in the early chapters of this book, students and executives often wonder why the climbing party did not clarify certain values at the base camp, before the climb. This would have been analogous to "orienting" the group, communicating the priorities that must govern behavior at 20,000 feet. Reell and Medtronic have "Base Camp

Agreements" that keep the purpose of the trip uppermost in their minds, lest the exigencies of the climb (business competition) lead to a kind of "forgetting."

The "vector" of corporate conscience is sometimes a *discovery* or rediscovery of a company's reason for being. Sometimes though, it is a group's decision (an *invention*) about such a reason. Together with an understanding of current attitudes and values, the vector is always a guide for *steering* the company when priorities need to be made clear. And this usually means economic success in the long term, as Bill George reminded us: "The best path to long-term growth in shareholder value comes from having a well-articulated mission that inspires employee commitment."

Location, Direction, Motivation: The Self-Assessment and Improvement Process[45]

One way of measuring the magnitude of the gap between an organization's actual values and its ideal values – and by implication, the perceived significance of that gap – is to use a process based on the Caux Round Table *Principles for Business* that was developed by a working group of practitioners and academics, a tool known as the Self-Assessment and Improvement Process (SAIP).

The Caux Round Table (CRT) *Principles for Business* originated in July 1994. The CRT, which had been founded in 1986 by a small group of Japanese, European, and American executives, embraced the mission of promoting *principled business leadership*. Each year, this group gathered in the peaceful village of Caux-sur-Montreux, overlooking Lake Geneva. The *Principles for Business* were fashioned in part from a document that one of the American members shared with the group – a document known as the *Minnesota Principles*, which came out of the Minnesota Center for Corporate Responsibility in 1992.[46]

The CRT *Principles* are a comprehensive set of ethical norms intended for businesses operating in diverse cultural environments. This meant that the framers of the *Principles* had to formulate them so that they were intelligible and acceptable from both Eastern and Western perspectives.

The *Principles* rest upon two basic ethical ideals – (1) the dignity of the human person, and (2) the Japanese concept of *kyosei*. The first ideal insists on valuing each human being as an end, implying that an individual's worth can never be reduced to his or her utility as a means to someone else's purpose. The ideal of *kyosei* was defined by Ryuzaburo Kaku, the late chairman of Canon, Inc., as "living and working together for the good of all." *Kyosei* is a concept that tempers individual, organizational, and even national self-interest by emphasizing more embracing "common goods."[47] In its July 2003 Global Dialogue in Switzerland, the CRT heard from three prominent representatives of Christianity, Judaism, and Islam about the strong fit between the CRT's foundational ideals and those underlying all three of these faith traditions, even though this fit was not a conscious part of the CRT design process.[48]

The CRT *Principles* express these two ideals in a format that progresses toward greater specificity. The document's *Preamble* asserts the vital need for corporate conscience in the modern business world. The *Preamble* is followed by seven *General Principles*, which apply the ideals of human dignity and *kyosei* to business practice in a global context. The third and final section of the CRT *Principles* invokes a stakeholder framework to spell out the *General Principles* even further. These *Stakeholder Principles*, as they are called, relate the ideals of human dignity and *kyosei* to a company's relationships with customers, employees, investors, suppliers, competitors, and communities. (The CRT *Principles for Business* appear as an Appendix to this chapter.)

Today, the CRT *Principles for Business* are a worldwide phenomenon. Available in 12 languages, they are acknowledged because of their origins in the business community itself – and textbooks in business administration present them as an example of how ethical norms can transcend cultures.[49] Harvard professor Lynn Sharp Paine refers in her recent book to the CRT *Principles for Business* as "among the best-known and more comprehensive statements to emerge in recent decades."[50] William Donaldson, former SEC Chairman, described the CRT Principles as having "energized thinking about ethical business practices not just in the United States, but throughout the world, with special emphasis in Europe and Japan."[51]

Since 2000 – as it turns out, years in which we have seen unprecedented business scandals – the CRT membership expressed strong interest in taking the principles further. At the 1999 CRT Global Dialogue, the followng sentiment was expressed and widely supported: "The mere *articulation* of principles does *not* carry aspiration into action. What is called for beyond articulation is the identification of objective criteria – what we are calling *benchmarks* – indicators that a company's acceptance of the Caux Principles is confirmed in practice."[52]

A Baldrige process for ethics?

A working group was formed after the 1999 CRT meeting to develop a set of benchmarks which came to be known as the SAIP (Self-Assessment and Improvement Process) and in the course of its deliberations, the group decided to model its efforts on the successful *Malcolm Baldrige National Quality Program* in the US.[53] The *Baldrige Quality Program* had a profound impact on American businesses, and its success in revolutionizing American industry led to its extension into education and healthcare, where it is exerting a similar positive influence. The inventors of the SAIP have attempted to build on this legacy by applying the Baldrige self-assessment model within the arena of business ethics.[54] In the words of three members of the inventor group, the Baldrige Criteria for Performance Excellence serve as:

• a focused business excellence model;
• a realistic basis for self-assessment;
• a comprehensive communications vehicle;
• a mechanism for continual improvement; and
• a framework for learning.

The inventors continue:

> Consistently applied, the Baldrige Criteria provide a model for assessing the current state of business performance and a roadmap to performance excellence. Similarly, the SAIP can be viewed as a large open book test on business ethics, encompassing all the corporate social responsibility questions business leaders now feel compelled to ask – a kind of *corporate* examination of conscience. The goal of the SAIP is an ethical reengineering of the corporation in the same sense that the Baldrige Criteria helped reengineer corporate performance.[55]

The SAIP is essentially a structured inventory of questions designed to reveal to corporate leaders and boards of directors the degree to which their organizations have institutionalized aspirations like those embodied in the CRT *Principles*. The seven CRT *General Principles*

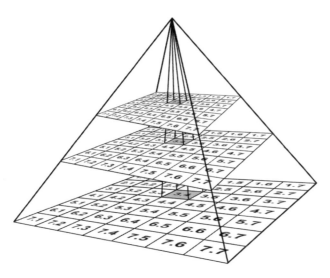

Figure 5.3 The SAIP Inventory Matrix in three progressively detailed versions

are arrayed, along with the *Stakeholder Principles* in a 49-cell matrix of self-assessment questions. But since collecting meaningful data in response to such a set of questions can take a significant amount of time, the SAIP inventory has been formulated in three versions, each progressively more detailed (and time-consuming) than its predecessor (see Figure 5.3). Version I (top layer) is the SAIP *Executive and Board Survey,* designed for a relatively quick (3 hour) "impression" of the company's performance with a single score associated with one question in each cell of the matrix. Version II (middle layer) is the Senior Management Survey, which calls for a more elaborate set of questions (and scoring procedures) and can take a few days or weeks to complete. Finally, Version III (bottom layer) is the complete (or "long form") version of the matrix, involving 275 benchmarks and a time investment of several months.

Beta-testing of the SAIP inventory has been progressing on several fronts since 2002, including companies in the US, Europe, and Asia. In Japan, two large companies are involved; in Germany, a middle-sized company; and in the US, two small-to-mid-sized companies.[56] A number of lessons have already been learned during this testing process, and the inventor group expects to be able to improve all three versions of the inventory considerably before its formal roll-out in 2006. Already apparent, however, are certain strengths, weaknesses, opportunities, and threats to the success of the SAIP effort, which I will take up next.

Strengths, weaknesses, opportunities and threats

Among the basic *strengths* of the SAIP, we can mention four. First, the deliberate modeling of the SAIP on the Baldrige process is a powerful and *practical foundation*. Recently, Jeffrey E. Garten, Dean of the Yale School of Management in his book *The Politics of Fortune: A New Agenda for Business Leaders* had this to say about the Baldrige process and ethics (subsequent to the SAIP development indicated above):

> American presidents bestow the Baldrige Award to companies that demonstrate the highest quality of products and services. Why not similar accolades for business leaders of character? The media fixates on CEOs whose share prices soar; why not give more attention to those whose ethical values are models for others?[57]

Second, the fact that the Caux *Principles* are the content platform for the SAIP inventory matrix affords it a significant level of *global credibility*. The CRT Principles were developed *by* business leaders *for* business leaders, facilitating their acceptance (and translation into 12 languages). Thus it is no accident that during the beta testing phase for the SAIP, enthusiastic efforts to translate and test the inventory were forthcoming from both European and Asian companies.

A third – and related strength – is the *comprehensiveness* of the SAIP inventory, rooted as it is in the comprehensiveness of the CRT *Principles* themselves. Unlike various auditing tools that might have special purposes, for example, to scan environmental or labor practices, the SAIP provides an overview of a company's ethical posture as well as its attitudes toward compliance with law and regulation. This allows boards of directors and senior executives to respond constructively, especially in the US context, to recent legal (Sarbanes-Oxley) and regulatory (2004 Revised Federal Sentencing Guidelines, see below) initiatives.

A fourth strength of the SAIP is *adaptability*. This strength manifests itself in three ways that are likely to appeal to business leaders and boards. As we have seen, the SAIP inventory, because it is designed with three levels of specificity, can be used by an organization gradually. It allows for the management of the costs of executive time.

Another form of adaptability comes from the possibility of applying the SAIP inventory to specific business units within large global organizations, rolling it out to the whole organization if the smaller-scale application warrants it. Finally, the SAIP, even though it was designed for use with the CRT *Principles for Business*, is adaptable for use with other norms and codes that align well with the CRT *Principles*, such as the *UN Global Compact* and the *OECD Corporate Guidelines*.

There are two *weaknesses* of the SAIP inventory that merit attention. The first is simply that it is not yet widely adopted and so it does not yet provide the kind of global business standard that will give companies the confidence they need to "join the party" so to speak. Beta-testing on three continents so far gives reason for optimism about overcoming this weakness. A second weakness is methodological. As it is currently conceived, the SAIP is essentially a *private* tool for companies to use, without oversight if oversight is not desired. This fact reduces barriers to using the inventory due to apprehension about both public relations and competitive advantage. On the other hand, the privacy of the SAIP's use raises questions about the objectivity of self-scoring (not present, we may note, in the context of the Baldrige process because it called for an external panel to do the scoring for the *awards* process).[58]

Furthermore, the benefits of less privacy, in addition to objectivity in scoring, might also include wider "best practices" learning within and between industries, beyond the longitudinal learning that SAIP companies achieve *internally* over time. Of course, companies have little to gain and much self-awareness to lose from "fudging" their own scoring, but the public policy possibilities of an SAIP used with – for example – SEC reporting standards and oversight are attractive in the long term. Jeffrey Garten might as well have been referring to the SAIP when he wrote:

> The next stage in corporate citizenship – indeed, it has already arrived – is for companies to allow their community and social policies to be audited by represented third parties. This will require the development of a common framework for how to measure different kinds of progress, in place of the wide variety of measurement techniques that companies use now.[59]

As to *opportunities*, several have already been anticipated. From the point of view of public policy, the SAIP might eventually provide a powerful template for ethical reporting and comparisons among companies. Indeed, beyond regulatory interests, such as the SEC and other agencies, there are the interests of "social investors" who would benefit from reliable quantification of corporate ethical values.

From the point of view of the companies actually *using* the SAIP, of course, there are other opportunities. First among them is self-awareness leading to self-improvement. But there are also the newly mandated requirements of the Sarbanes-Oxley Act (2002) and the newly revised Federal Sentencing Guidelines (2004). Sarbanes-Oxley calls not only for expanding the roles of corporate Audit Committees, removing conflicts of interest on the part of external auditors, and new duties for analysts and attorneys.[60] It also establishes new executive responsibilities and restrictions for CEOs and CFOs. These include, among other things, responsibility for establishing and maintaining the company's internal controls and demonstrating "that the internal controls have been designed, established, and maintained for the purpose of providing material information to them about the company and its subsidiaries." The SAIP is a tool that could play a significant role in such a demonstration – both to corporate officers and boards of directors.

Similarly, the newly revised Federal Sentencing Guidelines for Organizations (FSGO) call for changes that the SAIP could in fact help to bring about. For example, the report of the Ad Hoc Advisory Group on the Organizational Guidelines (October 7, 2003) suggests the following modifications and additions, among others, to the original 1991 Federal Sentencing Guidelines:

- Emphasis on the importance within the guidelines of an *organizational culture* that encourages a commitment to compliance with the law;
- Specification of the *responsibilities* of an organization's *governing authority and organizational leadership* for compliance;
- Addition of "*periodic evaluation of the effectiveness of a program*" to the requirement for monitoring and auditing systems;
- Inclusion of the phrase "seek guidance about potential or actual violations of law" within the criteria in order to more specifically encourage *prevention* and *deterrence* of violations of law as part of compliance programs;
- Provision for the conduct of *ongoing risk assessments* as part of the implementation of an "effective program."

Because the SAIP represents – ultimately – a cultural discipline within an organization, it can provide an implementation vehicle as well as an early warning system for many of the items listed above, especially where I have added emphasis using italics.[61]

Charles M. Denny, former CEO of ADC Telecommunications, Inc., summarized the opportunities afforded by the SAIP eloquently:

> The only way a director can totally understand the behavior of a company is to shake it from top to bottom, by means of a thorough and systematic assessment like the SAIP. Performing just such an assessment is critical if directors are to assure themselves that the company for which they are responsible is performing as they believe it should.[62]

Finally, as to *threats*, perhaps the most significant lies with a problem identified in the revised FSGO as the "litigation dilemma." This threat comes not from a conflict *within* the organizations to which the FSGO apply, but from *outside*. In the words of the Ad Hoc Advisory Group, the dilemma arises in this way:

> [T]he institution of truly effective programs, the auditing and monitoring that such programs require, and the training and internal reporting systems that such programs contemplate, all create a real risk that information generated by these admirable practices will be used by other potential litigants to harm the organization. This situation is often referred to as the "litigation dilemma," and it is recognized as one of the major greatest impediments to the institution or maintenance of truly effective compliance programs.

What a paradoxical situation seems to have been created in US society – a situation in which organizations seeking to develop information to improve their behavior have to fear that such information might actually be used against them! This amounts to an incentive *not* to be responsible – at least not in a systematic way that could be effective, such as the SAIP. If an "examination of conscience" is an effective tool for self-assessment and improvement – and it is – then we have to find a way to remove the hazard of "discoverability" from such examinations. The Ad Hoc Advisory Group acknowledged: (a) that this threat was real; and (b) that it would probably take the US Congress to remove it:

Recognizing that the litigation dilemma cannot be resolved within the organizational sentencing guidelines themselves, the Advisory Group is compelled by practicality to signal the pivotal role that the organizational sentencing guidelines play in this dilemma. Consequently, the Advisory Group recommends that the Sentencing Commission initiate and foster further dialogue toward a resolution of the "litigation dilemma" with appropriate policy makers, including Congress . . .[63]

Conclusion

No tool, including the SAIP, can by itself orient corporate conscience. But it seems reasonable to suggest that honest, forthright application of the SAIP could help to uncover behavior and tendencies like those that undermined Enron, Andersen, and other companies. It profiles a company's current "location" (self-assessment), allows for quantifying a company's "destination" (improvement), and identifies the magnitude of the gap between them. The SAIP goes some distance toward realizing Lynn Paine's call in her book *Value Shift*:

> What's needed is a method for integrating the moral point of view into the management decision process. A structured process for identifying and evaluating moral concerns can correct for the blind spots inherent in many conventional frameworks and help decision makers more effectively link the values they espouse with the choices they actually make.[64]

When the task of orienting values is approached in this way, the SAIP's probing questions can function not only for gathering information, but for raising awareness and anticipating future ethical challenges. As Sam Goldwyn once said: "For your information, let me ask you a question." This kind of *orientation* sets the stage naturally for *institutionalization*, as we shall see in Chapter 6. Let me conclude with a remark from Jeffrey Garten that is reminiscent of Reell's co-CEO Steve Wikstrom on the idea of a moral compass:

> In other words, CEOs and their boards need a "true north" – a clear sense of who they are, what their company stands for, and what obligations it has, not only to shareholders but also to stakeholders around the world. These views should be clearly articulated to all constituencies – not as rhetorical mush, but as guidelines for operations. The purpose is to set realistic expectations for all concerned.[65]

Appendix: The Caux Round Table Principles
– *Business Behavior for a Better World*

Section 1: Preamble

The mobility of employment and capital is making business increasingly global in its transactions and its effects. Laws and market forces in such a context are necessary but insufficient guides for conduct. Responsibility for a corporation's actions and policies and respect for the dignity and interests of its stakeholders are fundamental. And shared values, including a commitment to shared prosperity, are as important for a global community as for communities of smaller scale. For all of the above reasons, and because business can be a powerful agent of positive social change, we offer the following principles as a foundation for dialogue and action by business leaders in search of corporate responsibility. In so doing, we affirm the legitimacy and centrality of moral values in economic decision-making because, without them, stable business relationships and a sustainable world community are impossible.

Section 2. General Principles

Principle 1. The responsibilities of corporations: Beyond shareholders toward stakeholders

The role of a corporation is to create wealth and employment and to provide marketable products and services to consumers at a reasonable price commensurate with quality. To play this role, the corporation must maintain its own economic health and viability, but its own survival is not an end in itself. The corporation also has a role to play in improving the lives of all of its customers, employees, and shareholders by sharing with them the wealth it has created. Suppliers and competitors as well should expect businesses to honor their obligations in a spirit of honesty and fairness. And as responsible citizens of the local, national, regional, and global communities in which they operate, corporations share a part in shaping the future of those communities.

Principle 2. The economic and social impact of corporations: Toward innovation, justice and world community

Corporations established in foreign countries to develop, produce, or sell should also contribute to the social advancement of those countries by

145

creating jobs and helping to raise their purchasing power. They should also give attention to and contribute to human rights, education, welfare, vitalization of communities in the countries in which they operate. Moreover, through innovation, effective and prudent use of resources, and free and fair competition, corporations should contribute to the economic and social development of the world community at large, not only the countries in which they operate. New technology, production, products, marketing, and communication are all means to this broader contribution.

Principle 3. Corporate behavior: Beyond the letter of law toward a spirit of trust

With the exception of legitimate trade secrets, a corporation should recognize that sincerity, candor, truthfulness, the keeping of promises, and transparency contribute not only to the credit and stability of business activities but also to the smoothness and efficiency of business transactions, particularly on the international level.

Principle 4. Respect for rules: Beyond trade friction toward cooperation

To avoid trade frictions and promote freer trade, equal business opportunity, and fair and equitable treatment for all participants, corporations should respect international and domestic rules. In addition, they should recognize that their own behavior, although legal, may still have adverse consequences.

Principle 5. Support for multilateral trade: Beyond isolation toward world community

Corporations should support the multilateral trade system of GATT/World Trade Organization and similar international agreements. They should cooperate in efforts to promote the judicious liberalization of trade and to relax those domestic measures that unreasonably hinder global commerce.

Principle 6. Respect for the environment: Beyond protection toward enhancement

A corporation should protect, and where possible, improve the environment, promote sustainable development, and prevent the wasteful use of natural resources.

Principle 7. Avoidance of illicit operations: Beyond profit toward peace

A corporation should not participate in or condone bribery, money laundering, and other corrupt practices. It should not trade in arms or materials used for terrorist activities, drug traffic or other organized crime.

Section 3. Stakeholder Principles

Customers

We believe in treating all customers with dignity and that our customers are not only those who directly purchase our products and services but also those who acquire them through authorized market channels. In cases where those who use our products and services do not purchase them directly from us, we will make our best effort to select marketing and assembly/ manufacturing channels that accept and follow the standards of business conduct articulated here. We have a responsibility:

- to provide our customers with the highest quality products and services consistent with their requirements;
- to treat our customers fairly in all aspects of our business transactions, including a high level of service and remedies for customer dissatisfaction;
- to make every effort to ensure that the health and safety (including environmental quality) of our customers will be sustained or enhanced by our products or services;
- to avoid disrespect for human dignity in products offered, marketing, and advertising;
- to respect the integrity of the cultures of our customers.

Employees

We believe in the dignity of every employee and we, therefore, have a responsibility:

- to provide jobs and compensation that improve and uplift workers' circumstances in life;
- to provide working conditions that respect employees' health and dignity;
- to be honest in communications with employees and open in sharing information, limited only by legal and competitive constraints;
- to be accessible to employee input, ideas, complaints, and requests;
- to engage in good faith negotiations when conflict arises;
- to avoid discriminatory practices and to guarantee equal treatment and opportunity in areas such as gender, age, race, and religion;

- to promote in the corporation itself the employment of handicapped and other disadvantaged people in places of work where they can be genuinely useful;
- to protect employees from avoidable injury and illness in the workplace.;
- to be sensitive to the serious unemployment problems frequently associated with business decisions and to work with governments and other agencies in addressing these dislocations.

Owners/Investors

We believe in honoring the trust our investors place in us. We, therefore, have a responsibility:

- to apply professional and diligent management in order to secure a fair and competitive return on our owners' investment;
- to disclose relevant information to owners/investors subject only to legal and competitive constraints;
- to conserve and protect the owners/investors' assets;
- to respect owner/investor' requests, suggestions, complaints, and formal resolutions.

Suppliers

We begin with the conviction that our relationship with suppliers and subcontractors, like a partnership, must be based on mutual respect. As a result, we have a responsibility:

- to seek fairness in all our activities including pricing, licensing, and rights to sell;
- to ensure that our business activities are free from coercion and unnecessary litigation, thus promoting fair competition;
- to foster long-term stability in the supplier relationship in return for value, quality and reliability;
- to share information with suppliers and integrate them into our planning processes in order to achieve stable relationships;
- to pay suppliers on time and in accordance with agreed terms of trade;
- to seek, encourage, and prefer suppliers and subcontractors whose employment practices respect human dignity.

Competitors

We believe that fair economic competition is one of the basic requirements for increasing the wealth of nations and ultimately for making possible the just distribution of goods and services. We, therefore, have responsibilities:

- to foster open markets for trade and investment;
- to promote competitive behavior that is socially and environmentally beneficial and demonstrates mutual respect among competitors;
- to refrain from either seeking or participating in questionable payments or favors to secure competitive advantages;
- to respect both material and intellectual property rights;
- to refuse to acquire commercial information by dishonest or unethical means, such as industrial espionage.

Communities

We believe that as global corporate citizens we can contribute, even to a small extent, to such forces of reform and human rights as are at work in the communities in which we operate. We, therefore, have responsibilities in the communities in which we do business:

- to respect human rights and democratic institutions, and to promote them wherever practical;
- to recognize government's legitimate obligation to the society at large and to support public policies and practices that promote human development through harmonious relations between business and other segments of society;
- to collaborate in countries and areas which struggle in their economic development with those forces which are dedicated to raising standards of health, education, and workplace safety;
- to promote and stimulate sustainable development;
- to play a lead role in preserving the physical environment and conserving the earth's resources;
- to support peace, security, and diversity in local communities;
- to respect the integrity of local cultures;
- to be a good citizen by supporting the communities in which we operate; this can be done through charitable donations, educational and cultural contributions, and employee participation in community and civic affairs.

6

Institutionalizing Corporate Conscience

Once corporate leaders achieve an *orientation* for their companies, clarifying the direction they wish to take – the process of *institutionalization* becomes paramount. How can the corporate mission and values be made part of the operating consciousness of the company? How can they be written into the incentive structure of the organization, alongside financial goals and performance criteria of other kinds? If the "first nature" of the corporation is economic, how can corporate conscience become "second nature"?

Giving Substance to the Type 3 Organization: The H. J. Heinz Case

The H. J. Heinz Company needs little introduction to most observers of the business world – or to most consumers of ketchup. Headquartered in Pittsburgh, Pennsylvania, Heinz was a large, divisionalized producer of food products (Heinz, Starkist, Oreida), but also diversified into food-related services (Weight Watchers). Like many large companies since the mid-1970s, Heinz had an ethics code, a management incentive system with annual bonuses, and relatively decentralized operations by division. In 1980, senior management at Heinz went through a scandal – not of the magnitude of the Enron and WorldCom scandals two decades later – but a scandal nonetheless. It was revealed that corporate earnings reports had been inaccurate for a number of years due to deliberate under-reporting of earnings by several divisions. After an investigation, the company acknowledged to the IRS and to the SEC that there had been a "loss of control consciousness" in a number of its divisions. Besides having to restate its financials for an 8-year period, the company's reputation with its shareholders and with government agencies suffered a blow.

At the time, Heinz was pursuing a strategy of smooth, predictable earnings growth. There was an incentive system for division managers with goals set automatically by corporate headquarters each year: last year's earnings plus 15 percent. And there were significant consequences for not making one's goals, with the annual bonus as much as 40 percent of compensation. The decentralized corporate structure included the financial reporting function. Managers had to sign off annually on a formal ethics code that specifically mentioned honesty in financial reporting, but there were informal norms understood by staff and division leadership which seemed to contradict the ethics code.

Apparently, the pressure to reach annual goals, together with the regular incrementing of those goals based on performance, led a number of division managers to use illegal methods of reducing reported earnings, once their basic targets had been met. The motive was to avoid excessive increases in performance expectations for the subsequent year through an "insurance policy" based on prepaid expenses and delayed invoices.

In discussions of the Heinz case over many years, I have found it useful to invoke the so-called "Seven S" framework for general management developed by McKinsey and published by Pascale and Athos in *The Art of Japanese Management* (1981).[1] The basic idea is that effective general management pays attention to seven dynamic aspects of the organization which need to be mutually reinforcing and which can work *against* one another if they are not harmonized (see Figure 6.1).

It becomes clear in analyzing the case that a certain *superordinate goal* (the company's *orientation*, to use the language of the previous chapter) guided the Heinz *strategy* of smooth, predictable earnings growth in a decentralized *structure* with incentive and goal-setting *systems* that created considerable pressure on *staff*, whose *skills* and *style* developed to mitigate the pressure through dishonest behavior. The trouble was that the *superordinate goal* was apparently not the company's original one of selling wholesome food products, but instead a financial one: satisfying Wall Street analysts.

It also becomes clear that the solution, culturally, to the Heinz problem will need to be thoroughgoing, attending to the relationships

151

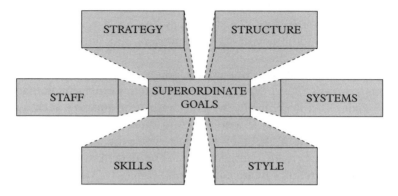

Figure 6.1 McKinsey's "Seven S" framework for general management

among all of the "Seven S" variables. To the extent that *teleopathy* infected – indeed, was *institutionalized* in – the Heinz culture, the development of *conscience* would have to be at least as pervasive. More on this point later in this chapter.

Lessons from the Heinz case

There are a number of lessons to take away from the H. J. Heinz case. One lesson is that managing organizations is like managing ecosystems. As environmentalists often remind us, "everything is connected to everything else." A management incentive system designed to "smooth" earnings to meet Wall Street's expectations had significant side effects. The company's decentralized structure provided the occasion and managers' risk-averse style provided the motivation. The result was systematic misrepresentation to shareholders over 8 years.

Another lesson from the Heinz case is that leadership influences the seriousness with which employees interpret value messages. Chagrined over the scandal, some senior managers appeared not to view the illegal behavior as significant. As a result, certain needed cultural changes at Heinz may well have been delayed, if they ever were implemented.

The most important lesson taught by the Heinz case, however, is this: *There are two languages of ethics in every organization.* There is the language of espoused values articulated in corporate codes of conduct and credos; and there is the language of values-in-action, driven by the incentives, rewards, hiring and promotion systems of the organization. When the two come into conflict, the second language inevitably prevails.

The Story of Beowulf

In his book, *The Heart Aroused*, David Whyte retells the story of the Old English epic of *Beowulf* with application to modern corporate life. Beowulf, a sixth-century "consultant," went from kingdom to kingdom solving problems.

> Hearing that Hrothgar, King of Denmark, was suffering the predations of Grendel, a diabolical swamp creature, he presented himself in Hrothgar's hall as the answer to his problems. Apparently, at night, after the feasting and gift-giving was done, a large green creature smeared with mud would emerge from the lake, enter the hall, fight off Hrothgar's best warriors, tear men and women limb from limb, and drag their remains back to the swamp . . .
>
> Beowulf is welcomed by Hrothgar, and that night lies in wait for Grendel with his men . . . [When Grendel appears] Beowulf mortally wounds Grendel who then staggers back to die in the mere.
>
> That night there is tremendous feasting and gift-giving. The problem, it seems, has been solved in one swift movement. But that night, as Beowulf sleeps with his men in a different hall, something else comes from the swamp . . . fights off the best warriors, and retreats with its human victim. Grendel's *mother*.
>
> The message in this portion of the poem is unsparing. It is not the thing you fear that you must deal with, it is the *mother* of the thing you fear. The very thing that has given birth to the nightmare.[2]

Whyte uses the poem to illustrate the power of fear in preventing individuals and groups from confronting the sources of their problems, the sources that often lie beneath the waters of dark lakes. Despite the objections of the people in Hrothgar's kingdom, Beowulf dives into the lake and kills Grendel's mother in her very lair, fighting without taking a breath. The monster-slaying analogy calls for serious conversations in the workplace – possibly revealing gaps between espoused organizational values and day-to-day incentives and behaviors. Unless the corporate culture permits – indeed, *encourages* – regular conversations that identify inevitable institutional barriers to its stated ethical aspirations, it is foolish to believe that those barriers will not eventually dominate the language of "espoused values." In the language of the epic, companies can "die on the shore," fearful of courageously diving into the lake:

> At night, that lake
> Burns like a torch. No one knows its bottom,
> No wisdom reaches such depths. A deer,
> Hunted through the woods by packs of Hounds,
> A stag with great horns, though driven through the forest
> From far away places, prefers to die
> On those shores, refuses to save its life
> In that water. It isn't far, nor is it
> A pleasant spot![3]

Minding the Gap: The Heinz Syndrome and "Hypocrisy Exercises"

In my work with a number of organizations, the third lesson mentioned above (about the two languages of ethics in every organization) has given rise to an interactive exercise that invariably yields practical insight to executives. We first discuss the H. J. Heinz case study, diagnosing the problem and suggesting ways to repair the situation culturally within the organization. Then, after sharing the Beowulf story (to urge courageous conversation) and defining the "Heinz Syndrome" *as a relatively stable tension or lack of congruence between the two languages of ethics in the organization,* I invite participants to look at their own organizations with this pattern in mind.

The signs on the train platforms in the London Underground warn: "Mind the gap!" Figuratively speaking, this warning applies as well to the relationship between espoused values and values-in-action. Each participant is asked to reflect on a grid as it applies in his or her own situation. Then small groups (6–8 persons each) are asked to discuss and surface for the large group the most significant examples of gaps between espoused values and values-in-action. I make it clear that this is not an exercise in corporate "gossip" and that the purpose is to learn a certain kind of discernment that all effective leaders must develop.

Using the template in Figure 6.2, executives are "given permission" to find and articulate hypocrisy gaps (1a and 2a) as well as *bridges* for those gaps (1b and 2b). This exercise is usually carried out in the presence of a senior leader who might be able to explain certain apparent anomalies or to address them in a practical way once they

HYPOCRISY EXERCISE TEMPLATE	
Building upon our discussion of ethical decision-making, especially the H. J. Heinz case series, turn now to your experience within this company. In the spaces provided below, try to identify:	
1a. An example from your past or current experience in which company values pointed one way and internal work incentives pointed another.	**1b.** What is the most realistic and responsible way to resolve or remove the disparity in 1a?
2a. An example from your past or current experience in which company values pointed one way and external sanctions/incentives pointed another.	**2b.** What is the most realistic and responsible way to resolve or remove the disparity in 2a?

Figure 6.2 Hypocrisy exercise template

have been identified. The distinction between 1a and 2a examples is significant, and helpful to the exercise. To fill the "1a" box, participants are looking for Heinz-like examples in which the company's own espoused values are out-of-synch with actual incentives, policies, reward systems, sanctions, etc. Sales incentives, for example, may be awarded quarterly, leading to urgent discounting and "loading" of products onto customer shelves, despite the counter-productive implications of the discounting and the potential for questionable financial reporting associated with "loading."

Reporter Tim Huber noted in February 2004 that Minneapolis-based General Mills had received a warning of a civil action by the Securities and Exchange Commission for violating federal securities laws.[4] One infraction thought to be part of the problem was known as "loading – or sending extra product to retailers so General Mills could book sales and meet quarterly revenue and profit goals." A former General Mills manager who was fired during 2003 alleged in an interview with the Associated Press "that General Mills has engaged in loading since 1998 and stepped up the practice in early 2003 because its share price affected how much it had to pay Diageo PLC for Pillsbury." The former employee alleged that General Mills "routinely shipped as much as 20 weeks worth of products to customers who wanted perhaps only a two-week supply."

To fill the "2a" box, participants are asked to look *outside* the company for incentives or sanctions that work against the best efforts of the company as it seeks to live up to its espoused values. Often examples in this area will come from competitive pressures (*"they do it, so we* have *to do it or lose business"*) or corruption in the political arena (bribery, demands for kickbacks, etc.). "2a" problems remind us that the social and political environment of business can attach serious costs to company integrity, both in relation to the attraction of customers and in relation to compliance with laws and regulations. And often these costs are levied when market competition and legal obligations have maximum leverage in the direction of compromise.

The "2a" and "2b" elements of the exercise allow participants to see espoused values as under pressure from the outside, while the "1a" and "1b" elements invite them to see the pressures as self-imposed, from the inside. The self-imposed pressures are often easier to recognize, culturally, than those that are imposed from the outside, but this is not always the case. And it is gratifying to listen to a group of thoughtful executives come up with ethically creative *responses* to such pressures, responses that can ultimately transform the "playing field" with the right degree of courage and patience.

Bill George comments in his book, *Authentic Leadership*, that identifying this kind of information is critical for developing a culture of trust in the organization:

> When the company's leaders become role models for its values, the impact on the entire organization is tremendous. The trust of the leadership is earned through practicing the company's values every day, not just by espousing them. But when leaders preach one thing and practice another, commitment is quickly lost and employees become doubly cynical.[5]

Integrity Exercises

Ron James, President of the *Center for Ethical Business Cultures* (CEBC) at the University of St. Thomas in Minnesota, suggested in response to an earlier draft of this chapter that hypocrisy exercises can and should be balanced with exercises that identify *positive* fits between an organization's aspirations and its incentive systems. We might call these "Integrity Exercises" and use a template similar to the one depicted in the previous section. The idea would be to help executives identify not only gaps or misfits between the two languages of ethics in their organizations, but also to find examples of successes

– where the languages are "in synch" with one another. After all, *integrity* is in many ways the opposite of hypocrisy. It signals a basic *unity* between espoused values and values-in-action – so that the culture of the company is really *working* – in contrast to the friction signaled by hypocrisy.

Integrity exercises and hypocrisy exercises are hands-on tools for enhancing ethical awareness in organizations and they have tremendous power in advancing what we are calling *institutionalization*. It is crucial, of course, that CEOs and/or other senior leaders be present for such exercises, not only to signal that they take ethical awareness seriously, but also to be in a position to respond to any identified "gaps."

Bill George suggests that often gaps (and successes) between behavior and aspirations need to be shared openly.[6] Such messages from CEOs to leaders and managers throughout their organizations can have enormously salutary effects, but they can sometimes seem to CEOs like "jumping in Grendel's lake" since they invite subsequent candid and revealing conversations in the workplace. The alternative, dying on the shore like the deer in the Beowulf epic, can be tempting.

Harry Halloran, Jr., CEO of American Refining Group, Inc., jumped into Grendel's lake in 2002, when he decided to do an examination of corporate conscience using the Self-Assessment and Improvement Process (SAIP) described in Chapter 5.[7] The SAIP is an elaborate version of what I have been calling a "hypocrisy exercise" in the sense that it displays a gap between actual corporate behavior and a company's espoused values. The identification of opportunities for improvement, based on a company's self-assessment, functions in the same way as bridging the gaps described earlier under "1b" and "2b."

Halloran had a strategic opportunity to acquire a second refinery in Rouseville, Pennsylvania shortly after his company had implemented the SAIP process. This second refinery was about 80 miles distant from the company's main refinery in Bradford, Pennsylvania. The Rouseville acquisition had the potential to lead to 40 redundancies within the Bradford workforce. Instead of automatically embracing this potential cost savings, Halloran challenged the company's leadership to plan the Rouseville acquisition *without laying off a single Bradford employee*. In the spirit mentioned by Bill George, Harry Halloran viewed his company's commitment to employees as a value that needed to be maintained in the face of an easier, more conventional, layoff approach – and he did this in part because of having seen in the SAIP results an opportunity for corporate improvement in the area of employee confidence in management. (The SAIP Executive Survey is reprinted as an Appendix to this chapter.)

Leadership Modeling Decisiveness

If "actions speak louder than words," the actions of CEOs that have both wide visibility and clear ethical content speak louder than any other actions. Such actions serve as large-scale demonstrations to the rank and file of the seriousness and importance that senior management attaches (or not) to ethical values. Stories of such actions become part of the orientation of newcomers to the company, tools for cultural transmission. This is a key element of what I am calling *institutionalization*.

It is hard to overstate, for example, the significance of James Burke's decisiveness in his handling of the *Tylenol* poisonings in the 1980s. It sent a powerful message to employees and customers alike regarding the operating values of Johnson & Johnson. It is still used today – sometimes accurately and sometimes not – as an "ethics story" both inside and outside the company.

About the same time as the *Tylenol* case, I became aware of another example while writing a case study on the Duke Power Company. When CEO Bill Lee had been faced with a layoff involving 1,500 construction workers, he needed to decide between inverse seniority as a criterion and a mechanism that would permit the retention of many recently employed minorities. The company's affirmative action gains were at stake at a point in its history when past injustices could not be ignored. Lee's conviction led him to protect minorities with less seniority and to face criticisms of reverse discrimination.

Years later, there was another contraction of that company's work force. Because of Lee's courage six years earlier, affirmative action gains were not at stake. Lee shared the following reflection on the importance of his original decision for institutionalizing the core value of racial justice. Having bit the bullet earlier, he said, and being careful in subsequent re-staffing:

> We were able to lay off in inverse seniority without affecting minority percentage employment. The [earlier] experience gave a positive signal throughout all departments of the company that we really care about

affirmative action. I believe this helped set the stage of acceptance of upward mobility for minorities and females as one of our published corporate performance goals. Achievement of these goals would result in some financial reward to all employees at every level. It receives wide publicity and monthly progress reports to all employees.[8]

Henry Schacht of Cummins, Inc. modeled decisiveness as his "clear-eyed and hard-nosed approach to business" combined with "a tenacious adherence to principle." The following story illustrates.

Cummins in the late 1970s held a 20 percent share of the diesel engine market in South Africa, and was being encouraged by the government to build manufacturing facilities there. The company agreed, on condition that it be permitted to do business in South Africa the same way it did business everywhere else in the world: Cummins South Africa would have an integrated work force, supervisors of all races, and so on. Quickly, the word came back from the South African authorities. No; that would not be acceptable, and if Cummins should choose to stand on principle, a European diesel maker would be happy to go into South Africa in Cummins' place.

"And that's what happened," Henry Schacht later remembered. "We lost all the business. Our view was that you don't need to have all the business in the world. You have certain fundamental principles – and if they can't be followed, then it's not business you want." Schacht also recalls that it "didn't take five minutes of the board's time" to make this decision.[9]

In Chapter 11 of *Authentic Leadership*, Bill George relates ethical dilemmas he had to face as CEO. One involved the firing of a business executive in Europe whom Bill George himself had appointed. A due diligence audit had uncovered improper accounting involving a sham contract for marketing services. "When the controller was asked what the account was for, he refused to answer, saying that it was integral to doing business in Italy."[10] George became convinced that the money was being used to pay off Italian doctors for using Medtronic products. The European president was called to Minneapolis and confronted.

At this point he got very defensive, even hostile, saying, "That's the trouble with you Americans. You're always trying to impose your values on Europeans. Business is done differently in Europe." Finally, I said, "These are not American values. They are Medtronic values that apply worldwide. You violated them, and you must resign immediately."[11]

More recently, Bill George's successor, Art Collins, and Steve Mahle, head of Medtronic's Cardiac Rhythm Management division, had to face a product quality issue that called for courage and humility. The issue and their decisive response are summarized in the following company press release:

MINNEAPOLIS, February 11, 2005 – Medtronic, Inc., today said it is voluntarily advising physicians about a potential battery shorting mechanism that may occur in a subset of implantable cardioverter-defibrillator (ICD) and cardiac resynchronization therapy defibrillator (CRT-D) models. In a letter to physicians, Medtronic reported that nine batteries (0.01 percent, or approximately 1 in 10,000) have experienced rapid battery depletion due to this shorting action. If shorting occurs, battery depletion can take place within a few hours to a few days, after which there is loss of device function. There are no reported patient injuries or deaths . . .

ICDs shock or pace the heart into normal rhythm after patients suffer rapid, life-threatening heart rhythm disturbances originating in the lower chambers of the heart that can lead to sudden cardiac arrest (SCA). CRT-Ds can also provide electrical pulses to the heart's two lower chambers to improve heart failure symptoms. An ICD or CRT-D device is surgically implanted in the chest in a procedure typically lasting one to two hours.

"We were able to identify this possible risk through our stringent product testing," said Steve Mahle, president of Medtronic Cardiac Rhythm Management. "Even though the potential for rapid battery depletion is extremely low, we see it as our obligation to alert all implanting physicians to the potential issue and provide ways to help them and their affected patients successfully manage the situation."

Stories about decisiveness communicate in a special way the seriousness with which a company takes its moral values. They get repeated over time, helping to make those (and similar) values institutional.

The institutionalization of conscience, then, depends on the convictions of senior leadership expressed in action. But there is more to the story than this. For while high profile examples of values in action give energy to the process, employees need to learn how less visible, *but equally important,* ethical decisions fall within their own spans of control.

Other Tools for Institutionalization: Symbols, Ceremonies, Celebrations and Seminars

Hypocrisy exercises and messages from CEOs about the importance of such exercises are just two tools for institutionalizing corporate conscience. There are many others. Four other tools are *symbols* (and images), *ceremonies* (for new hires), *celebrations* (of the impact of the mission), and *seminars* (on ethical leadership). Notice that in the foregoing and in what follows, an underlying dynamic is this: an organization, through its leadership, articulates, symbolizes, celebrates, and reinforces the centrality of ethics to its operations. In doing so, it "puts out the word" that it wishes to take ethics seriously. *This creates the potential for shortfall.*

The "psychology" of corporate conscience – like the psychology of individual conscience – involves setting forth "talk" or external communications that the company's "walk" will then need to live up to. We deliberately expose ourselves to charges of hypocrisy in an effort to deter ourselves from meriting such charges! We cannot be hypocrites without espousing values that might differ from our behavior. We might say that human beings (and human organizations) are aspirational animals! Living *up* to aspirations is the way that conscience functions in our lives. Climbing involves reaching out (talk) and then converging on the destination point (walk). Someone once said that "walking is a series of arrested falls."

I will use Medtronic, Inc. as my primary illustration below because I am most familiar with the inner dynamics of that corporation, but the institutional strategies are quite generalizable.

Symbols

At Medtronic, Inc., the current company logo is adapted from a large mural painted on the original headquarters wall. The mural symbolizes "restoration to health" and depicts a recumbent figure arising from a bed and walking forward.[12] Capturing the elements of corporate values using art and symbolism is a communication tool used

161

by other companies as well. In the 1980s, I described in a Harvard case study how "The Beliefs of Borg-Warner" were transformed into artistic drawings at the request of then-CEO James Beré in an effort to engage the *imaginations* of his management team.[13]

Ceremonies

The symbolic image of the rising figure (first created in an oil painting by artist Alan O. Hage in 1968) is embossed on one side of a medallion, with the company's mission on the reverse side (see Figure 6.3). These medallions are presented personally to each newly hired Medtronic employee in formal ceremonies conducted world-wide by Earl Bakken, the founder of the company, or by the current Chairman and/or CEO. The medallion symbolizes Medtronic's mission to contribute "toward full life" of patients. Some companies give books to new employees recounting corporate history or plaques bearing the corporate credo or value statement. The signal that such ceremonies send to employees (both new and long-term) is that the company wishes to go on record publicly about its basic mission and values. Such actions risk both cynicism and criticism if the "walk" and the "talk" are seriously divergent. *Deliberately creating this risk* is a behavioral tool of great power if it is managed wisely.

Celebrations

Each year prior to Christmas, five or six patients, accompanied by their physicians, describe at a *holiday celebration* for employees how the efforts of those who work for Medtronic have changed their lives.[14] Initiating this practice, Founder Earl Bakken said, "We want our employees to have the reward of seeing patients restored to health." It is hard to overstate the impact that these emotional testimonials have on the employees *around the world* who hear them. It is also hard to overstate the organizational effort and expense that goes into communicating these messages globally, both through closed-circuit television and, when necessary, through geographic-ally separate additional celebrations. The significance of the work of the company to patients and their doctors is reinforced throughout the workforce by these events. They are a powerful reminder of the "purpose of the trip."

Other companies can and should consider such celebrations – essentially manifesting the human goods or services that explain what

162

(a)

(b)

Figure 6.3 Medtronic medallion: (a) Front: "Medtronic – Alleviating Pain – Restoring Health – Extending Life" (b) Back: "Contributing to human welfare in the application of biomedical engineering to alleviate pain, restore health, and extend life." Reproduced by permission of Medtronic, Inc.

the company is "for" and why its values are important.[15] Financial services make possible homes and dreams and the desire for retirement security. Food companies make possible nutrition and conviviality. Entertainment companies make possible creativity and enjoyment. And so on. Every major economic endeavor has (or should have) a link to human good, and companies need to rediscover, reaffirm, and celebrate their contributions in these terms. This will go a considerable distance toward institutionalizing ethical values. Recall Charles

Handy's observation quoted in the last chapter: "The purpose of a business . . . is not to make a profit, full stop. It is to make a profit so that the business can do something more or better. That 'something' becomes the real justification for the business."[16]

Seminars

Management development with an emphasis on ethical values is an important component – and an important *signal* – to those whose words and actions are ultimately the evidence of a company's sincerity about conscience. In the UK, apparently, there are problems linking the espoused values of companies with the educational efforts needed to make them practical. An article in the online version of the *Financial Times* reports that:

> Many leading companies are failing to train their workforce in ethical behaviour despite growing awareness of the need for strict codes of business conduct. . . . [A] survey of companies with ethics codes found half did not provide training for all staff in how to apply them, even though 60 percent required employees to obey the codes as part of their contracts.[17]

Simon Webley, research director of the Institute of Business Ethics and one of the co-authors of the survey report, is quoted in the same article as having said: "Expecting a business ethics policy to have any noticeable effect . . . when no training is provided . . . does not make any business sense." It is unlikely that this problem is unique to the UK.

Indeed, in the US, the revised Federal Sentencing Guidelines for Organizations (FSGO) include a directive to extend ethics training beyond management to leadership, and beyond leadership to the governance structure, including the board of directors:

> The organization shall take reasonable steps to communicate periodically and in a practical manner its standards and procedures, and other aspects of the compliance and ethics program, to [the Board and others] by conducting effective training programs and otherwise disseminating information appropriate to such individuals' respective roles and responsibilities.[18]

But companies have been slow to respond. A survey at the 2004 Ethics Officer Association annual conference found that:

Out of 69 respondents, only 29 (42 percent) said that their organizations provide ethics and compliance training for the board of directors. Twenty percent said they plan to introduce such training "within the next six months" and a further 17 percent "within the next year." However, 12 percent said their organizations had no current plans to do so.[19]

The difference between "training" and "education" in this arena is worth noting. Usually, the term "training" is reserved for activities involving the application to a specific organizational setting of codified laws or norms. "Education" typically has a broader and deeper meaning.[20] What Boards need in this context goes beyond training to education. There will be much more to say on this subject in Chapter 8.

Twice annually, 25 of the approximately 400 director-level executives in Medtronic gather together from around the world for a one-week retreat called "The Medtronic Leader," focused on the ethical challenges of leadership, the need for spiritual reflection, and the meaning of the Medtronic Mission Statement. The Chief Executive Officer speaks to the participants each time, and one member of the company's Executive Committee attends for the entire week to help communicate company history, culture, and values. As Bill George (former CEO and originator of the seminar) described it:

> We created an educational course for high-talent managers around the world called "The Medtronic Leader." The program focuses on leadership from the heart and developing the qualities of a leader, applying experiential learning. I participated in all these sessions, sharing my path to leadership and interacting with the group about the leadership issues they face. Enabling people to go inside to learn more about themselves, their strengths and weaknesses, and their impact on others is an important element of their leadership development.[21]

The current Medtronic CEO, Art Collins has himself never missed the seminar and continues to energize this important developmental experience. Seminars of this kind are clearly generalizable, and many companies have leadership initiatives that are similar – though Medtronic's emphasis on ethical values is bold and unabashed. One of the best ways for companies to develop such seminars is to make use of case studies – either studies of companies that make for good comparisons, or studies of one's own company.

The Seven S Framework Revisited

The process of institutionalization, as I indicated above in connection with the H. J. Heinz case, can be a force for good or ill. The Seven S framework is a useful lens for understanding the "ecology" of an organization's operating consciousness, but it is neutral with respect to whether the ecology is healthy or unhealthy. There was "dysfunctional synergy" among the seven elements for Heinz, which meant that the problem was unlikely to be resolved internally – the challenge would have to come from outside the "ecosystem."

And, of course, that is exactly what happened – during an antitrust suit filed by Heinz against the Campbell Soup Company. Heinz had accused Campbell of monopolistic practices in the canned soup market. Campbell countersued, charging that Heinz monopolized the ketchup market:

> Campbell attorneys, preparing for court action, subpoenaed Heinz documents reflecting its financial relationships with one of its advertising agencies. In April 1979, while taking a deposition from [the president] of the Heinz USA division, Campbell attorneys asked about flows of funds, "certain items which can be called off-book accounts."[22]

This being said, however, the Seven S framework can also help us to identify appropriate "levers of institutionalization" when our purpose is to make ethical values more operational in an organization. At the center, of course, are *superordinate goals* – what I would prefer to call the organizations *mission*, since "goals" at this level are much more embracing, inevitably connected to the economic, political, and social dynamics surrounding the corporation – not just to those that define the corporation in isolation. As we have seen, orienting precedes institutionalizing – and superordinate goals have a lot to do with corporate orientation. But their effective articulation is also the departure point for institutionalization.

Strategy, in the context of corporate conscience, has to do with achieving through market competition the very best for the various stakeholders of the enterprise – short term and long term. Strategy, in conjunction with the organization's mission, defines "rationality and respect" in the company's "mindset" (see Chapters 2 and 3). Leadership messages, symbols, ceremonies, and celebrations connect directly to mission and strategy as the leading edge of corporate conscience. Seminars and "hypocrisy exercises" bridge to the other five of the seven.

Structures and *systems*, the next two "Ss" in the framework, are ultimately in the service of mission and strategy, providing much of the "walk" in the company's "talk." An appropriately decentralized structure, for example, is important for a diversified organization, but the core values of the organization must be communicated and enforced across this structure and must transcend both business unit and geographical boundaries. *Systems* include not only financial controls, but also performance feedback, incentives, goal setting, legal compliance (more in a moment) and board oversight. If these systems are not aligned with the core espoused values of the company, they can easily distort them.

Staff, *skills* and *style*, the so-called "soft Ss" in the framework, relate to the talent that the company puts in the service of mission and strategy, and the way in which that talent is managed. The implications of these factors for corporate conscience are significant. In his penetrating *New Yorker* article diagnosing the culture of Enron before its collapse, Malcolm Gladwell identifies something he called "the talent myth" as a primary factor. He describes Enron's "mind-set" as part of "the new orthodoxy" of American management preached by McKinsey consultants. It justifies high premiums "on degrees from first-tier business schools" and lavish top executive compensation packages. The focus is not on the system or the team, but on "stars." Jeff Skilling, of course, was steeped in the McKinsey culture before joining Enron.[23]

It is perhaps ironic that McKinsey & Co. is the source of both the Seven S framework and the "talent myth" described by Gladwell. Nevertheless, his observations about the talent myth relate not only to staff, skills, and style, but indirectly to structure and systems as well:

> You can grade someone's performance only if you know their performance. And, in the freewheeling culture of Enron, this was all but impossible. People deemed "talented" were constantly being pushed into new jobs and given new challenges. Annual turnover from promotions was close to twenty per cent.[24]

In the end, of course, it is the staff, with their skills and their style, that administer the systems and structures of the organization – and that (eventually) decide on whether the strategies and superordinate goals of the organization will change or remain the same. The staff represents a powerful link between the consciences of individuals and the conscience of the corporation. The talent myth, Gladwell implies, can undermine the culture of the corporation, intentionally or not. In the language of this chapter, the talent myth can undermine the *institutionalization* of ethical values.

> The broader failing of McKinsey and its acolytes at Enron is their assumption that an organization's intelligence is simply a function of the intelligence of its employees. *They believe in stars, because they don't believe in systems.* In a way, that's understandable, because our lives are so obviously enriched by individual brilliance. Groups don't write great novels, and a committee didn't come up with the theory of relativity. But companies work by different rules. They don't just create; they execute and compete and coordinate the efforts of many different people, and the organizations that are most successful at that task are the ones where the *system* is the star.[25]

Gladwell points to the potential downside impact of staffing from the outside and style in relation to the talent myth. Charles Handy, on the other hand, points to the systematic impact of unsustainable work demands on managers:

> In the knowledge economy, sustainability must extend to the *human* as well as the *environmental* level. Many people have seen their ability to balance work with the rest of their lives deteriorate steadily, as they fall victim to the stresses of the long-hours culture. An executive life, some worry, is becoming unsustainable in social terms. We are in danger of populating companies with the modern equivalent of monks, people who forgo all else for the sake of their calling.[26]

Handy's comparison of modern managers to monks is unfortunate in this context. Indeed, if modern managers were to follow monks in "forgoing all else for the sake of their *calling*," we would see more – not less – balance. We would see less – not more – teleopathy.[27] It is not the "forgoing of all else" in itself that threatens an individual's or an organization's sanity, but "forgoing of all else" for the sake of something unworthy. Conscience is not about avoiding *devotion*; it is about avoiding *misplaced* devotion.[28]

Institutionalizing corporate conscience becomes an imperative for leaders once they have clarified their company's *orientation*. The Seven S framework offers a useful checklist for implementation. It is worth noting, however, that there is another "checklist" that aligns with this

US Federal Sentencing Guidelines – Seven Steps (1991 Guidelines, Revised in 2004)	
1. Establish standards and procedures to prevent and detect violations of law.	*STANDARDS AND PROCEDURES*
2. Assign specific individuals with overall responsibility for standards and procedures.	*RESPONSIBLE OFFICER*
3. Avoid delegation to individuals with propensity to engage in illegal activities.	*CAUTIOUS DELEGATION*
4. Effective communication of and training in standards and procedures.	*COMMUNICATION AND TRAINING PROGRAM*
5. Monitoring and auditing systems as well as employee reporting mechanism.	*MONITORING, AUDITING, AND REPORTING SYSTEMS*
6. Consistent enforcement and discipline for standards and procedures.	*ENFORCEMENT AND DISCIPLINE SYSTEM*
7. Effective response and prevention steps after detection of a problem.	*RESPONSE AND PREVENTION SYSTEM*

Figure 6.4 Federal guidelines

framework, a fact that may add to our confidence in its value. I refer to the seven elements in the US Federal Sentencing Guidelines for Organizations (FSGO), originally promulgated in 1991 and renewed in 2004. The FSGO were and are an unusual approach to public sector regulation of private sector behavior. This is due to the fact that instead of mandating a complex set of rules for corporate behavior, they mandate, in effect, certain elements of corporate *systems and structures*, trusting that these elements will in turn influence behavior.[29] Companies that wish to avoid strict liability under federal law and distance themselves from any illegal behavior of their managers or other employees must demonstrate that they have (had) in place an effective compliance system. The seven defining elements of such a system are presented in Figure 6.4.

While the 1991 version of the FSGO is aimed at legal compliance more than ethical values per se, it contains an implicit theory of how an institution's culture is effectively shaped and influenced. In November 2004, the revised FSGO introduced explicit new requirements calling (among other things) for corporate cultures that encourage *ethical conduct*, not simply observance of law. The business scandals of 2001 and 2002 had clearly indicated the prior influence of a firm's *ethical* values on its compliance culture.

The first step in the FSGO list is to create and articulate a set of standards and procedures. This step maps rather directly onto both *superordinate goals* and *systems* in the Seven S framework. The second and third steps map onto *staff* and *skills* in the Seven S framework – putting in place a key "ethics officer" and avoiding the delegation of decisions to staff or "agents" who might reasonably be expected not to live up to the standards. The fourth, fifth, and sixth steps in the FSGO link directly to *systems*. Executive and employee education, audit systems, hotlines for "internal whistle blowing," and clear rewards and sanctions all involve systems that Heinz (as we saw earlier) did *not* have in place in a meaningful way.

Finally, the seventh FSGO step – a feedback loop that fosters organizational learning in the event of an offense – involves a response-prevention *strategy*, *system*, and *style*. Bill George alludes to such a response-prevention approach in his comments about a systemic problem (though not, strictly, a legal compliance issue) within Medtronic that needed his attention:

> In taking specific issues raised by our customers back to Medtronic's engineers, I found a high level of ignorance and even denial that the problems actually existed. Why? As well intentioned as they were, the engineers were not spending any time with customers and were insulated from product problems. By the time the problems reached them, they had been filtered by many different organizations. The engineers tended to deny the design flaws, often blaming physicians for not using the products correctly.[30]

Every company will, because of its special history, industry, and culture, address ethical codes and audits somewhat differently. Nevertheless, certain elements will be common to the process of institutionalization in any firm. A statement of standards or values or beliefs along with a monitoring process is one of these common elements.

The Dow Corning Corporation
Case – Best of Intentions

Dow Corning Corporation passed through an enormous product safety controversy during the 1990s. Litigation over silicone breast implants eventually led the company into Chapter 11 bankruptcy.

Eventually too, scientific studies have come down on Dow Corning's side, though the evidence was slow in coming. For a time, barely 1 percent of the corporation's business brought down 100 percent of its operations.

All of this was in many ways a sad irony. For no company during the 1980s was more celebrated and accomplished for its "institutionalization" of conscience than Dow Corning. The company had gone to great lengths to develop a process for self-improvement. This story has been eclipsed by the controversy surrounding one of its smaller and (in the 1980s) newer acquisitions in medical devices (breast implants). This business unit failed either to ask or to answer questions on which the FDA would eventually focus extraordinary attention. And the rest, as they say, is history.

Almost two decades before the implant controversy, in 1976, Jack Ludington was CEO of Dow Corning Corporation. He asked four senior corporate managers to serve as a Business Conduct Committee (BCC), reporting to the Audit and Social Responsibility Committee of the board of directors. The BCC was charged with developing guidelines that would help communicate ethical standards to company sites around the world and a workable process for monitoring, reporting, and improving business practices. Once a *corporate* code was drafted, "it was sent to area managers with instructions that they develop their own codes, paying particular attention to their unique concerns. The only constraint was that area codes not conflict with the corporate code."

Ludington had, as we have recommended, done an informal scan or "sounding" of top managers and key outside sources as he identified corporate values. He even involved line management further by asking for area-specific codes consistent with the (more general) corporate code. But he did not stop there.

The code of business conduct was reviewed every two or three years, with an eye to improving its coverage of issues that either corporate or area management thought important. The principal vehicle for this process was a series of regular "Business Conduct Audits." These audits were undertaken by senior corporate managers on a rotating basis at company offices worldwide.

Area managers were asked to prepare for the audits by using "worksheets" that encouraged concreteness and detail regarding each of the topics raised by the code of conduct. In effect, "cases" were being reported in real time for review by the BCC. Particularly serious issues that emerged from these sessions – issues like questionable

171

payments and abuse of proprietary information – were presented for discussion by the BCC annually to the Audit and Social Responsibility Committee of the board.

In this way, corporate leadership informed both itself and the relevant employees of the specific nature and extent of the company's ethical concerns. Regularly those concerns involved what I have called teleopathy: How will we let competitive pressure lead us in this kind of situation? What about our "technically legal" practices in that situation? Two-way communication made the implications of the code of business conduct quite concrete. There was, in other words, an attempt at a thoughtful balancing of purpose.[31]

Summary – Beyond the Operational – Making It Last

Over three decades ago, Harvard's Kenneth Andrews emphasized the impotence of even the strongest convictions when they are not institutionalized, i.e., tied to structural and cultural incentives:

> It is quite possible . . . and indeed quite usual, for a highly moral and humane chief executive to preside over an "amoral organization" – one made so by processes developed before the liberalization of traditional corporate economic objectives. The internal force which stubbornly resists efforts to make the corporation compassionate (and exacting) toward its own people and responsible (as well as economically efficient) in its external relationships is the incentive system forcing attention to short-term quantifiable results.[32]

Without a willingness to reward performance based on contributions to the *quality* as much as the *quantity* of profits, the Seven S approach and the FSGO steps will accomplish very little. Bill George points out that in recent years "many companies have 'sold out' to the financial community in a never-ending quest to drive their stock price higher. Once a company does so, it is extremely difficult to regain a sense of purpose."[33]

I have characterized the ethical challenge to corporate leadership as involving three imperatives – orienting, institutionalizing, and sustaining shared ethical values. Since the efforts of even the best leaders to act on the first two of these imperatives are subject to a kind of winding down or wearing out, we must now turn to the challenge of sustaining corporate values over time.

Appendix to Chapter 6: Self Assessment & Improvement Process™ Executive and Board Survey[34]

Company Information

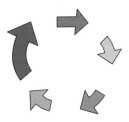

Company Name (Optional): _____

Date Established (Optional): _____

Chief Product/Service: _____

Annual Revenue: _____

Number of Employees: _____

Publicly Traded: ☐ Yes ☐ No

All company data will be held in the strictest confidence.

Instructions

This survey is designed to help you perform a preliminary assessment of how your company addresses issues of corporate responsibility. More specifically, it invites you to examine the *approach* your company takes to 49 criteria for responsible conduct, and to consider how well *developed* this approach is. By "approach," we mean *the method, process, or practice your company uses to address a specific criterion*. The 49 criteria are based upon the Caux Round Table *Principles for Business*, a comprehensive standard for ethical business behavior. They also incorporate other important norms for responsible corporate conduct.

STEP 1. Please complete the company information.
STEP 2. For each criterion, please rate the <u>level of development</u> attained by your company's approach on a six point scale. Please mark your rating in the blank adjacent to the criterion.

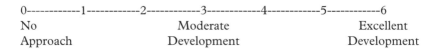

0------------1------------2------------3------------4------------5------------6
No   Moderate   Excellent
Approach   Development   Development

Please base your rating on the following questions:

- Does your company have a process or a practice that addresses the criterion's requirements?
- Is the process documented?
- Is the process effective? Does it achieve its intended purpose?
- Does your company have a way to evaluate and improve the process over time?

To the extent your answer to each of these is affirmative, your company's approach will qualify for a higher rating on the scale.
These following guideposts may be helpful to your evaluation:

0 points	No process or practice.
1–2 points	Some evidence of a policy or practice. Documentation may be outdated or rudimentary at best.
3 points	A documented policy or practice exists, with some evidence of its effectiveness.
4–5 points	A documented policy or practice exists. There is evidence that this approach has proven largely effective over time. The organization has examined and modified the approach to enhance its effectiveness, although a formal improvement mechanism has not been established.
6 points	The company has implemented a proven, documented approach that is supported by a systematic improvement methodology.

Do not attempt to be overly precise in your rating. Simply assign a score that indicates your assessment of your company's approach in light of the four questions and the guideposts, given your present knowledge of your firm's activities.
Note: You may encounter criteria that are inapplicable to your company, due to the current nature of your firm's operations. In such cases, do not rate your company against that criterion. Simply mark "N/A" in the adjacent blank.

STEP 3. Once you have completed your ratings, transfer them to the *Executive Summary Scorecard*[TM] (see Figure 6.5). **Total both rows and columns.** This will enable you to see how your company fares against the aspirations articulated in both the seven *General Principles* contained within the Caux *Principles for Business* (rows), and the more specific *Stakeholder Principles* (columns).

174

Self Assessment and Improvement Process – Board & Executive Survey Scorecard

COMPANY NAME:

Stakeholders / Principles	1. Fundamental Duties Max. Pts.	Score	2. Customers Max. Pts.	Score	3. Employees Max. Pts.	Score	4. Owners/ Investors Max. Pts.	Score	5. Suppliers/ Partners Max. Pts.	Score	6. Competitors Max. Pts.	Score	7. Community Max. Pts.	Score	Performance by Principle Max. total points	Total score
1. Responsibilities of Businesses	$\frac{1.1}{6}$		$\frac{1.2}{6}$		$\frac{1.3}{6}$		$\frac{1.4}{6}$		$\frac{1.5}{6}$		$\frac{1.6}{6}$		$\frac{1.7}{6}$		42	
2. Economic/ Social Impact of Business	$\frac{2.1}{6}$		$\frac{2.2}{6}$		$\frac{2.3}{6}$		$\frac{2.4}{6}$		$\frac{2.5}{6}$		$\frac{2.6}{6}$		$\frac{2.7}{6}$		42	
3. Business Behavior	$\frac{3.1}{6}$		$\frac{3.2}{6}$		$\frac{3.3}{6}$		$\frac{3.4}{6}$		$\frac{3.5}{6}$		$\frac{3.6}{6}$		$\frac{3.7}{6}$		42	
4. Respect for Rules	$\frac{4.1}{6}$		$\frac{4.2}{6}$		$\frac{4.3}{6}$		$\frac{4.4}{6}$		$\frac{4.5}{6}$		$\frac{4.6}{6}$		$\frac{4.7}{6}$		42	
5. Support for Multilateral Trade	$\frac{5.1}{6}$		$\frac{5.2}{6}$		$\frac{5.3}{6}$		$\frac{5.4}{6}$		$\frac{5.5}{6}$		$\frac{5.6}{6}$		$\frac{5.7}{6}$		42	
6. Respect for Environment	$\frac{6.1}{6}$		$\frac{6.2}{6}$		$\frac{6.3}{6}$		$\frac{6.4}{6}$		$\frac{6.5}{6}$		$\frac{6.6}{6}$		$\frac{6.7}{6}$		42	
7. Avoidance of Illicit Operations	$\frac{7.1}{6}$		$\frac{7.2}{6}$		$\frac{7.3}{6}$		$\frac{7.4}{6}$		$\frac{7.5}{6}$		$\frac{7.6}{6}$		$\frac{7.7}{6}$		42	
Performance By Stakeholder	Max. total points 42	Total score	Max. total points 42	Total score	Max. total points 42	Total score	Max. total points 42	Total score	Max. total points 42	Total score	Max. total points 42	Total score	Max. total points 42	Total score		294

Figure 6.5 SAIP Executive Summary Scorecard

Please note that the maximum possible score for your company will be reduced by 6 points for each inapplicable criterion. For example, if you encounter two inapplicable criteria, the maximum total score your company could attain is 294 minus (2 × 6), or 282 points.

Stakeholder: Fundamental Duties

Score (0–6)

Criterion 1.1 *Principle: Beyond Shareholders towards Stakeholders*

How does the company manage its fundamental duty to provide products and/or services that promote the common good and human dignity?

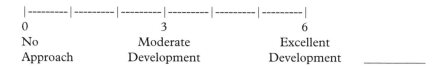

|--------- |--------- |--------- |--------- |--------- |--------- |
0   3   6
No   Moderate   Excellent
Approach   Development   Development   _____

Criterion 2.1 *Principle: Economic/Social Impact of Business*

How does the company promote economic and social advancement in the countries in which it develops, produces, or sells?

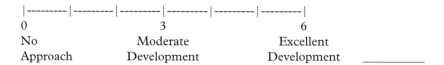

|--------- |--------- |--------- |--------- |--------- |--------- |
0   3   6
No   Moderate   Excellent
Approach   Development   Development   _____

Criterion 3.1 *Principle: Business Behavior*

How does the company achieve trust with its stakeholders (e.g., through honesty, transparency, candor, promise-keeping, and reliability)?

|--------- |--------- |--------- |--------- |--------- |--------- |
0   3   6
No   Moderate   Excellent
Approach   Development   Development   _____

176

Score (0–6)

Criterion 4.1 *Principle: Respect for Rules*

How does the company manage compliance with the letter and spirit of national and international rules?

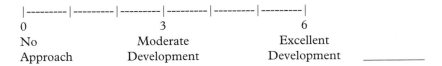

0		3		6	
No		Moderate		Excellent	
Approach		Development		Development	_____

Criterion 5.1 *Principle: Support for Multilateral Trade*

How does the company support international agreements on multilateral trade and promote the liberalization of trade (e.g., by supporting fair trade policies and discouraging protectionism)?

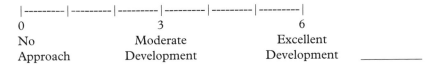

0		3		6	
No		Moderate		Excellent	
Approach		Development		Development	_____

Criterion 6.1 *Principle: Respect for the Environment*

How does the company manage and assure the environmental sustainability of its operations, products, and services?

0		3		6	
No		Moderate		Excellent	
Approach		Development		Development	_____

Criterion 7.1 *Principle: Avoidance of Illicit Operations*

How does the company take action, by itself or collaboratively, to prevent illicit and corrupt activities (e.g., money laundering, drug trafficking, organized crime, insider trading)?

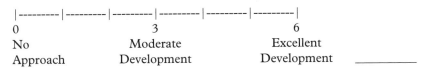

0		3		6	
No		Moderate		Excellent	
Approach		Development		Development	_____

TOTAL SCORE (maximum possible points = 42)

177

Stakeholder: Customers

Score (0–6)

Criterion 1.2 *Principle: Beyond Shareholders towards Stakeholders*

How does the company provide quality products and services which maximize their value to the customer while assuring respect for human dignity?

```
|---------|---------|---------|---------|---------|---------|
0                   3                   6
No                  Moderate            Excellent
Approach            Development         Development        _____
```

Criterion 2.2 *Principle: Economic/Social Impact of Business*

How does the company assure protection for its customers, and demonstrate respect for their cultures in its marketing and communications?

```
|---------|---------|---------|---------|---------|---------|
0                   3                   6
No                  Moderate            Excellent
Approach            Development         Development        _____
```

Criterion 3.2 *Principle: Business Behavior*

How does the company elicit the trust of customers (e.g., through responsible advertising, warranty fulfillment)?

```
|---------|---------|---------|---------|---------|---------|
0                   3                   6
No                  Moderate            Excellent
Approach            Development         Development        _____
```

Criterion 4.2 *Principle: Respect for Rules*

How does the company manage compliance with the letter and spirit of national and international customer-related rules?

```
|---------|---------|---------|---------|---------|---------|
0                   3                   6
No                  Moderate            Excellent
Approach            Development         Development        _____
```

Score (0–6)

Criterion 5.2 *Principle: Support for Multilateral Trade*

How does the company support its customers throughout the world, and improve the cost and quality of its good/services through international trade?

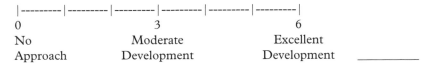

0	3	6
No	Moderate	Excellent
Approach	Development	Development

Criterion 6.2 *Principle: Respect for the Environment*

How does the company manage customer-related environmental issues (e.g., health and safety, "green design," recycling)?

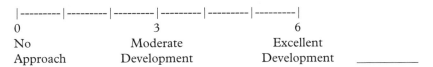

0	3	6
No	Moderate	Excellent
Approach	Development	Development

Criterion 7.2 *Principle: Avoidance of Illicit Operations*

How does the company take action to prevent such illicit activities as deceptive sales practices and sales to inappropriate customers?

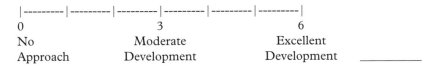

0	3	6
No	Moderate	Excellent
Approach	Development	Development

TOTAL SCORE (maximum possible points = 42)

Stakeholder: Employees

Score (0–6)

Criterion 1.3 *Principle: Beyond Shareholders toward Stakeholders*

How does the company recognize employee interests and take steps to improve employees' lives, individually and collectively?

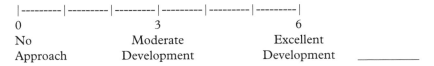

0	3	6
No	Moderate	Excellent
Approach	Development	Development

Score (0–6)

Criterion 2.3 *Principle: Economic/Social Impact of Business*

How does the company create employment and employability, and honor human rights within its operations?

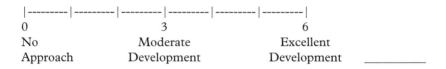

0	3	6
No	Moderate	Excellent
Approach	Development	Development	_____

Criterion 3.3 *Principle: Business Behavior*

How does the company elicit employee trust (e.g., through effective communication and dialogue, credible evaluation systems)?

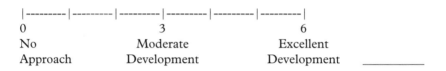

0	3	6
No	Moderate	Excellent
Approach	Development	Development	_____

Criterion 4.3 *Principle: Respect for Rules*

How does the company manage compliance with the letter and spirit of national and international employee-related rules?

0	3	6
No	Moderate	Excellent
Approach	Development	Development	_____

Criterion 5.3 *Principle: Support for Multilateral Trade*

How does the company develop its human capital globally while attending to employee needs domestically?

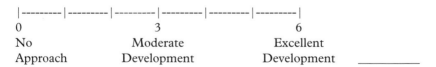

0	3	6
No	Moderate	Excellent
Approach	Development	Development	_____

Score (0–6)

Criterion 6.3 *Principle: Respect for the Environment*

How do employee policies and practices help prevent environmental damage and promote sustainability?

| --------- | --------- | --------- | --------- | --------- | --------- |
0   3   6
No   Moderate   Excellent
Approach   Development   Development   _____

Criterion 7.3 *Principle: Avoidance of Illicit Operations*

How does the company take action to prevent illicit activities by employees (e.g., offering/accepting bribes, violating licensing or copyright restrictions)?

| --------- | --------- | --------- | --------- | --------- | --------- |
0   3   6
No   Moderate   Excellent
Approach   Development   Development   _____

TOTAL SCORE (maximum possible points = 42)

Stakeholder: Owners/Investors

Score (0–6)

Criterion 1.4 *Principle: Beyond Shareholders towards Stakeholders*

How does the company's governance structure assure the health and viability of the business, and respond to the concerns of current owners/investors and other stakeholders?

| --------- | --------- | --------- | --------- | --------- | --------- |
0   3   6
No   Moderate   Excellent
Approach   Development   Development   _____

Criterion 2.4 *Principle: Economic/Social Impact of Business*

How does the company use its resources to enhance the economic and social value of its products/services (e.g., through the development of new products/services, new applications for existing products, new production processes)?

| --------- | --------- | --------- | --------- | --------- | --------- |
0   3   6
No   Moderate   Excellent
Approach   Development   Development   _____

Score (0–6)

Criterion 3.4 *Principle: Business Behavior*

How does the company elicit the trust of owners/investors (e.g., through responsible disclosures, timely and complete responses to shareholder/investor inquiries, governance policies and practices)?

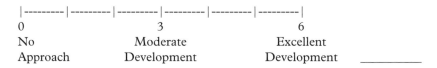

| --------- | --------- | --------- | --------- | --------- | --------- |
0   3   6
No   Moderate   Excellent
Approach   Development   Development   _____

Criterion 4.4 *Principle: Respect for Rules*

How does the company manage compliance with the letter and spirit of national and international owner/investor-related rules?

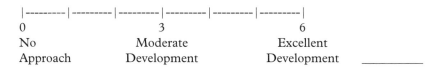

| --------- | --------- | --------- | --------- | --------- | --------- |
0   3   6
No   Moderate   Excellent
Approach   Development   Development   _____

Criterion 5.4 *Principle: Support for Multilateral Trade*

How does the company avail itself of international business opportunities for the benefit of owners/investors?

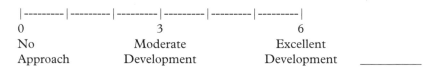

| --------- | --------- | --------- | --------- | --------- | --------- |
0   3   6
No   Moderate   Excellent
Approach   Development   Development   _____

Criterion 6.4 *Principle: Respect for the Environment*

How does the company manage environmental issues that impact owners/investors (e.g., health and safety risks, legacy issues, litigation and financial risks)?

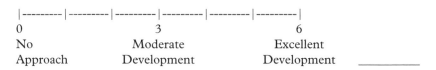

| --------- | --------- | --------- | --------- | --------- | --------- |
0   3   6
No   Moderate   Excellent
Approach   Development   Development   _____

Score (0–6)

Criterion 7.4 *Principle: Avoidance of Illicit Operations*

How does the company take action to prevent such illicit activities as insider trading and fraudulent reporting?

```
|---------|---------|---------|---------|---------|---------|
0                   3                   6
No                  Moderate            Excellent
Approach            Development         Development          _____
```

TOTAL SCORE (maximum possible points = 42)

Stakeholder: Supplier/Partners

Score (0–6)

Criterion 1.5 *Principle: Beyond Shareholders towards Stakeholders*

How does the company assure the practice of honesty and fairness in supplier/partner relationships (e.g., including, but not limited to, issues of pricing, technology licensing, right to sell)?

```
|---------|---------|---------|---------|---------|---------|
0                   3                   6
No                  Moderate            Excellent
Approach            Development         Development          _____
```

Criterion 2.5 *Principle: Economic/Social Impact of Business*

How does the company assure stable supplier/partner relationships, and the prudent and innovative utilization of resources by supplier/partners?

```
|---------|---------|---------|---------|---------|---------|
0                   3                   6
No                  Moderate            Excellent
Approach            Development         Development          _____
```

Criterion 3.5 *Principle: Business Behavior*

How does the company achieve trust with supplier/partners (e.g., through integrity in the bid evaluation process, protection of proprietary innovations)?

```
|---------|---------|---------|---------|---------|---------|
0                   3                   6
No                  Moderate            Excellent
Approach            Development         Development          _____
```

Score (0–6)

Criterion 4.5 *Principle: Respect for Rules*

How does the company manage compliance with the letter and spirit of national and international supplier/partner-related rules?

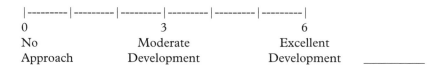

|---------|---------|---------|---------|---------|---------|
0   3   6
No   Moderate   Excellent
Approach   Development   Development   _____

Criterion 5.5 *Principle: Support for Multilateral Trade*

How does the company seek and utilize international suppliers, in both its domestic and non-domestic operations?

|---------|---------|---------|---------|---------|---------|
0   3   6
No   Moderate   Excellent
Approach   Development   Development   _____

Criterion 6.5 *Principle: Respect for the Environment*

How does the company manage environmental performance standards on a comparable basis throughout its supply chain?

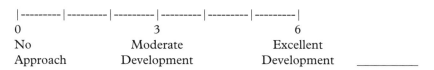

|---------|---------|---------|---------|---------|---------|
0   3   6
No   Moderate   Excellent
Approach   Development   Development   _____

Criterion 7.5 *Principle: Avoidance of Illicit Operations*

How does the company implement corrective action when it uncovers illicit activities by a supplier/partner?

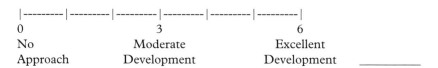

|---------|---------|---------|---------|---------|---------|
0   3   6
No   Moderate   Excellent
Approach   Development   Development   _____

TOTAL SCORE (maximum possible points = 42)

Stakeholder: Competitors

Score (0–6)

Criterion 1.6 *Principle: Beyond Shareholders towards Stakeholders*

How does the company assure honesty and fairness in its relationships with competitors?

```
| --------- | --------- | --------- | --------- | --------- | --------- |
0                       3                       6
No                      Moderate                Excellent
Approach                Development             Development         _____
```

Criterion 2.6 *Principle: Economic/Social Impact of Business*

How does the company promote free and fair competition in its home market and in other countries in which it operates?

```
| --------- | --------- | --------- | --------- | --------- | --------- |
0                       3                       6
No                      Moderate                Excellent
Approach                Development             Development         _____
```

Criterion 3.6 *Principle: Business Behavior*

How does the company achieve trust with competitors (e.g., by demonstrating respect for confidential competitor information, preventing the acquisition of commercial information by unethical means)?

```
| --------- | --------- | --------- | --------- | --------- | --------- |
0                       3                       6
No                      Moderate                Excellent
Approach                Development             Development         _____
```

Criterion 4.6 *Principle: Respect for Rules*

How does the company manage compliance with the letter and spirit of national and international competitor-related rules?

```
| --------- | --------- | --------- | --------- | --------- | --------- |
0                       3                       6
No                      Moderate                Excellent
Approach                Development             Development         _____
```

185

Score (0–6)

Criterion 5.6 *Principle: Support for Multilateral Trade*

How does the company take action to generally promote the opening of new markets to free and fair trade?

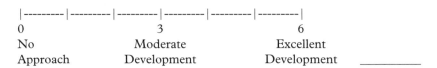

```
|---------|---------|---------|---------|---------|---------|
0                   3                   6
No                  Moderate            Excellent
Approach            Development         Development        _____
```

Criterion 6.6 *Principle: Respect for the Environment*

How does the company participate in the development of industry-wide standards for environmental management, promoting both performance measurement and compliance?

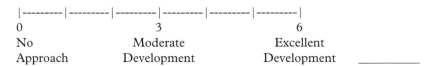

```
|---------|---------|---------|---------|---------|---------|
0                   3                   6
No                  Moderate            Excellent
Approach            Development         Development        _____
```

Criterion 7.6 *Principle: Avoidance of Illicit Operations*

How does the company take action to prevent illicit competitive activities (e.g., illegal payments to secure a competitive advantage, collusion with competitors)?

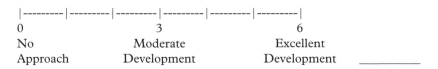

```
|---------|---------|---------|---------|---------|---------|
0                   3                   6
No                  Moderate            Excellent
Approach            Development         Development        _____
```

TOTAL SCORE (maximum possible points = 42)

Stakeholder: Communities

Score (0–6)

Criterion 1.7 *Principle: Beyond Shareholders towards Stakeholders*

How does the company demonstrate respect for the integrity of local cultures and for democratic institutions?

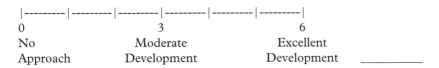

0	3	6
No	Moderate	Excellent
Approach	Development	Development	_____

Criterion 2.7 *Principle: Economic/Social Impact of Business*

How does the company contribute to the social and economic advancement of the communities in which it operates (e.g., promoting human rights, employability, the community's economic vitalization)?

0	3	6
No	Moderate	Excellent
Approach	Development	Development	_____

Criterion 3.7 *Principle: Business Behavior*

How does the company identify important constituencies within its communities, eliciting trust from them (e.g., through effective dialogue, responsible disclosures)?

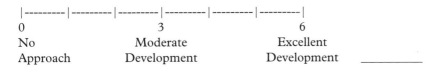

0	3	6
No	Moderate	Excellent
Approach	Development	Development	_____

Score (0–6)

Criterion 4.7 *Principle: Respect for Rules*

How does the company manage compliance with the letter and spirit of national and international community-related rules (e.g., the Worker Adjustment and Retraining Notification Act, OECD Guidelines for Multinational Enterprises)?

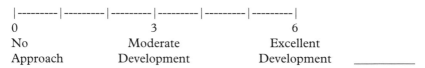

0	3	6
No	Moderate	Excellent
Approach	Development	Development

Criterion 5.7 *Principle: Support for Multilateral Trade*

How does the company manage the impact of international trade upon its communities (e.g., issues related to increased or decreased employment levels, capital mobility and labor immobility)?

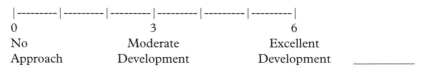

0	3	6
No	Moderate	Excellent
Approach	Development	Development

Criterion 6.7 *Principle: Respect for the Environment*

How does the company manage community-related environmental impacts (e.g., land management, water contamination, air pollution, noise pollution)?

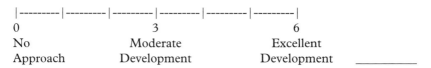

0	3	6
No	Moderate	Excellent
Approach	Development	Development

Criterion 7.7 *Principle: Avoidance of Illicit Operations*

How does the company take action to prevent such illicit activities as illegal campaign contributions and the avoidance of legitimate taxation?

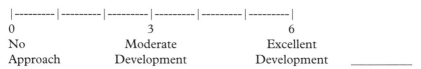

0	3	6
No	Moderate	Excellent
Approach	Development	Development

TOTAL SCORE (maximum possible points = 42)

For More Information

If you are interested in learning more about the *Self Assessment and Improvement Process*, or in exploring the possibility of utilizing the tool within your company, the following individuals can provide you with additional information:

T. Dean Maines
Global Project Director
Self Assessment and Improvement Process,
and
Research Associate,
Koch Chair in Business Ethics
University of St. Thomas
1000 LaSalle Avenue
Minneapolis, Minnesota 55403-2005
USA

Web: www.stthomas.edu/cob/about/ethics/resources/saip.asp
Telephone: +1.651.962.4261
Facsimilie: +1.651.962.4208
Email: tdmaines@stthomas.edu

Kenneth E. Goodpaster
Professor and Holder of the Koch Chair in Business Ethics,
University of St. Thomas
1000 LaSalle Avenue
Minneapolis, Minnesota 55403-2005
USA

Web: www.stthomas.edu/cob/about/ethics/about
Telephone: +1.651.962.4212
Facsimilie: +1.651.962.4208
Email: kegoodpaster@stthomas.edu

7

Sustaining Corporate Conscience

As an organization acquires a self, a distinctive identity, it becomes an institution. This involves the taking on of values, ways of acting and believing that are deemed important for their own sake. From then on self-maintenance becomes more than bare organizational survival; it becomes a struggle to preserve the uniqueness of the group in the face of new problems and altered circumstances.

Philip Selznick[1]

Reell Revisited

In Chapter 1, we saw how a mountain climbing experience became – in the mind of Bowen McCoy and in the minds of many students of business ethics since – a *parable*, a pattern that could teach larger lessons. It became a touchstone for the occupational hazard that I called *teleopathy*.

In this chapter, another experience – a journey if not a mountain climbing one – may serve as a parable to communicate the challenges associated with sustaining a corporate conscience. I have already introduced parts of this narrative in Chapter 5, illustrating various aspects of *orienting* corporate conscience within Reell Precision Manufacturing, Inc. (RPM). In the present context, however, we can use the dynamics of the Reell case to learn some larger lessons.

To do this, we need to go back to the beginning of the journey, in 1970. The following paragraph appears in a document called the *Founders' Statement*, that hangs on a wall in the company headquarters:

190

The three of us, Dale Merrick, Lee Johnson, and Robert L. Wahlstedt, became acquainted through business associations between 1955 and 1960. This acquaintance developed into a business relationship which resulted in the incorporation of RPM in 1970. Partly as a result of this business relationship and partly through the influence of other friends, each of us found something else – a personal commitment to God, revealed in Jesus Christ. As this has grown, we have found that the operation of a business on Judeo-Christian values is not only possible, but also an invigorating and rewarding experience. It is our intent that RPM be a place where you will find no conflict between your work and your moral and ethical values.

Understanding the faith-based entrepreneurial dream of these three executives (whose denominational affiliations were different from one another, but whose hopes were congruent) takes more discernment than we find among present-day religious stereotypes. The founders sought to *orient, institutionalize,* and ultimately to *sustain* a business that walked some daring talk. At the time, the "talk" was distinctive because of its *reach*, its aspiration to anchor an enterprise in some unequivocal moral convictions. It was not an evangelizing community. Manufacturing constant torque hinges was the principal economic activity. But the spirit in which this fledgling business was born was unapologetically rooted in the Judeo-Christian tradition.

The new company faced several challenges in its first 20 years. Quality manufacturing lessons had to be learned. Religious enthusiasms of certain employees had to be moderated so as not to become distractions in the workplace. The articulation of a Direction Statement was important for orientation – both among the company's leaders and in the hiring process. Care was taken to develop and maintain a culture within the company that stayed true to the founders' ideals as scores of new employees were attracted to it.

Employee comments about working at Reell were almost uniformly positive. Some examples:[2]

- "This is a people company. The little guy gets listened to. It's easier to be happy here because there is a fundamental trust."
- "There is a people difference here. As an African American, it was not what I was expecting. The emphasis is on personal growth. Conflict resolution is an important part of what we learn."
- "I had heard about this place several years before I was hired. It is for real here!"

191

- "There is a community that cares here – and it helps a person to take it home. Reinforcement."
- "The attitude around here: How can we help you to succeed?"
- "The intent around here is to balance the needs of the corporation with the needs of the person – sometimes to a fault!"

As the first founder retired in 1991 and the second prepared for retirement by 1996, the company's Direction Statement was put on the table for either re-affirmation or revision. The vast majority (over 95 percent) of the 120 employees of the successful firm were quite positive about the statement, but there were a few who had reservations about the legality and morality of mentioning "Judeo-Christian" values in the statement, along with references to the "will of God" and "the character of our Creator."[3] They were concerned that the statement might lead to discrimination against those who did not share the faith that inspired it. The company's leaders had to decide how to handle both the small minority of dissenters *and* the large majority of supporters. Where did *internal* alignment between the corporate value system and employees' values lie when there was not unanimity? The company's leaders also had to decide whether institutions *external* to the company would be so out of alignment with the company's aspiration that they (the law and the courts) would render that aspiration *unsustainable*.[4]

The opinion of the company's outside legal counsel was not encouraging to management:

> Certainly no prohibition exists restricting RPM management and employees from expressing their commitment to Christian values and ideals; however, incorporating these beliefs into the company's Mission and Direction Statements verges on appearing to exclude non-Christian beliefs. While the Mission Statement indicates: "[i]t is our intention that RPM be a place where you will find no conflict between your work and your moral and ethical values . . ." this may not be true for non-Christians. The interview process affords you an opportunity to determine whether or not an individual possesses the personal morals, ethics, and integrity that you seek in an employee. However, the risk I see in your Mission and Direction Statement is that you appear to exclude individuals who may possess acceptable morals, ethics, and integrity if they do not also possess Christian religious beliefs.

The attorney then concluded:

My recommendation to you is that you modify your Mission and Direction Statements somewhat to eliminate references to religion. You may want to substitute these references with references to cultivating an atmosphere of conducting business in compliance with sound moral and ethical values, without regard to religion.[5]

Many believed that at Reell there was something of value that needed to be sustained, once the company became a going concern – something beyond high-quality constant torque hinges – something that arguably contributed to its survival and growth from the outset. But sustaining that "something" would require attention to stresses within the organization as well as stresses between the organization and the wider social systems within which the organization needed to function.

Ten years later

In 2004, ten years after the original Reell case study was written, I returned with a colleague and a research assistant to study some new developments. During the intervening years since the company's Direction Statement had been reaffirmed, growth and diversity among employees had led to problems. Reell's new leaders (the founders having retired to the board) listened to concerns raised by some employees and job applicants about the Direction Statement's reference to the Judeo-Christian religious tradition. Some asked whether there was a religious requirement in order to work at the company, and after a new worker orientation, another wrote:

> While I do have religious beliefs and principles, I do not try to impose them on others . . . I would like to request that Reell be considerate of not trying to proselytize religion; I feel that religion is a personal thing and should not be imposed on anyone. When we state Judeo-Christian values we may be offending our fellow man by not stating Hindu, Moslem, skeptics and agnostics as part of that statement. It could be interpreted that only people who adhere to Judeo-Christian values have good character and principles (or that they have a preferred place or status within the organization).[6]

The three founders, whose influence was still strong in the company, were not of one mind about changing the Direction Statement to make it more inclusive. Their 35-year business journey together had been deeply connected to their Christian faith. As they relinquished

Figure 7.1 Illustration of the adaptation between employee values and company values as well as between company values and the values in its social environment

leadership control over the company, except indirectly as shareholders, their devotion to Reell was not unlike that of parents seeking to set a direction for a child.

Nevertheless, the majority of the voted shares favored more expansive (less explicitly Judeo-Christian) language in the Direction Statement.[7] The leadership and the employees had adapted the orienting document of the company ten years later, despite some strenuous objections. Reell's orientation – for good or ill – was not static, it was dynamic. A moral equilibrium, of sorts, was sought first, between employees and the company, and second, between the company and the surrounding society (see Figure 7.1)

The new leaders saw the Direction Statement not as a threat to employees' religious liberty, but as a public standard of Reell's commitment to treat all co-workers, customers, suppliers, and other business partners with the highest degree of integrity. The *wording* of the Direction Statement had become a concern which they felt obliged to address. They sought to express better the link between spiritual inclusivity (where all employees could bring their whole selves to work and their religious liberty would be respected) and the original religious source of the company's guiding values. In their words: "We wanted the Direction Statement to invite people into the conversation, not shut the conversation off. We had strong convictions about the role of spirit in business. But how do you write about it so it becomes attractive?"

A faith-based, American entrepreneurial dream had been sustained – in a society conflicted about the place of faith in its public square.[8] But not without some degree of adaptation to its internal and external environments. Co-CEO Bob Carlson put the central question of the "parable" this way in a 2004 speech: "How does one articulate the unifying spirit of an enterprise while at the same time respecting the diversity that its very success ushers in?" The story of Reell is a macrocosm of the story of many families, and perhaps also a microcosm of the story of the nation in which it was born.

Sustaining Corporate Conscience

What can the "parable" of Reell teach us about corporate leadership? Sustaining a company's conscience by communicating it to the next generation of managers as well as to the wider socioeconomic system constitutes the third imperative of the leader's moral agenda. It is true that values get communicated (and often reinforced) within a company "by example" whenever they are practiced. Individuals discover the implicit ethical values of an organizational culture and either conform to them, try to change them, or exit the organization.

Similarly, other organizations and society at large perceive a company to have certain ethical values and may be positive, negative, or neutral toward those values. If positive, a company can expect "good press" and perhaps easier sledding in both the marketplace and the regulatory environment. If negative, a company can expect resistance in the form of regulation, litigation, boycott or minimally, bad public relations. If neutral, sustaining the company's values will receive neither support nor resistance from its external environment. This leaves the matter largely to whatever energy there may be *internally* to keep the ethical aspects of the culture alive. Of course, if there is no *internal* support for sustaining the values of the organization, those values – however oriented and institutionalized – can be expected eventually to fade away.

We can distinguish between orienting and institutionalizing ethical values in an organization on the one hand, and deliberately seeking to *sustain* those values over time, on the other. Sustaining involves *clarity* about orientation, *effectiveness* at institutionalization – but also success at two major tasks: (1) *imparting* the ethical values to the next generation of company leadership; and (2) *confirming* the ethical values of the company in the economic and social environment outside the organization.

The former task, when it is directed toward organizational members and subgroups, includes such activities as hiring and recruitment, management selection and development, executive succession, board oversight, and (in the case of large corporations) acquisition and divestiture of business units. The latter task includes corporate

Figure 7.2   The head of Janus
Source: Dr. *Vollmer's Wörterbuch der Mythologie aller Völker*. Stuttgart:
Hoffmann'sche Verlagsbuchhandlung, 1874

communication, business–government relations, and company participation in its various communities, local and global.

The third imperative, then, has to do with leadership actions aimed at a kind of congruence – what Chester Barnard referred to as "fit" – between the mindset of the organization and the mindsets of both its future leaders and its wider institutional environment.[9] Without some degree of ethical fit or congruence, the corporate mindset simply cannot survive or replicate itself. It will fail to sustain itself from within, or it will be eliminated or transformed by forces outside itself. We might think of the dual leadership role in this context as similar to that of Janus, the ancient Roman god "of doorways, of beginnings, and of the rising and setting of the sun." Janus was usually represented as a figure at city gates, with one head and two faces back to back, one looking outward and the other inward (see Figure 7.2).

In the next section, I will expand on the ideas of "mindset stability" and "degrees of fit" among mindset types *as theoretical constructs*. These constructs are later illustrated using case studies. Finally, I consider some challenges that confront the corporate leader who seeks to sustain ethical values in his or her organization.

Theories of Mindset Stability and Degrees of Ethical "Fit"

It is essential for sustaining a company's ethical values that the consciences of its future leaders and the values of its surrounding social environment be "hospitable" or "aligned" *to some degree* with those of the company. These are, after all, the factors that tend to reinforce or resist the corporate conscience over the long term. But if some degree of "ethical fit" is needed, the question naturally arises: How much? In answer to this question, leaders may choose along a spectrum of alternatives, ranging qualitatively from *low* through *medium* to *high* degrees of congruence. If there is a most desirable *degree of fit*, we can then think about strategies for achieving that degree of fit.

I must emphasize at this point that value congruence and mindset stability are – for the moment – being considered independently of the *content* of those values or mindsets. A dysfunctional set of values might be sustained and stabilized (for a time) if the leadership groomed similarly dysfunctional successors and the system surrounding the organization was itself receptive to such dysfunction. Whether such dysfunction could be sustained indefinitely, of course, is quite another matter. Presumably the answer is negative, which is why we use the word 'dysfunctional.'[10]

In the *low* range, there would be little or (at the limit) no similarity (fit) – either between employee values and organizational values (*microfit*) or between organizational values and the values of the wider social system (*macrofit*). From the point of view of the individual in the organization or the organization in the community, the low range implies a maximal degree of *pluralism* and a minimal degree of *consensus*. Looking in the other direction, from the system to the organization and from the organization to the individual, the low range implies – at its limit – a kind of "ethical anarchy." Sustaining an organizational mindset seems impossible in the low range, since the forces tending to dismantle it (a moral analogue to entropy) are at their strongest both from within and from without.

Imagine that the hiring process of an organization paid little or no attention to microfits. This might mean reluctance to look for value fit or alignment between the ethical culture of the organization and the values of the candidate. Eventually, that ethical culture would simply dissipate. Or imagine an organizational culture whose values are antithetical to those of the surrounding culture. Perhaps a company with strong and explicit Christian principles in a secular society; or a company with strong racist values, like the Ku Klux Klan, in a society that is repulsed by such values. Again, it is hard to imagine such companies *sustaining* their shared values over time.[11]

In the *high* range, on the other hand, there is strong congruence (fit) among the values in question. The individual is ethically aligned with the company's values (is an ethical "organization person") and

197

the organization is in strict ethical accord with its surrounding institutions. We might expect stability in such circumstances, but this may depend on how the "fit" has been achieved. If, for example, the price of such high congruence has been rigid dogmatic enforcement, stability may be somewhat illusory. If the reason for the congruence is more "natural" (not simply "coerced"), stability might be quite strong.[12] It would be useful to study totalitarian systems in these terms, and also organizations that imitate totalitarian practices in relation to their members (e.g., what are sometimes called "cults"). The rigidity, perhaps even tyranny, of the *high* range stands in dramatic contrast to the ethical anarchy of the *low* range.

The *medium* range seeks varying points of balance between too much and too little congruence. Corporate leaders in this range will try to respect individual moral differences, *but within the limits of a reasonably well-defined corporate value structure*. Likewise, the corporation's moral initiative in the wider socioeconomic system will be substantial but limited.

These ranges of "fit" help clarify the idea of mindset *stability* much as the typology in Chapter 3 clarified the ideas of mindset *orientation*. They provide a map of the generic options without prescribing which option should be pursued in a given corporate environment.

An image for understanding mindset congruence

A corporate mindset, then, might or might not resemble the mindsets of key individuals within the organization as well as institutional structures surrounding the organization. Such a phenomenon was explored visually by the famous Dutch artist M. C. Escher as shown in Figure 7.3. Escher's study of "Fishes and Scales" suggests three features of mindsets that help us to interpret mindset stability: mindsets are *nested, self-similar,* and *dynamic*.[13]

The active figures are drawn at different scales with a medium degree of similarity to one another, like the ethical values of individuals within organizations – and organizations within a surrounding social system. The smaller fish, while *similar* to the larger fish, are *nested* as "scales" on the surfaces of the larger fish. The entire diagram, in addition to having the *nested* and *self-similarity* properties, also communicates a certain *dynamism* – the fish (like mindsets) are in *motion*. Part of the aesthetic appeal of Escher's drawing may stem from the fact that the artist avoids *both* dissonance between levels *and* rigid conformity, i.e., he finds a middle range of "fit."

Figure 7.3 M. C. Escher's "Fishes and Scales"
Source: © 2005 The M. C. Escher Company-Holland. All rights reserved.
www.mcescher.com

The Escher image is a helpful aesthetic reminder of the challenges facing organizational leaders seeking to sustain ethical values. They must ask:

- What is an appropriate degree of "value tolerance" in an organization, avoiding both indifference (chaos, complete dissimilarity) and dogmatism (complete similarity with no variation)?
- What is an appropriate degree of "value tolerance" in a social system made up of public, private, and independent sector organizations? How can the social system avoid both indifference to the values of the organizations that it supports and dogmatism about those values at the same time?[14]

We can use another Escher-like image (called a "fractal") to visualize how part of an object can be similar in shape to the object itself, and how the object itself can be similar in shape to ("fit in with") those in its wider environment.[15]

The questions above, when approached from the perspective of the individual or the organization looking outward (Figure 7.4, left), call to mind issues of free expression and assembly as well as civil disobedience. Do/should the ethical "contours" of the individual or

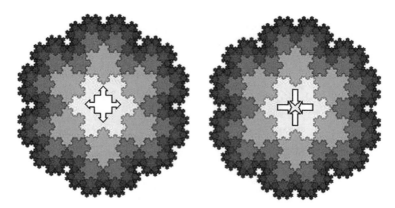

Figure 7.4 A fractal "snowflake" viewed from center outward and periphery inward

the organization shape (partially or completely) the ethical "contours" of the surrounding organization or society, respectively? Do members of organizations (and organizations themselves) deserve broader protections than those currently accorded by law? What does this mean for the traditional "termination at will" doctrine? For "whistle-blowing" and civil liberties in (and of) the corporation?[16]

When approached from the opposite direction, from the perspective of the more embracing group looking inward (Figure 7.4, right), these questions call to mind classical issues in political and legal theory about the merits of constitutional democracy, due process, and pluralism. Do/should the ethical "contours" of organizations or the wider society shape (partially or completely) the ethical "contours" of the individuals and organizations, respectively, which they surround? What limits can society legitimately place on corporations (and corporations on their members) in view of the exclusively economic function that has traditionally defined their relationships in the past? Are these limits changing? How and why?

Mindset Stability in Practice:
Some Case Illustrations

In Chapter 3, cases were presented to clarify each of the mindset types in various business settings. Here I will use cases to illustrate different degrees (low, medium, and high) of ethical congruence along with their implications for such issues as employee rights and public/private sector relationships. Then, I will address the problems associated with the low range of congruence as well as the high range, especially when Type 3 values are the leader's goal.

Microfit: The organization and its members

From the perspective of top management, sustaining a company's mindset (achieving mindset stability) depends on what we are calling *microfit* and *macrofit*. The pursuit of *microfit* includes a number of strategies. The most obvious is *succession planning* for the CEO and other top officers with company ethical values in mind. Another is the use of mission or values *statements* to provide long-term vision when founders or key leaders have long since retired.[17] *Board oversight* is a third strategy, one that has particular salience in the wake of the corporate scandals of 2002. A fourth strategy has to do with *recruitment, hiring,* and *promotion* of employees; while a fifth strategy relates to *merger and acquisition criteria* that can influence the culture of the corporation going forward. *The common element in microfit strategies is that they are aimed at maintaining a company's cultural commitment to core ethical values over time.* The leadership imperatives of orienting and institutionalizing values relate mostly to the past and the present, while *sustaining* company values relates primarily to the future.

In relatively small, entrepreneurial organizations, where the influence of the leader is most direct, a company's mindset pattern (whether it includes respect as a fundamental value or not) depends primarily on the values of the person at the helm. We saw this in the Reell case at the beginning of this chapter. In such companies, sustaining or passing on the corporate mindset to the next generation amounts to identifying and grooming a successor for the president who will preserve the company's value orientation.

In larger organizations, however, or as smaller companies grow, this task becomes much more complicated. While succession to the top remains a major factor, management development throughout the hierarchy is critical. "As an organization grows larger and as operations become more decentralized," Kenneth Andrews points out, "the power and influence of the chief executive are reinterpreted and diffused."[18] There must be a pool of talented managers in the domain of what we have been calling rationality-oriented values who are capable of joining them to respect-oriented values – and in a way that preserves with some degree of fidelity the interpretations of the chief executive officer. Developing and maintaining this pool is an ongoing leadership challenge.[19]

I am aware of one chief executive of a Fortune 100 company who responded to this challenge with great care and self-awareness. Not only did he monitor personally and regularly the progress of 75 key managers in his corporation, he did so with explicit attention to the congruence between their beliefs and attitudes and the overall corporate value system. In one case, an otherwise very strong executive who was considered in line to be CEO was asked to resign for reasons related directly to his cynicism about the company's stated philosophy of human values. It should be added that this decision was made with the full understanding, counsel, and support of the board of directors.

Another chief executive officer worked with his board of directors in developing a set of criteria for appraising the character traits and qualifications of candidates for leadership roles in the corporation. The criteria include not only experience, intelligence, and economic performance, but also integrity, maturity, balance, and community service.

Medtronic's Bill George says of the succession issue that "At the end of the day, leaders must pave the way for a successor to lead the company in the next generation while they move on to their next set of challenges."[20] This meant insuring that the values of the company as expressed in its Mission Statement were held as passionately by his successor, Art Collins, as they were by Bill George himself and the Medtronic board.

In these three examples, the leaders involved were, by their own accounts, protecting and sustaining a mindset orientation by paying close attention to the values of identifiable individuals who were candidates for future leadership roles. Another approach to what we might call the "succession of ethical values" in an organization is for the leader to focus on a written statement – of mission, or direction, or belief – that is intended to carry forward the ethical elements in the culture.

Some case illustrations will help clarify the leadership implications of this second approach to microfits, i.e., to achieving internal mindset stability over time.

We have already examined with some care the case of Reell Precision Manufacturing in the opening discussion of this chapter. A somewhat parallel case illustration comes from a British company,

Lex Service Group.[21] Lex was a highly diversified provider of industrial transport equipment and services. The company's CEO, a devout Jew, wanted to leave behind at his retirement a company whose values, particularly as they related to the treatment of employees, would continue after him. In the mid-1980s, he gathered a number of key managers together and crafted a set of *Guidelines for Conduct* that captured not only ethical ideals about employee security, but also economic ideals about company leverage and long-term profitability.

During the year following the adoption of the guidelines, several difficult situations arose which appeared to put the economic and the ethical provisions in the guidelines at odds with one another: an employee's safety versus his job security; the sale of an unprofitable transportation depot versus the layoff of a substantial number of its employees.

The Reell and Lex cases – controversial as they always are in MBA classrooms – profile two very different companies each seeking a way to *sustain* corporate values into the future using creed-like vehicles as tools for the purpose. Both companies were reasonably successful at achieving consensus around their value statements, but not completely successful. Both faced puzzling challenges of application subsequent to the affirmations of their corporate values.

Few corporate decisions have larger consequences for the values and cultures of a company than decisions to acquire or merge with other companies. And these decisions require not only senior leaders, but also board involvement. Financial "fit" between two organizations can look wonderful on paper – and even after the modest amount of due diligence that can be accomplished *quietly* before an acquisition or a merger is announced. Recounting certain acquisitions that did not "work out," Bill George remarks in his recent book:

> In my experience acquisitions often fail, not because of the financials or lack of a strategic rationale, but because of cultural clashes. . . . If you can reach agreement first on a common vision, values, and organization structure, the negotiations over money will go a lot faster.[22]

Unfortunately, the need for a great deal of secrecy and confidentiality during the "dating game" between two companies leads paradoxically (and often tragically) to blindness regarding *cultural* fit between them. It is perhaps no wonder that the vast majority of mergers fail.

An old classic

It is interesting to recall, as a final case illustration and as a transition to the next section, that some corporate leaders have drawn a sharp ethical line between *microfits* and *macrofits*. One such leader was described by my mentor, John B. Matthews, in a classic Harvard Business School case dating back over four decades. His name was Arthur Wiebel, President of Tennessee Coal and Iron (TCI), an acquired division of United States Steel Corporation. In the early 1960s, Wiebel was very active in support of civil rights for blacks both as a private citizen of Birmingham, Alabama, and as an able leader of TCI. He initiated broad changes in discriminatory labor agreements and sent strong signals to managers and employees regarding fairness in hiring, promotion, and job assignments with the company. He sought energetically to bring about a fit between his and TCI's commitment to the value of racial justice and the decision-making of those within the company.

When asked obliquely by the Kennedy administration to use TCI's substantial influence to improve racial justice in the Birmingham community, however, Wiebel backed away:

> As individuals we can exercise what influence we may have as citizens, but for a corporation to attempt to exert any kind of economic compulsion to achieve a particular end in a social area seems to me to be quite beyond what a corporation can do. I believe that while government may seek to compel social reforms, any attempt by a private organization like TCI to impose its views, its beliefs, and its will upon the community would be repugnant to our American constitutional concepts and that appropriate steps to correct this abuse of corporation power would be universally demanded by public opinion.[23]

Wiebel apparently had two *different* standards regarding value fit – one for a company and its employees, and another for a company in relation to its surrounding community. Debates during the 1980s about responsible business activity in South Africa and debates during the 1990s about the effects of globalization suggest that internationally at least, Wiebel's "TCI distinction" is still very much alive. Let us now take a closer look at the challenges facing corporate leaders (both nationally and internationally) as they consider *external* value congruence as a factor in sustaining corporate conscience.

Macrofits: The organization
and the wider community

Sustaining a corporate mindset requires not only the achievement of reasonable fit between the values of an organization and those of its present and future leaders. It also requires a reasonable fit in the direction of the larger network of organizations and institutions that we refer to collectively as "society" or the socioeconomic system. Just as one would expect an individual in an organization to have some impact, however limited, on the values of the organization as a whole – even if the influence in the opposite direction is likely to be stronger – so it is with an organization in its societal context.[24]

In order for a set of corporate values to continue for any significant period of time, it must not only be affirmed by individuals who share those values achieving leadership positions, it must also be supported from the outside by a value system that accords it validity and respect. Otherwise, the law, the regulatory process, industry competition, and public pressure will probably undermine its stability. This was the principal argument used by critics of Arthur Wiebel's position in the TCI case.

Corporate values within the social system, like individual values within the organization, *can* have very real influence. This was evident in a situation that confronted Northern States Power Company (now called Xcel Energy).[25]

The case describes a situation that confronted the Minnesota Public Utilities Commission (PUC) in November 2000. The PUC was responsible for ensuring that Minnesota utilities provided consumers with safe, adequate, reliable electrical service at fair and reasonable rates. As a part of this charge, the Commission oversaw energy sourcing agreements entered into by Minnesota utilities, including Northern States Power (NSP). NSP had recently petitioned to renew a sourcing arrangement with Manitoba Hydro, a Canadian crown corporation operated by the Province of Manitoba. Large-scale construction projects implemented in the late 1960s and early 1970s resulted in surplus hydroelectric generating capacity for Manitoba Hydro, enabling it to export power to Minnesota-based utilities.

The new dams and reservoirs were located on the traditional hunting and fishing grounds of five indigenous Cree nations. Their operation had significantly affected the ecology of the surrounding territory, as well as the culture of the indigenous peoples. Having failed to obtain satisfactory compensation for this damage through negotiations with Manitoba Hydro and the governments of Manitoba and Canada, the Pimicikamak Cree Nation (PCN) – sometimes referred to as the Cross Lake Cree Nation because of its location – brought its case to the Minnesota Public Utility Commission. Specifically, it requested that the Commission delay the renewal of Manitoba Hydro's contract with NSP until all the environmental and socioeconomic costs associated with the Canadian utility's bid were accounted for. Several Minnesota environmental groups – although conflicted because of their support for "green" hydroelectric power over more conventional forms of electrical power generation – endorsed the Pimicikamak Cree's contention that the Commission needed to consider these externalities to fulfill its responsibilities.

However, the four remaining Cree nations dissented strongly from this position. They urged the PUC and, by implication NSP, to move forward with the contract since (a) they had settled equity agreements with Manitoba Hydro, and (b) jobs and other economic returns to their nations were critical to the health of their tribes. Chief Jerry Primrose, speaking for these tribes at the PUC hearing said that there was a 75 percent approval rate for the Manitoba Hydro agreements, and to the Pimicikamak Cree's contentions, he responded:

> Our community was not bought-out. The community made the decision, based on negotiations and information provided by our local negotiation team and our legal counsel. I have tried to listen respectfully to PCN's story, about the social devastation that Manitoba Hydro has caused on PCN, the suicides, the hopelessness, the despair. As leader of my community, I must speak out. All of the socioeconomic difficulties facing the Cree in Manitoba or any other Canadian Aboriginal peoples cannot be blamed on specific entities or, in this case, Manitoba Hydro.[26]

The PUC eventually decided to allow the contract to go forward, but did insist upon further study of the socioeconomic impacts of such purchases. The issue continues at this writing, with the tactics of the PCN shifting from the PUC to shareholder resolutions at the annual meetings of Xcel Energy.

What are the lessons to be learned from this case about *macrofits*? First, it is clear that the ethical values of NSP as a corporation were being challenged in relation to the ethical values of the community surrounding the company. If a lack of congruence had been found, the likely outcome would have been for the company values to give way.

Initially, the institution representing the surrounding community was the PUC, the *regulatory agency* to which the PCN made its appeal. Eventually, the institution representing the surrounding community was *the company's own shareholder group*, to which the PCN directed its efforts when unsuccessful at the PUC. Quite apart from the merits of the PCN's case, it is clear that a lack of "fit" was alleged between the company's ethical values and those of the surrounding community. The issue: *doing business with suppliers alleged to be unjust, thereby benefiting economically from that injustice.*

The company (NSP) has so far been vindicated in its insistence that there is not a lack of "fit" between company values and the values of the community. NSP representative Jim Alders said at the PUC hearing that "NSP does not consider itself as a mediator in this situation," and that:

> There are details and history that can only be overcome through the interactions of Manitoba Hydro, the First Nations, and the provincial and national governments of Canada. NSP has encouraged Hydro and Cross Lake to get to 'yes.' Given all the dynamics, as a purchaser of that power I ask myself, can I bring any value to that complex set of negotiations? I keep coming up with 'no.' As a practical matter there's very little I can do other than to publicly encourage the parties to reach an agreement. Not to buy that power is detrimental to our customers and shareholders. It is our obligation to meet our customers' demand for electricity as cost effectively and as environmentally sensitively as we can.[27]

Perhaps the most important outcome here resides in the background. For the principle acknowledged by *all* parties to the dispute is *the relevance of the ethics of suppliers in economic relationships.*[28]

A macrofit challenge was discernable during 1983 and 1984, when Velsicol Chemical Corporation attempted to initiate industry self-regulation in the export of hazardous chemicals by proposing a "One World Communication System" for pesticide labeling. The idea was to create an industry-wide system of pictograms to convey information on the safe use of pesticides – especially for the small farmer who was illiterate or could not understand the precautionary information on current labels.

The social values of both the industry and regulatory environment were not, however, congruent. Enthusiasm for Velsicol's initiative was not sufficient to move the idea forward, with the result that the CEO decided on economic grounds not to continue the project. A number of managers, discouraged by this decision, left the company.[29]

In general, corporate *lobbying*, in relation to public-sector statutes and regulations (state or federal), is a way of trying to manage the macrofits between organizations and their legal environment. To be sure, lobbying has a "mixed" reputation because it is often thought to be simply a self-serving activity on the part of an industry or even a single corporation. But viewed more dispassionately, lobbying is a form of mutual accommodation between organizations and their societies, sometimes leading to good for *both*. I have often remarked that we do not pay sufficient attention to the idea of "lobbying in the public interest" as a corporation's way to eliminate competitive dilemmas that undermine the common good, e.g., mileage or emissions regulations for automobiles; safety regulations for consumer goods.

Another form of managing macrofits is industry activity independent of the public sector. Industry associations can be a vehicle for the private sector to reduce competitive behavior that does not *fit* with society's expectations. The Velsicol case, of course, is an example of a company's lack of success in influencing its industry association. But there are many cases of effective industry collaboration on this front. One recent example is the voluntary "Code of Ethics on Interactions with Health Care Professionals" adopted by the *Advanced Medical Technology Association* ("AdvaMed") in January 2004.

Medical device manufacturers had for many years experienced considerable competitive pressure in connection with business practices aimed at attracting and retaining physician loyalty to their branded products. The incremental escalation ("one-upsmanship") in this arena was leading to questionable behaviors (e.g., travel inducements and perks for physicians and their spouses) that were neither socially good nor in the interests of the industry competitors generally. Medtronic, under the leadership of Art Collins, guided the development and adoption of the AdvaMed Code of Ethics, the *Preamble* of which reads as follows:

["AdvaMed"] is dedicated to the advancement of medical science, the improvement of patient care, and in particular to the contribution that high quality, cost-effective health care technology can make toward achieving those goals. In pursuing this mission, AdvaMed members ("Members") recognize that adherence to ethical standards and compliance with applicable laws are critical to the medical device industry's ability to continue its collaboration with health care professionals. Members encourage ethical business practices and socially responsible industry conduct related to their interactions with health care professionals. Members also respect the obligation of health care professionals to make independent decisions regarding Member products. Consequently, AdvaMed adopts this voluntary Code of Ethics, effective January 1, 2004, to facilitate Members' ethical interactions with those individuals or entities that purchase, lease, recommend, use, arrange for the purchase or lease of, or prescribe Members' medical technology products in the United States ("Health Care Professionals").[30]

The AdvaMed Code is just one of many examples of industry self-regulation efforts that are ultimately aimed at securing macrofits between society's ethical expectations and corporate behavior *when marketplace pressures lead in a dysfunctional direction.* The lesson is not just that accommodation or fit between the organization and the wider system is desirable, but that some companies succeed in influencing this fit while others do not. And it is not self-evident, Arthur Wiebel's views notwithstanding, that corporations should eschew moral influence. Philip Selznick in his 1959 classic, *Leadership in Administration* reminded us of the dynamics of macrofits:

> From the standpoint of social systems rather than persons, organizations become infused with value as they come to symbolize the community's aspirations, its sense of identity. Some organizations perform this function more readily and fully than others. An organization that does take on this symbolic meaning has some claim on the community to avoid liquidation or transformation on purely technical or economic grounds.[31]

The fate of the Arthur Andersen company illustrates the tragic potential of a discontinuity between corporate values and societal values.[32] Indeed, in the wake of the corporate scandals of 2002, and the passage of the Sarbanes-Oxley act, it seems clear that the systems surrounding corporations will attempt to *legislate* a "macrofit" if there is a perceived breakdown.

Balancing microfit and macrofit

The cases we have been discussing are not simple ones. Their complexity comes from fundamental values that come into play as well as the tensions that arise when internal and external pressures conflict. A powerful illustration of the perennial nature of the *macrofit* issue can be seen in another classic Harvard case from 40 years ago, "The Individual and the Corporation."[33]

After John F. Kennedy was assassinated in 1963, Donald Singleton, senior vice-president of a large oil company based in Dallas, Texas, wrote an article for *Look* magazine reflecting on the meaning of the event. He took a position that caused vexation in the Dallas business community. Though Singleton did not mention his affiliation in the article, the company received a number of negative letters and even some returned credit cards. Singleton himself received numerous letters and phone calls, most of which praised his insight and courage. The pressure on the company from the community eventually led to Singleton's resignation. His own description of that result was as follows:

> When I resigned, the impression got around that [the company] asked for my resignation because it disagreed with what I wrote. This is not what happened and obscures the basic decision that most company men have to make, at one moment or, more likely, on the installment plan. About a month after the article, and hours after the *Dallas Morning News* took me to its editorial-page woodshed a second time, I was suddenly confronted with a company demand: I must agree never to comment publicly without formally clearing each word in advance and in writing. The issue was not *what* I said, but whether I could say anything at all.

The challenges of microfit and macrofit come together and interact in this case on the subject of free speech.[34] There is the question of value fit between Donald Singleton and the corporation *as well as* the question of value fit between the corporation and its social environment, locally and nationally. In the absence of strong corporate leadership, we can see how pressures from the latter flow through to the former (and back again).

Over the years, many students have argued that the corporation "caved in" to one set of pressures in the process of rigidly imposing another set on the individual. Others have argued that Singleton either underestimated the need for congruence or overestimated his power to achieve it. The tragedy, if that is an appropriate description, came from the lack of "space" for moral initiative that both the corporation and the individual were given. I am convinced that this drama has been and continues to be played out all too frequently in today's business world. The tragedy is that experienced and insightful executives often lose the ability to share their experience and insight as they succeed and rise to positions of responsibility in corporate life.

The Challenge to Leadership

Two basic *empirical* questions that this discussion of mindset stability raises for future research are:

1   How do the moral values of managers and business units at various levels in the corporate hierarchy influence the moral values of the company as a whole (and conversely)?
2   How do the moral values of the wider society influence the moral values of the corporation (and conversely)?

Other questions raised, however, are *ethical* questions for business leaders.

Leaders who would sustain shared values face something of a paradox, one that is both philosophical and practical. If mindset stability (the preservation of corporate conscience) is truly an imperative, then it would seem that values should be encouraged in a way that commands maximum adherence among managers and employees (internally) and society (externally). Yet such a demand can seem imperious and dogmatic, contrary to the spirit of the moral point of view. In Chapter 4, I discussed this problem in connection with what I called the *employee-based objection*. Let us here refer to it as the *paradox of paternalism*:

> It seems essential for sustaining a group conscience, yet coercive, to seek to dictate the value orientation of others, whether inside the corporation or outside.

Resolving this paradox in practice is one of the chief marks of responsible leadership, so let us take a closer look.

The tension created by the paradox of paternalism springs from two sources: the type of mindset orientation in question (content) and the way in which congruence or fit is pursued (process). And the content issue (e.g., Types 1, 2a, 2b, or 3) will influence the

211

process by which the company encourages both internal and external fit. Recall some of the cases discussed in Chapter 3.

Companies with a Type 1 mindset – Enron and WorldCom may have been recent examples – would presumably *not* encourage their managers (or the surrounding community) to adopt a similar orientation (self-interest alone), since it would be in the company's interest for these parties to be relatively selfless. In the spirit of Machiavelli, an ethic of company loyalty, rather than a Type 1 mindset, would seem to be called for. Similarly, a company like Exxon (in relation to the Valdez oil spill) with a Type 2a or 2b mindset would want its employees (and surrounding institutions) to be guided by loyalty to its competitive advantage within the constraints of the law and the regulatory process. *Only in the case of a Type 3 corporate orientation does it seem realistic and consistent to advocate congruence among mindset levels (employees, organization, community).*

Type 3 thinking escapes the charge of fostering a double standard for employees and the community in a way that the other mindset types do not.[35] But there is more to the paradox than this content issue. *Process* is also important. Even with Type 3 organizations, if corporate advocacy is highly specific and inflexible, the danger of what some call "moral imperialism" is real. Both executives and the community can feel threatened by too much moral pressure. We saw this in the context of the Reell case with which we opened this chapter. It was also an issue in the widely discussed 1987 case of Dayton Hudson Corporation.[36]

Between June 11 and June 25, 1987, Dayton Hudson Corporation (DHC, today Target Corporation), was under threat of hostile takeover by the Dart Group, headed up by Herbert Haft and his son Robert. In a period of just 14 days, DHC managed to persuade the governor to re-convene the State Legislature for a special session in which a new law was passed, making the takeover of DHC by Dart much more difficult than it otherwise would have been. The company accomplished this with support from the general population of Minnesota, no doubt because of the good will that it had generated over many decades of customer satisfaction and community involvement.

It was clear that DHC saw itself as upholding a tradition of strong ethical values as it sought a high degree of congruence between those values and the wider community. Lobbying effectively for the new anti-takeover law (a law similar to one that it had actually opposed some years earlier) was an extraordinary example of proactively seeking macrofit in the name of corporate survival. Most saw the company's use of its influence as justified. But there were some who viewed DHC's exercise of economic power in the public policy arena with alarm.[37] The paradox of paternalism was very much in evidence.

In search of pluralism

I remember well a speech at the Harvard Business School in the mid-1980s by James F. Beré, Chairman and Chief Executive Officer of Borg-Warner Corporation. Beré spoke of the importance of both flexibility and patience in communicating shared values to those who would eventually carry them on. Referring to his company's "Beliefs" statement (mentioned earlier in Chapter 3), he said:

> The very last thing we want at Borg-Warner is to have our people marching in *lockstep*. Managers at all levels must make their own decisions in dealing with specific needs. The *Beliefs* do not provide rules. They do provide standards against which individuals can test the actions that seem necessary. They raise the ethical questions that should be asked as part of any decision making. And they will invariably be interpreted differently at different locations, depending on the background, the traditions, and the mindset of each individual. It may take a decade before a true commonality of attitude develops.[38]

Beré's remarks indicate an understanding of value stabilization not only as an exercise of influence by the corporation on its future leaders, but also as a process that can move in the reverse direction, i.e., from individual values to the larger organization. For in the development of what Beré called "a true commonality of attitude" (what we have called *microfit*) both parties should be capable of accommodation. Only the medium-range approach, it seems, allows for the latter possibility. The low range fails at influence in either direction, while the high range involves the "lockstep" that Beré is rejecting.

Specific company policies can help facilitate "microfit" by encouraging exchanges between individual employees and the organizations for which they work. For example, long-standing standards for conduct within Cummins, Inc., direct employees *not* to perform an action if they have doubts about its ethical propriety. Instead, employees are asked to raise their concerns with management, so that open discussion about the issue can take place. The necessary

213

conditions for such dialogue are safeguarded by the organization's pledge to ensure that "no employee is put at a career disadvantage because of his or her willingness to raise a questions about a corporate practice or unwillingness to pursue a course of action which seems inappropriate or morally dubious" – a commitment the firm's management has worked hard to meet throughout the company's history.

At the conclusion of his speech, Beré revealed an awareness of the corresponding macrofit challenge:

> I find a changing attitude *outside* the company equally encouraging. When the *Beliefs* were first announced, they were greeted with snickers by a few of my peers. That has stopped. Now I am frequently asked by my CEO's how we developed and introduced the *Beliefs*. People may be waiting to see how the fruit ripens, but they are no longer dismissing the idea out of hand. I think the climate is changing throughout industry.

Beré's remarks were prophetic in the context of globalization at the close of the twentieth century. As Yale's business school Dean observed:

> In the future, the most effective global CEOs will give more attention to the relationships between their companies and the societies in which they operate. These executives will think about corporate citizenship and social responsibility, not just as philanthropy and good public relations, but as an integral part of their business strategy. They should be careful not to over-promise, but they should also not shy away from using their considerable energies and talents to invest in the full development of the society around them.[39]

How and with what kind of forbearance should a company try to influence future leaders and the wider community in the direction of a given Type 3 orientation? Once we ask this question, we begin to see that Type 3 thinking and the medium range of mindset congruence go together in a natural way. The company that values respect *for* others will be more likely to respect the values *of* others.

The medium range is the only range within which Type 3 values can effectively be sustained – in contrast not only with Type 1 and Type 2 values, but with high and low range efforts to advocate Type 3. This is due to the way in which respect figures so centrally in the orientation of the Type 3 leader. *Respect fosters a self-moderating moral pluralism. The high range is too dogmatic to be respectful, while the low range it too relativistic to be stable.* If the value orientation of a corporation governs the strategy adopted for sustaining it (a reasonable assumption in the absence of hypocrisy), then medium-range Type 3 thinking will help the leader to manage, if not resolve, the paradox of paternalism.

Conclusion

We need to understand the relationships among the three levels of ethical decision-making (person, organization, wider community) if we are to clarify the leader's moral agenda. This agenda requires not only *orienting* and *institutionalizing* corporate conscience. It also requires *sustaining* it by attending to the fit between the company's values, the values of the individuals who will (or will not) carry them forward, and the values of the community that will (or will not) be supportive. When rationality and respect are basic to corporate values, the degree of fit that the leader seeks will tend to avoid paradox by striking an appropriate balance.

In the next chapter, I will apply some of the lessons learned about the moral agenda of corporate leadership in this and the previous two chapters to the educational institutions that serve as the "formation" system for business. As we shall see, the "moral agenda of business education" bears remarkable similarities to the agenda for corporations.

8

Conscience and Three Academies

As we have seen in Chapters 5, 6, and 7, business leaders are the principal architects of corporate conscience. They are the ones who must manage the challenges associated with pursuing profit while maintaining integrity. They are the ones most responsible for delivering on the moral agenda of the corporation.[1] And that agenda includes three primary imperatives: *orienting*, *institutionalizing*, and *sustaining* ethical values within the corporate culture.

But there must be another – supplementary – item on the moral agenda. For without *educational support structures* for the moral agenda of corporate leaders, there is little hope of *passing on* these values to the next generation of business professionals. I will refer to these educational support structures as the "three academies" (see Figure 8.1). All three of these academies must come to terms with Plato's classical question in his dialogue, the *Meno* – "Can virtue be taught?" – if they are to avoid defaulting on the moral formation of future leaders.[2]

- The *first academy* is the modern business school, including undergraduate, MBA, and doctoral programs. After describing a strategy for integrating ethics into the curriculum, I will argue that the three imperatives of *corporate* leadership (orienting, institutionalizing, and sustaining ethical values) have mirror images that are rarely implemented in business schools: the need to initiate, integrate, and continue ethics education beyond graduation.[3]
- By the *second academy*, I mean corporate management and leadership development programs *embedded within their organizations*. This academy too must address the moral agenda – both in

216

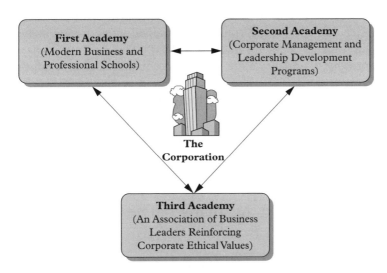

Figure 8.1   Three academies

general and as it relates to company-specific values. Corporate management and leadership development programs are in many ways business schools in their own right, often employing educators from the first academy, and they need to incorporate ethics education for the same reasons.

• By the *third academy*, I mean a global association of business leaders that reflects actively on corporate responsibility, with emphasis on cross-cultural principles and *methods for making such principles operational*. Such an "academy" does not exist today for business as a single unified institution. What we have today is a *set* of organizations sharing a common aspiration – not unlike the first and second academies. Examples of such institutions are the Caux Round Table,[4] the International Society for Business, Economics and Ethics (ISBEE) the Aspen Institute, and the Center for Ethical Business Cultures. As the professions of law and medicine have their associations which act as forums for standards and oversight, as well as state-of-the-art discussions of principles and practices, so too with the profession of management, especially in a global economy.

There are two features shared by the three academies: (1) each supports conscience in the individual *and* in the corporation (because each is concerned with leadership development); and (2) each is a reminder that supporting conscience (individual and organizational) is a life-long process for those involved. The process starts with undergraduate and graduate academic education. But it continues after conventional schooling with education in one's own workplace culture and eventually with participation in global dialogues *across* workplaces. Without *seeking* the support of the three academies, individuals and organizations risk the attractions of teleopathy. Without *providing* this support, educational institutions, corporations, and "civil society" enhance that risk.

The First Academy – The Modern Business School

Yale professor Robert J. Shiller recently wrote that: "Education molds not just individuals but also common assumptions and conventional wisdom. And when it comes to the business world, our universities – and especially their graduate business schools – are powerful shapers of the culture."[5]

Powerful shapers indeed; especially when there is empirical evidence that the culture attributed to business by the schools of the first academy is *not* congruent with the culture actually current in business practice. How destructive is it for schools to actually *prepare* students for a world with less integrity than they will actually see, once they arrive? It is reminiscent of Machiavelli's advice in *The Prince* that leaders should prepare themselves by "learning how not to be good."[6] Many times I have observed cynicism about business ethics from undergraduate students with little or no business experience discussing the *same cases* as graduate students attending evening classes while working. Unless faculty adjust for such naïveté, they risk fueling a self-fulfilling prophecy. Respected business researcher Jim Collins helps to anchor this point: "Contrary to business school doctrine, *we did not find 'maximizing shareholder wealth' or 'profit maximization' as the dominant driving force or primary objective through the history of most of the visionary companies.*"[7]

AACSB

The Association to Advance Collegiate Schools of Business (AACSB International) is the principal accrediting organization for business schools in the US and abroad. In 2003, partly in response to the corporate scandals of 2002, AACSB leadership appointed a special task force to recommend ways to improve ethics education in AACSB accredited institutions. The report of that task force is before the AACSB Board at this writing. The following two paragraphs in the report are particularly noteworthy:

> Few professions have been immune from public embarrassment and accusations, but some – such as business – have become the target of highly visible publicity in the wake of travesties like those at Enron, WorldCom, and Parmalat. Some critics have charged business schools with teaching students to bend the rules to make the numbers. Others have maintained that business schools glossed over ethical conduct in examining business transactions and might go so far as to encourage students to bypass policies, procedures, and even the law, to ensure favorable financial results.
>
> To be sure, business schools cannot be expected to assume total responsibility for ethical debacles in corporations and throughout the business world. Education is hardly the sole determinant of human behavior, and responsibility for ethics education is not the exclusive province of business schools. Nonetheless, ethics education has always been part of business curricula, and AACSB International accreditation standards have long mandated that ethics be taught as part of management degree curricula.[8]

In essence, the AACSB Task Force acknowledges that business schools – while not *determinative* of individual or corporate ethical values – are *contributory*. And as contributory, they need to take a close look at their treatment of ethics, lest a message be sent by silence or neglect that ethical values are peripheral to business success. To quote the AACSB task force again:

> This report is based on the premise that the time has come for business schools – supported by AACSB – to renew and revitalize their commitment to the centrality of ethical responsibility at both the individual and corporate levels in preparing business leaders for the twenty-first century.[9]

But what do "renew and revitalize" mean in institutional terms? What are some reliable methods for making ethical values a central factor in the administration and curriculum of what I am calling the first academy? Support for blending management education with ethics education manifests itself institutionally in three broad arenas:

(1) integration *within* the curriculum; (2) emphasis from what we might call the "*extra-curriculum*"; and (3) in the *mindset* or culture of the school as a whole.[10] Just as corporate conscience is much more than an individual matter, so too the ethical commitment of a business school is much more than an individual matter. Let us look at (1), (2), and (3) in the sections that follow.

Ethics in the First Academy curriculum:
A preamble and a strategy

A curricular strategy that emphasizes ethical management and leadership must start with a fundamental commitment by administration and faculty to the importance of the task. Without such a commitment, any such strategy is doomed to failure. At the University of St. Thomas today, the mission is made clear in all of our promotional literature and on the walls of all of our classrooms: "To educate highly-principled, global business leaders." But this is not a new commitment. In 1990, UST students, faculty, and administrators formulated a mission-like document, which we called a "Preamble," that articulated the institution's commitment to the importance of ethics in the curriculum:

> Business education is commonly aimed at the knowledge needed to perform effectively and efficiently in the business world. We at the University of St. Thomas are committed to that objective and more: encouraging serious consideration and application of ethical values in business decision-making.
>
> Since business ethics can mean different things to different people, we want to specify the assumptions that guide our efforts. Responsibility for one's actions and respect for the dignity of others are fundamental, both for the content of our approach to ethics and for the process by which we teach it. In this approach, dogmatism is as inappropriate as relativism.
>
> Our emphasis, therefore, is on the importance of dialogue for developing mature moral judgment both personally and in group decision-making. In our view, this maturity includes the exercise of certain virtues in the workplace, such as honesty, fairness, empathy, promise keeping, prudence, courage, and concern for the common good. It also includes interaction between the cognitive and emotional dimensions of conscience (i.e., both "head" and "heart") and the need for congruence between judgment and action. We believe such moral development is a life-long process.

> Our goal [at St. Thomas] is to encourage this development in the context of sound policies and practices. We affirm the legitimacy and centrality of moral values in economic decision-making because without them, business relationships and strong communities are impossible.[11]

This statement served the institution well for over a decade, providing a magnetic North for its curricular compass when either the graduate or the undergraduate business programs needed (recalling the "Parable of the Sadhu") to "remember the purpose of the trip." In the spirit of such a "Preamble," business schools can and should formulate *curricular strategies* that avoid the false dilemma of "Should we have a special course or should ethics be in every course?" Too often, this kind of question leads to *compartmentalizing* ethics education (if the first horn of the dilemma is chosen)[12] or to *diluting* it (if the second horn of the dilemma is chosen).

Professor Robert Shiller, quoted at the beginning of this chapter, reminds us that:

> ... some business school curriculums have been improving over the years. Many schools now offer a course in business ethics, and some even try to integrate business ethics into their other courses. But nowhere is ethics seen as a centerpiece or even integral part of the curriculum. And even when business students do take an ethics course, the theoretical framework of the core courses tends to be so devoid of moral content that the discussions of ethics must seem like a side order of some overcooked vegetable.[13]

An alternative (and more effective) strategy consists of four principal steps in a cycle, each called for by the step preceding and each leading to the step following (see Figure 8.2). These are the steps to be applied to the *core* curriculum:

1 *initiation,* an introductory module or "half-course" to foster a common language among students in addressing ethical aspects of business;
2 *inclusion* of ethics cases and readings in the main functional courses in the curriculum, e.g., marketing, finance, accounting, management, business law, and entrepreneurship;
3 *consolidation* of functional applications of ethics in a special course on ethics and governance, or in the business capstone; and
4 *feedback* from alumni of the program and leaders in the wider business community to improve methods and teaching materials

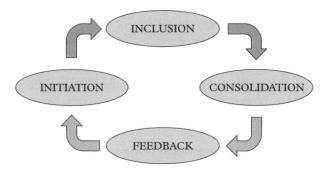

Figure 8.2 Four steps to ethics integration in the curriculum

for the next generation of students, returning us naturally to the initiatory stage.

Initiation

One can *initiate* through a required module, deliberately limited in length, at both graduate and undergraduate levels. This module signals early on that ethical values are central to the entire curriculum, but it also signals (by its limited length) that true integration will take a lot more than a single exposure.

Corresponding to *orientation* in the corporate arena, there needs to be an introduction to ethical values early on in the management curriculum. The language of ethics needs to become part of the student's and the faculty's vocabulary from the beginning. If possible, this initiatory experience should include an indication of the relevance of ethics to each of the main categories of the curriculum that lies ahead, for example, marketing, accounting, finance, law, organizational behavior, international business. Unfortunately, some schools offer an introduction or initiation of this kind and never broach the subject again. This is analogous to a corporation that puts mission, vision, and values statements on a wall or in a handbook, never to revisit them.

Inclusion

Inclusion is sought through course design workshops within departments, including Marketing, Finance, Accounting, Management, Business Law, and Entrepreneurship. The goal in working with each

222

of the departments is to *encourage* and *empower* faculty in the core subject areas to include ethical frameworks alongside the conventional frameworks in these areas – and to develop case studies that illustrate the relevance of ethical awareness to their disciplines in management education.

One of the notable advantages of including ethics in the curriculum using the *case method* is that it can enable the teacher to add ethical themes into an already content-packed course, permitting the analysis of conventional business problems that also have significant ethical dimensions. We might think of this as a kind of "curricular multi-tasking."

Consolidation

At or near the conclusion of the curriculum, efforts to include an ethics theme in all of the core courses can and should be *consolidated* in the capstone course, usually a course aimed at synthesizing the learning that has gone before. Alternatively, a special course on ethics and corporate governance can perform this consolidating function, in tandem with the capstone course.

Consolidation calls for working with the capstone course faculty. The hope is to offer the students who are completing the business curriculum a significant exposure to ways of blending strategic and ethical considerations in decision-making, as a general manager would be expected to do.

Other forms of consolidation (as indicated below under the "extra-curriculum") might involve "business and society" elective courses or, as we do at St. Thomas, a *Great Books Seminar,* modeled on the *Executive Seminar* offered for over a half-century by the Aspen Institute. It should be remembered, however, that the function of consolidation cannot be performed in a curriculum by *elective* courses alone. It must be anchored in the *core* curriculum.

Feedback

As a means to the end of deepening and continuing a school's efforts to institutionalize ethics in the curriculum, *alumni* have a unique role to play. Most schools turn to their alumni for financial support, and this is as it should be. But I dare say that most schools do not ask *enough* of their alumni unless they consult with them systematically about the ethical challenges they face and the kind of preparation they would recommend. The experiences and the wisdom of alumni are a fertile ground for case studies and classroom testimony about the reality of ethical challenges in management.

Feedback includes (a) holding alumni workshops and (b) tapping graduates (after they have had substantial business experience) for contributions to ethics-related course development. This represents a generous investment on their part in future students, and it completes the circle, bringing us back to initiation again as we constantly revitalize the opening module.

Ethics course content

Business ethics courses, whether we are talking about the initiatory module or a fuller-scale course later in the sequence, should offer a set of cases and readings aimed at joining ethical reflection to business decision-making. Several criteria can guide the selection and organization of these materials: *topical relevance* to the modern manager, *curricular relevance* to the required core courses that will follow, and *conceptual relevance* to applied ethics.

Topically, the idea is to examine current and significant management challenges such as product safety, honesty in marketing, environmental protection, transparent financial reporting, and international business in diverse cultures. From the perspective of *curricular* relevance, the course materials should display breadth and richness of a different kind. The principal subject areas in the curriculum should be represented: management (human resources, operations, strategy), marketing, finance, accounting, entrepreneurship, and business law. The third criterion – *conceptual* relevance in applied ethics – draws attention to several levels at which ethical concepts can be applied to business activity: the level of the individual (managerial decisions and virtues), the level of the organization (policy formulation and implementation), and the level of the society as a whole (democratic capitalism nationally and globally). Other conceptual questions in the background include: What is "the moral point of view" in a postmodern world? What avenues or frameworks are available for making responsible decisions? Can ethical principles and values transcend cultural boundaries?

The search for *excellence* in such coursework calls for a team effort by the faculty. The *flow* of the course, after some introductory material, goes from "Ethics and the Individual," to "Ethics and the Organization," to "Ethics and the Market System." In each of these parts of the course – and thus at each of these three levels of analysis –

instructors and learners examine cases and readings with attention not only to "stakeholder" thinking but also virtue-based (or, in relation to companies and societies, culture-based) thinking. Course objectives include:

- enhancing learner awareness of the importance of ethical values for individual and organizational success;
- stimulating a positive attitude in learners toward incorporating virtue-based and stakeholder analysis throughout business decision-making; and
- providing a process for thinking through the economic and non-economic implications of strategies and implementation plans in realistic business situations.

Ethical awareness and sound moral judgment are not, of course, substitutes for basic business skills in the functional areas (marketing, finance, accounting, etc.). But it is becoming increasingly clear, that the exercise of basic managerial skills in an atmosphere of uncritical moral and social premises leads not only to expanding external regulation and adversarialism, but to a widespread and reasonable lack of trust in institutional forms of all kinds: economic, political, academic, and even religious. As Bennis and O'Toole put it in "How Business Schools Lost Their Way":

> If the purpose of graduate business education is to develop executives – leaders – then the faculty must have expertise in more than just fact collection. The best classroom experiences are those in which professors with broad perspectives and diverse skills analyze cases that have seemingly straightforward technical challenges and then gradually peel away the layers to reveal hidden strategic, economic, competitive, human, and political complexities – all of which must be plumbed to reach truly effective business decisions.[14]

Students need to engage in case method dialogue, allowing their preparation, energy, and willingness to learn from peers to produce genuine moral insight. They can then take what they have learned and carry it into each of the courses that make up their business curriculum. Ultimately, students must be *challenged* to go beyond specific issues and courses to develop a responsible business philosophy of their own.

The extra-curriculum

Beyond the regular curriculum, wrapped around it in concentric circles as it were, there can be many "extra-curricular" activities that support a *culture of relevance* for ethics and the case method. In addition to core courses, there are elective courses, guest speakers, colloquia, alumni seminars, and various Internet-based enhancements to learning:

- *Elective courses*: Making all ethics-related courses in the curriculum *required* courses is probably unwise, never mind that it would be politically impossible in most colleges and universities. But a menu of elective courses that relate in various ways to business ethics (e.g., a seminar on *Spirituality and Management* or a *Great Books* seminar for graduate students and alumni or a *Case Research* practicum) carries an important message to teachers and learners alike about the importance the institution assigns to the ethics agenda.
- *Guest speakers*: Regular guest speakers addressing ethics-related themes are also a powerful signal of an institution's commitment, especially if the audience is "town and gown," i.e., not only faculty and students, but also business persons in the college or university community.
- *Colloquia*: Another type of extra-curricular integration of ethics is the systematic dialogue or colloquium. Colloquia can involve students, faculty, and executives. Individual and panel presentations can include prepared papers or case studies.
- *Alumni seminars*: While alumni are natural participants in both guest speaker events and colloquia, events held especially for alumni provide an opportunity for both alumni and their *alma mater* to share important information. Lifelong learning for alumni is increasingly valuable to them, of course, but less noticed is an *institution's* need for lifelong learning by sharing the experiences of its alumni, often in the form of case studies. Without tapping such information, an institution risks lack of currency and eventually irrelevance in its professional education programs.
- *Internet-assisted learning*: Virtual classrooms offer new techniques for ethics education both inside and outside the curriculum. Internet-based case studies, often available on CD-ROMs, provide more than conventional case text. They also provide audio-visual examples of case facts and hyperlinks to relevant case information

on various Internet sites. Distance learning courses in ethics are a recent development, but they will be a growing pedagogical tool. Geographical dispersion and asynchronous delivery can be seen as limitations on ethics education – but they can also provide new opportunities. A case discussion in ethics is never richer, for example, than when the participants come from different cultural backgrounds, which the Internet makes possible. In a new distance course that this writer has recently developed, something called the "C.A.T. Scan" (Case Analysis Template, see Figure 8.3) has been automated as a learning tool for participants and as a way for instructors to regularly monitor participants' understanding

"CAT Scan" [*Case Analysis Template*]				
CASE ANALYSIS STEPS (5 D's)	*INTEREST-BASED OUTLOOK*	*RIGHTS-BASED OUTLOOK*	*DUTY-BASED OUTLOOK*	*VIRTUE-BASED OUTLOOK*
DESCRIBE	How did the situation come about? What are the key presenting issues? Who are the key individuals and groups affected by the situation, the *stakeholders*?			
	Identify interests.	Identify rights.	Identify duties.	Identify virtues.
DISCERN	What is the most significant of the "presenting issues" – the one that might lie underneath it all? And who are the core stakeholders involved in the case?			
	Are there conflicting interests with respect to this issue, and how basic are they?	Are there rights in conflict with interests or with other rights? Are some weightier than others?	Does duty come into the picture – and are there tensions with rights or interests? Can I prioritize?	Is character an issue in this case – habits that bring us to this point or that will be reinforced later?
DISPLAY	What are the principal realistic *options* available to the decision maker(s) in this case, including possible branching among sub-options – leading to a set of action plans?			
DECIDE	What is my *considered judgment* on the best option to take from those listed above?			
DEFEND	Which of the avenues predominates in my choice of options above, and can I give *good reasons* for preferring the ethical priorities I have adopted in this case that are consistent with other such cases? What would an imaginary jury of the four "voices" decide and why? What is my moral framework?			

Figure 8.3 Case Analysis Template ("CAT Scan")

of ethics case materials.[15] The "C.A.T. Scan" was developed to echo the four avenues of ethical analysis described in Chapter 3.

The business school mindset or culture

Teleopathy can manifest itself in the life of the academy as much as in the life of a corporation. This includes, in the present context, business schools. Like corporations, schools as organizations can "forget the purpose of the trip," becoming fixated on goals far from their original mission. In an effort to cultivate donors, high rankings, or tuition dollars, schools of business (among other professional schools) can actually *manifest* teleopathy while advertising a curriculum that stands for avoiding it! Yale's Schiller: "[T]he view of the world that one gets in a modern business curriculum can lead to an ethical disconnect. The courses often encourage a view of human nature that does not inspire high-mindedness."[16]

When the first academy claims to offer knowledge and skill in a certain professional domain – especially ethics – it is reasonable to ask whether such knowledge and skill should be demonstrated not only in the *curriculum*, but modeled by the school *as an organization* made up of faculty, administration, and students. It is reasonable to measure the effectiveness of ethics education by asking how much business schools are able to "walk their talk" – to evidence their own abilities to live out the managerial virtues that they would foster in their students. The *culture* of an academic institution is more than just the *curriculum* of that institution.

The AACSB International Task Force Report referred to earlier is emphatic about the importance of the cultures of business schools:

> Another way students learn about ethical behaviors is through the ethical culture they observe in their respective business schools. Students cannot be expected to internalize the importance of ethics and values unless business schools demonstrate such commitment within their own organizations. This means that business school deans need to think of themselves as ethical leaders who communicate regularly about ethics and values; who model ethical conduct; and who hold community members – faculty, staff, and students – accountable for their actions. Academic policies and systems should clearly be an integral, living part of the school's culture, and not simply a stack of documents in the file drawer.[17]

Business ethics education can only be effective if it is supported widely by the faculty and administration of the school. Responsibility for ethics in the business curriculum must be borne by the entire business faculty, not outsourced or handled by one or two specialists or "gurus." The risk associated with outsourcing (e.g., from a philosophy department) is the same as the risk associated with special "gurus" – *compartmentalization*. Compartmentalization means that ethical issues that arise in other parts of the business curriculum are "referred to the experts," sending the wrong message to students as future ethical decision-makers.

My former Harvard colleague, John B. Matthews, Jr., used to observe that business school faculty carried a powerful "eraser" when it came to the seriousness with which students took ethical considerations in their courses. The work of colleagues committed to the ethics in management could be "erased" by quips and body language by instructors in certain "tough minded" courses that signaled "softness" or "sentimentality" in ethical business decision-making. Students read more than books and case studies in business school – they read the *faculty* with great attention.

Emphasis on ethics education must come from the school's leadership, but must also be built into the hiring, promotion, and other incentive systems of the school. Key faculty resources must be identified to model the desired curricular initiatives and search committee criteria must include attention to ethics. Regular audits of faculty can ask how ethics is worked into the various core course syllabi. Student course evaluations can include questions about the degree to which the course addressed the ethical aspects of the subject matter.[18]

Let us return in conclusion to the Task Force Report quoted earlier:

> AACSB must support and encourage a renaissance in ethics education and exercise its leadership role to ensure the commitment of business schools. We must strengthen ethics components of our curricula in all disciplines to emphasize the importance of individual integrity and corporate responsibility to business success. We must offer courses that introduce ethical frameworks to help challenge students to resolve business and managerial problems; courses that lay out the larger societal context in which business operates; and seminars and workshops that bring executives to campus to focus on the link between leadership and values. We must work to build a community of scholars and students in which ethical principles are not platitudes, but reality.[19]

Just as we remind our *students* that their management education does not end with a degree or a diploma, we must remind *ourselves* that education in ethical awareness must continue and be strengthened over time. This means not only that faculty and administrators need continuing education and outside speakers, but also that faculty need to be supported in research and case writing on the ethical aspects of their respective specialties.

If ethics is not woven into the fabric of business education (and I am talking about more than simply the addition of a course), the business academy runs the risk of encouraging (rather than discouraging) teleopathy in its *hidden* curriculum (the curriculum that often forms the philosophical outlook of the graduates). Schools speak not only by the way in which they make decisions generally – but also by the way in which they design priorities into their curricula. Silence can be an eloquent teacher. Eventually, of course, the business school passes the baton of ethics education to the second academy.

The Second Academy – Corporate Ethics and Leadership Development Programs

In a recent *Harvard Business Review* article, Professors Warren Bennis and James O'Toole wrote provocatively:

> Today, business practitioners are discovering that B school professors know more about academic publishing than about the problems of the workplace. It's no wonder there's been such a marked increase in the number of in-house corporate universities and for-profit management education organizations.[20]

In 2002, in the US, over 2,400 colleges and universities had business programs. More than 100,000 students were pursuing MBA degrees, 25 percent of all graduate students.[21] But corporations were educators of their own employees in even larger numbers:

> Companies themselves are also providing formal education for their own executives; General Electric's campus at Crotonville, New York, is perhaps the most famous and has become a model for many others, such as Motorola, PepsiCo, Goldman Sachs, Sun Microsystems, Inc., Johnson & Johnson, and Siemens.[22]

According to a survey conducted by Fairfield Research, Inc., and *Chief Learning Officer* magazine, US companies with $500 million or more in sales spent $11.5 billion on learning and training in 2002, or an average of $3.7 million per firm. Aggregate spending within this sector is expected to increase to $14 billion by 2007.[23]

The American Society for Training and Development's 2004 *State of the Industry Report* estimates that, on average, US firms spend 2.5 percent of their payroll costs on training and learning. The same report estimates that "training investment leaders" – companies with an outstanding, demonstrated commitment to learning, and the effective alignment of learning with business needs and individual employee needs – invest even more, 4.2 percent.

So we turn to what I have called the second academy. The corporation is a business school in its own right, and needs to incorporate ethics education just as the first academy does. The second academy must support the development of conscience individually and organizationally – but it does so as a training or educational function within the workplace itself, not as an independent source of knowledge outside.

In many ways, of course, we have already discussed the second academy in Chapters 5, 6, and 7, but here it is useful to focus on the specifically educational aspects of the leadership imperatives. Corporate Ethics and Leadership Development Programs not only orient, institutionalize, and sustain an organization's conscience, they inevitably serve as "continuing education" for many managers who continue their careers in other companies. In that respect, such programs are quite analogous to private business schools. Indeed, when corporate programs are either "outsourced" or "insourced" they actually make use of the intellectual capital of the first academy.[24]

Two engines in the second academy

There are two principal developmental engines for ethics within the second academy. The first has to do with the preparation of leaders within the organization to take over from the current generation, the "leadership pipeline" as some call it. Often, a company's senior vice-president for Human Resources will shoulder this responsibility. The second engine is normally the corporate ethics and compliance program, usually headed up by someone called an "ethics officer." This engine tends to be less about leadership development and more about company education around ethically and legally relevant norms for behavior.

Let us begin with the (second) "ethics and legal compliance" arena within the corporate academy, an arena that is growing dramatically, especially since the corporate scandals of 2001–2. Membership in the Ethics Officer Association "has risen more than 25% since 2003. Its more than 1,200 members include ethics officers representing about 40% of the Fortune 500."[25]

The US Federal Sentencing Guidelines for Organizations[26]

In 1987, Congress passed the Federal Sentencing Guidelines, a product of the work of a special commission set up for the purpose. The aim was to create more uniformity in sentencing (*individual*) criminals. In 1991, the US Federal Sentencing Commission submitted and Congress approved sentencing guidelines covering *organizational* offenders. The Federal Sentencing Guidelines for Organizations (FSGO) were "designed so that the sanctions imposed upon organizations and their agents, taken together, will provide just punishment, adequate deterrence, and incentives for organizations to maintain internal mechanisms for preventing, detecting, and reporting criminal conduct."[27]

The guidelines allowed the imposition of reduced penalties on companies with qualified corporate compliance programs. To qualify, such programs had to fulfill seven minimum requirements (see Chapter 6.) These included assigning "high-level personnel to oversee the compliance program, such as an ethics officer, ombudsman, or compliance officer."[28]

The revised FSGO (2004)

In May 2004, the US Sentencing Commission recommended to Congress certain modifications of the 1991 Federal Sentencing Guidelines for Organizations. The revised guidelines, which were approved and went into effect in November 2004, introduced new requirements designed to catalyze changes in corporate compliance programs. Three changes were particularly significant:

1 The revised guidelines mandated that companies periodically evaluate the effectiveness of their compliance programs. What was the likelihood that the program might fail to prevent illegal or unethical behavior? Companies were directed to use these risk assessments to improve their programs.

232

2   The revisions called for the promotion of an organizational culture that encouraged *ethical conduct* as well as observance of the law. This new provision recognized the significant influence of a firm's culture on employee behavior, illustrated by many of the business scandals that emerged in 2001 and 2002. It also formally introduced ethics as a key element in an effective compliance program.

3   The revised FSGO underscored the responsibilities of boards of directors and senior executives for a company's compliance program. Corporate directors needed to be knowledgeable about the content and operation of the organization's program, and had to receive training appropriate to their role and responsibilities. Company executives were held responsible for ensuring that the firm's compliance program was effective. This included providing the individual charged with day-to-day responsibility for the program (the "ethics officer") with adequate resources, authority, and access, including access to the board of directors or the appropriate board committee.

The role of the ethics officer

As a position that was fairly new to the business world, there was at first no standard definition of the tasks an ethics officer should undertake. However, most ethics officers provided support in four major areas: (1) serving as a resource to managers and employees on questions of ethics and legal compliance; (2) monitoring the corporation's policies and procedures; (3) developing ethics training programs; and (4) assisting with deliberations on ethical concerns. In the words of Edward Petry and Fred Tietz, the ethics officer "is expected to be confessor, corporate conscience, investigator, enforcer, and teacher, all rolled into one."[29]

In the US, the Ethics Officers Association (EOA) was created in 1991 to support occupants of this new position. From 12 charter members, the EOA had grown by 2005 to include over 1,200 companies in more than 35 different industries. Initially, its efforts focused on providing educational and networking opportunities. The EOA's initiatives have since expanded to include an annual conference addressing current issues facing ethics officers, as well as other opportunities for exploring ethics-related trends and practices.

The 2000 Annual Report of the Ethics Officer Association indicated that the average annual budget for ethics and compliance training within its member companies is $382,000. Among organizations with annual revenues between roughly $5.1 billion and $10 billion, this expenditure increased to $778,000 annually.

Ethics officers are not, however, the only ethics-related careers available. Some organizations name a compliance officer to oversee the legal aspects of an ethics officer's role in the organization, i.e. to ensure that the organization is not unknowingly violating any laws or regulations. Another position is that of the ombudsperson, a person appointed to investigate complaints against the firm as reported by employees.

An organization serving both ethics officers and compliance officers is the Society of Corporate Compliance & Ethics (SCCE). According to its mission statement, it "exists to champion compliance standards, corporate governance, and ethical practice in the business community and to provide the necessary resources for compliance and ethics professionals and others who share these principles." SCCE describes its key roles as:

- facilitating the development and maintenance of compliance programs;
- providing a forum for understanding the complicated compliance environment; and
- offering tools, resources and educational opportunities for those involved with corporate compliance.[30]

The ethics officer's position can be viewed as somewhat paradoxical insofar as it seems to involve being paid to "bite the hand that feeds it." However, this is a misperception that fails to appreciate the positive contribution an ethics officer can make. In many ways, the ethics officer assists with the critical task of forming what we have been calling the organization's "conscience."[31] The role helps foster an ethical environment, aids decision-making, and supports doing the right thing even though it may not always be financially or strategically ideal.

In view of the ethics officer's role, it is vital for its occupant to have access to the top of the corporation's hierarchy. Lacking this, he or she will lack the clout necessary to initiate change. "Recent surveys show that 50% of North America's biggest companies have ethics officers reporting to chief executives. And many experts believe that number will rise with the revision of the sentencing guidelines."[32]

Ethics officers are more frequently reporting to the CEO in order to be sure that their influence reaches as high as possible in their organizations:

> The latest push to put ethics officers in the executive suite . . . has been driven by the 2002 Sarbanes-Oxley Act, which defines and punishes corporate crimes much more explicitly, and by the revised US sentencing guidelines that took effect in November 2004. These require companies to make stronger commitments to ethical standards and prove they are living up to those commitments.[33]

Despite positional authority, however, it is important that the ethics officer not be identified simply as a member of upper management, since this could fracture communications with the rank and file. Instead, the ethics officer must be viewed as occupying a role at the center of the organization, accessible by employees at all levels and responsive to their concerns.

Ethics training

If the UK is any indication, it does *not* go without saying that companies with ethics or compliance officers and explicit codes and policies about ethical conduct offer solid training and ethics education to their employees. A recent survey by the *Financial Times* in the UK noted this incongruous – but real – state of affairs:

> Many leading companies are failing to train their workforce in ethical behaviour despite growing awareness of the need for strict codes of business conduct, a report will reveal today. The survey of companies with ethics codes found half did not provide training for all staff in how to apply them, even though 60 percent required employees to obey the codes as part of their contracts.
>
> Simon Webley, research director of the Institute of Business Ethics, a charity promoting high standards of corporate behaviour, and co-author of the report, said: "Expecting a business ethics policy to have any noticeable effect . . . when no training is provided . . . does not make any business sense."[34]

The explanation for the incongruity is not hard to discern – even if it is often hard to accept. The *Financial Times* report suggested the explanation was that senior managers were reluctant to approve expenditures on programs they thought did not have "a direct impact on profitability."[35]

Recent developments: US Supreme Court Ruling (January 2005)

Despite the positive power and influence that the US Federal Sentencing guidelines have had since 1991 – especially the guidelines for organizations – recent court challenges have raised problems. To what extent do the mandated sentences built into the guidelines infringe upon the right to a trial by jury (of both individuals and organizations)?

The Supreme Court issued a long-awaited decision on the constitutionality of the federal guidelines (individual and organizational) in *United States v. Booker*, US, No. 04-104, 1/12/05.

> A 5–4 majority of the court held that the federal guidelines violate the Sixth Amendment's right to trial by jury by requiring judges to increase sentences on the basis of facts not found by a jury. However, a slightly different five-member majority ruled that the remedy is for judges to treat the guidelines as advisory rather than mandatory.[36]

This somewhat surprising development has been a concern to some in the field of corporate compliance, especially those who celebrated the approval of the revised FSGO in November 2004. As it turns out, the significance of the High Court ruling is likely to be greater for the *individual* sentencing guidelines than for the *organizational* guidelines. While the guidelines shift from mandatory to advisory because of the ruling, their importance to corporations, even as advisory, remains. This is because company compliance programs are aimed at avoiding being *charged*, let alone being *sentenced*, and the Department of Justice continues to use the FSGO as highly relevant to prosecutorial decisions.[37]

Win Swenson, former deputy general counsel at the Sentencing Commission, predicted that the court's ruling would not have a significant impact on corporate sentencing. "The Supreme Court's decision doesn't make the federal guidelines irrelevant – in fact sentencing courts 'must consult' and 'take into account' the guidelines."[38] "Most important," Swenson explained, the Justice Department made clear that it will advocate that sentencing judges follow the guidelines: "Since most corporate cases are resolved through plea bargains negotiated by the Department, the Department's continued endorsement of the corporate guidelines virtually guarantees their continued relevance."[39]

236

Ethics and leadership education within the corporation

Let us now turn to the other developmental engine for ethics within the second academy, the preparation of leaders within the organization to take over from the current generation, the "leadership pipeline." Often this effort, which we first discussed in connection with "sustaining corporate conscience" in Chapter 7, is led by the senior vice-president for Human Resources. In addition to talent management – identifying and promoting key individuals in the pipeline – the task here is what used to be called "grooming." And grooming is frequently done through mentoring, coaching, and leadership seminars and programs.[40] These efforts need to be distinguished from "training" in the conventional sense. They are more about developing perspective, maturity of outlook, and character than they are about communicating rules and compliance norms.

Yale's Dean Jeffrey Garten expresses concern about leadership development at this level, including not only executives, but boards of directors:

> Today's system for educating business executives does not go far enough to train CEOs to be leaders in society. The educational process needs to be broader and to take place over a longer period. It needs to be aimed not only at a company's management but also at those who serve on the boards of directors. It needs to encompass not just MBA curricula but executive education programs, too.[41]

The corporate scandals of 2001–2003 in the US resulted in new requirements for education for senior leaders and board members, as we saw above in relation to the FSGO.[42] It is, therefore, in a company's self-interest, quite apart from more intrinsic motivation, to initiate and maintain solid, participative, senior leadership programs.

Taking time

What are the key elements that leadership development seminars in corporations need to include if they are to provide effective second academy engines for ethical values? There are numerous content possibilities and pedagogical approaches, but my experience with hundreds of executives has taught me that whatever the content and whatever the pedagogy, the key to effectiveness centers on *time*.

237

Books, articles, stories, case studies, video materials, small group projects, interactive exercises – all of these have a place, not to mention recreation: music, art, and physical activity. Indeed, not just any books, but *Great Books* (in the style pioneered by the Aspen Institute) offer tremendous leadership substance. The critical point, however, is to allow executives to *take time* both in solitude and together to be reflective and to pursue the *awareness* discussed throughout Chapter 3. Time – no doubt the most expensive investment that companies can make in senior executives – allows for reflection, communication, and ultimately moral renewal. David Whyte, whose poetry has enriched so many of my leadership seminars, makes the point eloquently:

> The core of difficulty at the heart of modern work life is its abstraction from many of the ancient cycles of life that allow the silence and time in which true appreciation and experience can take place. The hurried child becomes the pressured student, and finally the harassed manager. The process is begun very young, and can be so in our bones, depending on the pressure of our upbringing, that the inability to pay real attention to our world may be difficult to recognize.[43]

It is ironic indeed that the multitasking, high technology, modern executive – a supposed paragon of productivity – finds himself or herself unable "to pay real attention to our world." And it is more than ironic – it is tragic – to realize that such an inability can distort or suppress ethical judgment. My own senior executive seminars, therefore, always begin with one of Anthony DeMello's Zen poems inviting those present to truly *be* present. The familiar alternation takes place initiated by the seeker after enlightenment and responded to by the Zen master:

> "Where shall I look for enlightenment?"
> "Here."
> "When will it happen?"
> "It is happening right now."
> "Then why don't I experience it?"
> "Because you do not look."
> "At what?"
> "Anything your eyes alight upon."
> "Must I look in a special kind of way?"
> "No. The ordinary way will do."
> "But don't I always look the ordinary way?"

"No."
"Why ever not?"
"Because to look you must be here.
You're mostly somewhere else."[44]

It is not uncommon for executives to travel periodically to fairly exotic or upscale places to have "retreats." It *is* uncommon to design such retreats not as high-level work sessions but as genuine opportunities to re-connect with the company's mission and core values. This is particularly true when a company has gone through a period of significant growth, by acquisition or otherwise. Such re-connection calls for a change of *pace* and of conversational *topic*; ultimately, it calls for a kind of examination of *corporate* conscience in relation to *personal* conscience.

Parker Palmer, in his book *The Active Life*, shares a Taoist prose poem about Khing, the master woodcarver. In the context of a senior leadership retreat, this story (like David Whyte's emphasis on "paying attention" and Anthony DeMello's emphasis on "being here rather than someplace else") provides a powerful reminder of how stress (teleopathy) can be self-defeating. Few have trouble identifying with the Woodcarver and applying this story to their corporate lives:

> Khing, the master carver, made a bell stand
> Of precious wood. When it was finished,
> All who saw it were astounded. They said it must be
> The work of spirits.
> The Prince of Lu said to the master carver:
> "What is your secret?"
>
> Khing replied: "I am only a workman;
> I have no secret. There is only this:
> When I began to think about the work you commanded
> I guarded my spirit, did not expend it
> On trifles, that were not to the point.
> I fasted in order to set
> My heart at rest.
> After five days
> I had forgotten praise or criticism.
> After seven days
> I had forgotten my body
> With all its limbs.

239

"By this time all thought of your Highness
And of the court had faded away.
All that might distract me from the work
Had vanished.
I was collected in the single thought
Of the bell stand.

"Then I went to the forest
To see the trees in their own natural state.
When the right tree appeared before my eyes,
The bell stand also appeared in it, clearly, beyond doubt.
All I had to do was to put forth my hand
And begin.

"If I had not met this particular tree
There would have been No bell stand at all.

"What happened?
My own collected thought
Encountered the hidden potential in the wood;
From this live encounter came the work
Which you ascribe to the spirits."[45]

Palmer points out that the woodcarver is under serious pressure to "perform" in this feudal environment.[46] And for this reason, his decision to spend precious *time* collecting himself before undertaking the task at hand strikes most readers as both surprising – and wise. Indeed, the message that senior leaders are "away" spending time reflecting on their company's core values *in order that the bell stand might have real value* is not lost on them. Other insights usually emerge as well:

- that "fasting" can be "informational," not just nutritional – so constant email and cell phone communication with the office might defeat the purpose of the trip;
- that fear of disapproval and its consequences is not a solid motivational platform;
- that accomplishing organizational goals means finding the right "trees," recognizing and cultivating the talents of the people in one's "forest"; and
- that excellence attributable to "the work of spirits" comes from *relationships*, not from solo operators on ego trips.[47]

240

In summary, the second academy is a critical support system for corporate conscience, functioning within companies (1) as part of the ethics and compliance system, and (2) as part of the leadership development pipeline, especially as that pipeline seeks highly principled global leaders who are personally and culturally self-aware. Let us now turn to the third academy, perhaps more a dream than a reality at the moment, but a dream capable of coming true in our lifetimes.

In Search of a Third Academy – Associating Business Leaders

If business schools are to regain their relevance, they must come to grips with the reality that business management is not a scientific discipline but a profession, and they must deal with what a professional education requires.[48]

It is not a new question – whether business can be a profession like law and medicine. In fact, the founding of business schools in the late nineteenth century within the academic communities of universities, alongside and by analogy with professional law schools, medical schools, and schools of divinity, represents an important social *aspiration* if not a social *reality*. Wharton (at the University of Pennsylvania) and the Harvard Business School were early efforts at *professionalizing* commercial enterprise, an institutional mission that many would argue is still unrealized.

What makes a profession a profession? Clearly the paradigms of law and medicine suggest that a *body of knowledge* is a necessary condition, knowledge applied to the service of critical human needs (e.g., justice, health). This "knowledge-worker" condition helps to explain (and justify) the presence of professional schools on university campuses.[49] And if it were the only condition on an occupation being a profession, business schools would long since have been recognized for their professionalism by their legal and medical peers.

There is, however, at least one *other* necessary condition behind the scenes, a condition originally met most clearly by the priestly or ministerial profession even before law and medicine. The condition is that, in addition to mastering a body of knowledge, a profession embodies a personal and social mission ("vocation") which is highly valued by the society in which it functions. Such a mission carries

241

with it both rights and responsibilities – privileges, prestige, and expectations beyond simply the requirements of laws and statutes. Indeed, we can say that to be a profession, an occupation must be surrounded by *a culture of ethical expectations*.

Kenneth Dayton, former CEO of Dayton Hudson (now Target), once said: "I happen to think that being the CEO of a corporation, large or small, is every bit as high a calling as being an educator, or being in the field of religion, medicine, law or any other occupation." Why is it such a high calling? Dayton goes on: "The CEO has the opportunity to impact a community more than almost anyone else, and therefore it is an incredibly high calling and opportunity to make this community and this nation a better place."[50] There are no doubt many corporate leaders who would identify with the spirit of Dayton's words, which may be the clearest expression ever of what it is for business to be seen as a profession.

Robert Bellah once suggested that management might become a profession in the "older sense of the word," beyond standards of technical competence to standards of public obligation "that could at moments of conflict override obligations to the corporate employer." He then added:

> Such a conception of the professional manager would require *a deep change in the ethos of schools of business administration*, where "business ethics" would have to become central in the process of professional formation. If the rewards of success in business management were not so inordinate, then choice of this profession could arise from more public-spirited motives. In short, personal, cultural, and structural change all entail one another.[51]

Bennis and O'Toole, in the article cited earlier, refer to the elements of a profession as described by Harvard Business School associate professor Rakesh Khurana:

> [P]rofessions have at least four key elements: an accepted body of knowledge, a system for certifying that individuals have mastered that body of knowledge before they are allowed to practice, a commitment to the public good, and an enforceable code of ethics.[52]

If there has been controversy about the legitimacy of business schools during the twentieth century, it has centered on the suggestion that *careers* and *private* enterprises are very different from professions (*vocations*) and institutions that serve the *community*. "If you want to

242

enjoy the respect of a truly *professional* school," one can imagine critics insisting, "your discipline will have to demonstrate a collective conscience and a devotion to society that heretofore has eluded your cultural role." It is as if the traditional learned professions achieve their status as professions not just by having *schools in universities* (the first academy), nor simply by having *continuing education* in organizational settings (the second academy) – but by having *associations that articulate ethical norms that hold members accountable to their callings.* This is what I mean by a third academy, and this is what I hope to persuade the reader of this book is essential for the future of market-based economic systems.

Lifelong learning for leadership

While it is true that the American Medical Association (AMA) and the American Bar Association (ABA) have many functions, including examination, continuing education, and the articulation of professional norms, these academies also represent forums for communication among and recognition of exemplary leaders in their professions. There is not a similar association for business leaders – at least not as a unified institution – but the time has come for this to change.

There are approximations or gestures in the direction of the kind of third academy imagined here, both in the US and abroad. In the US, we find the Business Roundtable, the Chamber(s) of Commerce, and various industry-specific associations seeking to foster responsible leadership. And as business globalization continues to evolve, there are increasingly associations abroad that perform similar functions.[53] But none of these organizations has the standing in the "profession" of business that the AMA and ABA have in relation to their respective professions. As we conclude our discussion of conscience and corporate culture, I would like to suggest that there are institutional *intimations* that already exist (albeit separately) of a third academy. By considering the *elements* of these models, we may be able to trace the contours of a new academy – and eventually help it to happen. The intimations that I would invite the reader to consider are four, all global in their aspirations but relatively small in scale:

• The Caux Round Table (CRT)
• The International Society for Business, Economics, and Ethics (ISBEE)

- The Aspen Institute (AI), and
- The Center for Ethical Business Cultures (CEBC)

An institutional portrait of a third academy for business as a profession will incorporate aspects of all four of these organizations.

The Caux Round Table and the SAIP

As explained in Chapter 5, the Caux Round Table (CRT) was founded in 1986 by a small group of Japanese, European, and American executives who embraced the mission of promoting *principled business leadership*. The loosely defined group gathered annually in the village of Caux-sur-Montreux, overlooking Lake Geneva. The CRT *Principles for Business* originated in July 1994 in part from a document that one of the American members shared with the group – a document known as the Minnesota Principles. The Center for Ethical Business Cultures, described below, is the successor organization to the Minnesota Center for Corporate Responsibility which developed the Minnesota Principles in 1992.

In 1999, a working group of executives and scholars developed a set of benchmarks, modeling its efforts on the Baldrige National Quality Program. This Self-Assessment and Improvement Process (SAIP), described in Chapter 5, is a structured inventory of questions – a comprehensive ethics audit – designed to show corporate leaders and boards of directors how their organizations have (or have not) institutionalized aspirations like those embodied in the CRT *Principles*.

The CRT and the SAIP working group bring to the search for a third academy two important elements, beyond their history as initiatives by global business leaders: (1) a set of transcultural ethical principles, and (2) a process for implementing these principles, and assessing and improving performance in relation to them. If business is to be a profession, it needs a transcultural ethical base, analogous to the Hippocratic Oath in medicine.[54]

The International Society for Business, Economics, and Ethics

The International Society of Business, Economics, and Ethics (ISBEE) is the first world-wide professional association to focus exclusively on the study of business, economics, and ethics. Its professional membership includes not only academics, but also managers of corporations from around the world. ISBEE provides a global network of persons and organizations and a wide range of professional activities including quadrennial congresses, proceedings, and an elaborate website.

The mission of ISBEE is "to provide a forum for the exchange of experiences and ideas; to enhance cooperation in cross-functional and cross-cultural projects; and to discuss the ethical dimension of economic, social, and environmental issues which affect companies nationally and internationally."[55]

ISBEE's signature events are the World Congresses of Business, Economics, and Ethics, held every four years. Past congresses have taken place in Tokyo, Japan (1996), in São Paulo, Brazil (2000), and in Melbourne, Australia (2004). The next congress is scheduled to meet in South Africa in 2008.[56]

ISBEE brings to the search for a third academy a global convening function more extensive (but less frequent) than the reach of the Caux Round Table, but it also brings another special contribution. ISBEE periodically scans its membership to identify and describe major global challenges on the horizon for business ethics. As part of an agreement with the Caux Round Table, ISBEE now shares this periodic scan with the membership of the Caux Round Table and in turn, ISBEE gains from participation in the Annual CRT Global Dialogues with business leaders. The most recent of these agendas, was presented to the ISBEE World Congress in Melbourne, Australia in July 2004. It was called "Agenda 2004" and is described on the ISBEE website:

> Agenda 2004 . . . was launched with the ISBEE Task Force for Global Challenges in 2002 that consisted of Richard De George, Georges Enderle, Kenneth Goodpaster, Bryan Husted, Peter Koslowski, and Henk van Luijk. Based on the newly established affiliation between the Caux Round Table (CRT) and ISBEE, preliminary findings on emerging ethical challenges in international business were presented by Bryan Husted and Kenneth Goodpaster at the 2002 CRT Global Dialogue in Mexico and by Georges Enderle and Kenneth Goodpaster at the 2003 CRT Global Dialogue in Caux-sur-Montreux, Switzerland. Five topic areas were identified in the Interim Reports, which were further explored in consultation with the ISBEE Business Executive Advisory Board.

Agenda 2004 included five essays drafted by the scholars mentioned below and is available online from ISBEE:

245

Professor G. J. (Deon) Rossouw, Rand Afrikaans University, South Africa: "Corporate Governance and Trust in Business";

Professor Georges Enderle, University of Notre Dame, Indiana, USA: "Globalization and Global Ethics";

Dr. Marta Sañudo Velázquez, Universidad de Monterrey, Mexico: "Fairness in International Trade and WTO";

Emeritus Professor Henk van Luijk, Amsterdam, The Netherlands: "Place of Institutional Actors"; and

Professor Richard T. De George, University of Kansas, USA. "Ethical Implications of Contemporary Technologies".

The Aspen Institute

The Aspen Institute is perhaps best known for its Great Books seminars offered to business executives and leaders in government, education, and other societal sectors. Its principal locations in the United States are Aspen, Colorado and Wye, Maryland. Founded in 1949, it was guided intellectually by the talents of philosopher Mortimer Adler (1902–2001).

The mission of the Aspen Institute is "to foster enlightened leadership and open-minded dialogue." It does this through seminars, policy programs, research studies, conferences and leadership development initiatives.[57] The Aspen Institute and its international partners "seek to promote nonpartisan inquiry and an appreciation for timeless values."[58] Or in the words of Bennis and O'Toole:

> [W]hen executives are given excerpts from the classics of political economy and philosophy in seminars at the Aspen Institute, the intent is not to turn them into experts on Plato and Locke but to illuminate the profound recesses of leadership that scientifically oriented texts either overlook or oversimplify.[59]

The Aspen Institute brings to the search for a third academy a proven Socratic methodology for discussing leadership challenges and a resource base second to none in Mortimer Adler's 60 volume *Great Books of the Western World* (along with an extensive non-Western collection of literature).

The Center for Ethical Business Cultures

Of the four "intimations" of the third academy here under discussion, the Center for Ethical Business Cultures (CEBC) at the University of St. Thomas-Minnesota comes closest to achieving the ideal of our search. Its scale is not sufficiently large at the moment, but its *mission* is on the mark. CEBC is a non-profit organization whose mission is to "assist business leaders in creating ethical and profitable business cultures at the enterprise, community and global levels." It was founded by business executives in 1978 as the Minnesota Project on Corporate Responsibility, and is the oldest business-founded, business-led center focused on business ethics and corporate citizenship in the United States.

The philosophy of its founding members was clear: "The only reason for the existence of the free enterprise system is to serve society," said Kenneth Dayton of the Dayton Hudson Corporation. Judson Bemis (The Bemis Company) added that "the major problems of society cannot be solved without the direct participation and resources of business initiated and sponsored by active personal involvement of the Chief Executive Officer." Today, the Center's services enhance the creation and maintenance of ethical cultures.[60]

CEBC and the Third Academy

The CEBC is a unique bridge between the worlds of academia and the business community, linking research and theory with practice and application. What is striking about the way in which CEBC pursues its mission is the firm grasp that it maintains on (a) its origins as a business-led institution focused on the needs and responsibilities of business, (b) its support not only for the cultures of companies but also for *the culture of business itself* (as a profession), and (c) its communication with the academic community in support of preparing current and future business leaders. Four recent examples may help to illustrate this mission in action.

- *A forum for speaking out*: In 2003, several members of CEBC, led by David Koch, former CEO of Minneapolis-based Graco, Inc., decided that business leaders were being altogether too silent in the wake of corporate scandals like Enron, Andersen, WorldCom, Tyco, Adelphia, and others. Using CEBC as the convening vehicle, Koch held a number of extended dialogues among well-respected business leaders over a six-month period which resulted in a kind of "manifesto" to the public. (See the Appendix to this chapter for the full text.) This document – entitled "What We Believe" and signed by the participants – was published in full-page ads of the major metropolitan newspapers. It was a response of business

247

leaders (albeit a response local in scale) to *a crisis of confidence in their profession*. Additional forums have showcased leaders with "best practices" as well as "lessons learned" from convicted white collar felons, and created a safe learning opportunity for business leaders to grapple with emerging ethical challenges.

- *Tools for company self-awareness*: In an effort to support companies in the region that sought to assess and improve the ethical dimensions of their cultures, CEBC undertook several initiatives during 2003. First, partnering with Gantz Wiley Research, an international survey research consulting firm, it has developed the *CEBC Integrity Measurement Program*.™ The survey tools in this program "help organizations understand their ethical environments, promote principled organizational practices, and maintain their competitive advantages."[61] Second, CEBC licenses the Self-Assessment and Improvement Process (SAIP™) for use with companies in its geographical region.

  The CEBC partnership with Ganz Wiley has already begun to yield intriguing results by measuring the strength of ethical cultures and correlating that strength with variables like teamwork, employee satisfaction and retention, quality emphasis, and customer orientation. Differential perceptions of ethical culture are also emerging in comparisons between executives and non-managerial employees.

- *Bockelman book commissioned*: This is an example of supporting not only the cultures of companies but also "*the culture of business itself.*" In 1999 CEBC commissioned Minnesota author Wilfred "Bill" Bockelman to write *Culture of Corporate Citizenship: Minnesota's Business Legacy for the Global Future*. The 180-page book tells the story of Minnesota business leaders "whose commitment to community well-being was as firm as their commitment to profitability." As a professionally written history, the book documents the evolution of what I referred to above as *a culture of ethical expectations*.[62]

- *The next generation*: Finally, while we can say that CEBC's primary client is business as a profession, it has also aligned itself with the *next generation* of business professionals in its work with high schools, colleges, and graduate programs in business administration. In cooperation with Rotary International and with funding from court-awarded white-collar criminal penalties, CEBC offers numerous high school ethics education programs and several study-abroad opportunities for MBA students.

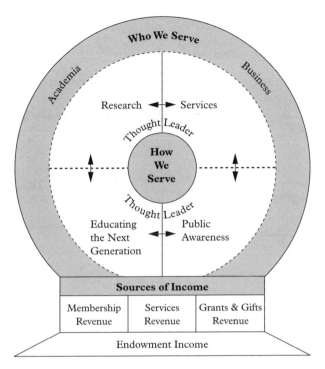

Figure 8.4 A depiction of the CEBC mission in action

The active mission of CEBC is depicted in Figure 8.4, suggesting a structure that may generalize to what I am here calling the third academy.

This section has been devoted to a "search" for the third academy. And while such an academy may not exist formally yet, its shape is at least discernable using the "intimations" of four important organizations: The Caux Round Table (CRT), The International Society for Business, Economics, and Ethics (ISBEE), The Aspen Institute (AI), and The Center for Ethical Business Cultures (CEBC). Each contributes several brush-strokes to the portrait of the third academy that I have begun to paint. Each offers a glimpse at an institutionalization of corporate conscience that takes us beyond the first academy of conventional business schools and the second academy of corporate compliance programs and leadership seminars. The moral agenda of the corporation requires scrutiny and steward-ship from the generation of leaders most experienced with its

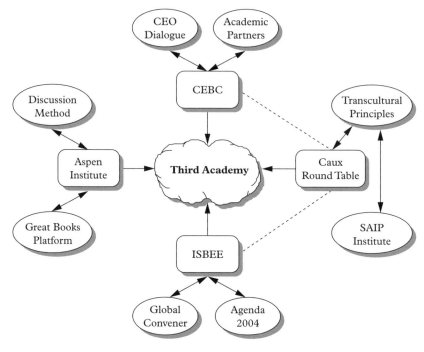

Figure 8.5   A portrait in draft: Intimations of a third academy

possibilities and challenges. Figure 8.5 summarizes the draft of the portrait which I now leave to the reader to pursue beyond these pages.

What a Third Academy could be

Borrowing key traits from the four organizations described above, we can see the contours of a third academy as (a) an association of distinguished corporate leaders, (b) in league with *academe* in various creative ways, (c) committed to a set of transcultural ethical principles for business, (d) with a measurement system, and (e) a Socratic method for global dialogue leading to (f) agendas and thoughtful recommendations to those who would embrace the *profession* of business administration. A third academy, so conceived, is an essential ingredient for realizing the aspiration of Robert Bellah:

Are business executives professionals? Do they have an ethical obligation beyond their own and their company's profit?.... I would like to answer rather vigorously, yes they are and they do. Such a position is grounded in the old Protestant notion, one shared in various degrees with all the Biblical religions, that the economy, like everything else on earth, belongs ultimately to God and that the businessperson is God's steward, with the obligation to make the economy serve everyone. That idea may seem quaint but, like the idea of the calling to which it is related, we need to revive it under present conditions.[63]

Summary and Conclusion

Integrating ethics into the business curriculum (especially using the case method) offers as clear an answer as possible to the question that spurred our inquiry at the beginning of this chapter: "Can you tell me, Socrates, whether virtue is acquired by teaching or by practice; or if neither by teaching nor practice, then whether it comes to man by nature or in what other way?" The answer seems to be this: "Virtue *is* acquired by teaching *and* by practice, assuming an honest desire by all parties to seek moral insight. *But there are three academies, not one, in which the teaching goes on.*"

A response to the occupational hazard of *teleopathy* calls for institutionalizing ethical awareness in the *classroom* (the first academy), the *corporation* (the second academy), and the *community* (the third academy) with parallel efforts. These support systems must introduce, establish or integrate, and see to the continuity of their commitments.

Emory University president James T. Laney observed two decades ago in an essay entitled "The Education of the Heart" (referring to the twentieth century):

> In many academic disciplines there has been a retreat from the attempt to relate values and wisdom to what is being taught. Not long ago, Bernard Williams, the noted British philosopher, observed that philosophers have been trying all this century to get rid of the dreadful idea that philosophy ought to be edifying. Philosophers are not the only ones to appreciate the force of that statement.... How can society survive if education does not attend to those qualities which it requires for its very perpetuation?[64]

251

Appendix: What We Believe: Minnesota Business Leaders Speak Out[65]

We in Minnesota are blessed to work and live in an exceptional community. Whether in the arts, education, the environment, civic engagement, business enterprise or progressive government, Minnesota has been a national leader in a country that leads the world.

Business has played an important role in the growth of what Minnesota has become. Through job creation, tax payments, volunteerism, philanthropy and executive involvement, business has helped to build the community.

However, during the past year, our American business system has taken a sharp blow to its integrity caused by the unethical actions of some including Enron, Tyco and WorldCom. This has caused an enormous breakdown in trust between the American public and American business.

While there have been swift legislative and regulatory responses, business voices have not risen to the same level. In the absence of a business voice, the public tars all businesses with the same brush.

We are business leaders in Minnesota, and we feel it important to speak up.

We believe that those who govern and lead corporations have not only a fiduciary responsibility, but also a responsibility to ensure that behavior is rooted in integrity and consistent with the company's purpose and values.

Those who invest in corporations deserve and should expect the following:

- *An accurate disclosure of information* from which to base investment decisions.
- *An alignment of the interests* of those who manage the company and those who invest in the company.
- *A fair return,* consistent with the risks, on their investments.

We believe that while businesses must meet the needs of their investors, they exist to serve multiple stakeholders including customers, employees, suppliers and the community while balancing short-term gain and long-term value creation.

Concerned about the breakdown in trust between business and its constituents, four current or former chief executive officers – David

Koch, Chuck Denny, Dick McFarland, and Dale Olseth – convened a group of 30 business executives to address issues of corporate responsibility, corporate governance, executive compensation, and balancing short-term gain and long-term value creation.

The Center for Ethical Business Cultures (CEBC), which is affiliated with the business schools at the University of St. Thomas and the University of Minnesota, facilitated, recorded and reported the group's deliberations. Here are the key themes.

Corporate governance

The headlines identify many ethical and legal breakdowns in corporate America. And the breakdowns can ultimately be traced to failures in corporate governance and integrity. Good corporate governance starts with the board of directors.

To restore trust, board members must be independent and not influenced by other relationships with the company that might affect their ability to impartially represent the shareholders' interests. Where conflicts of interest exist, they should be fully disclosed.

CEO selection is critical as the CEO is a key to building a culture of integrity in the organization and setting the tone of ethical behavior at the top.

Boards should utilize a non-executive board chair, or a lead director when the same person serves as CEO and chairman of the board.

Boards should install feedback mechanisms to ensure the integrity of the organization as well as its progress toward meeting strategic, operating, and financial goals.

Boards will need to invest in upgrading their skills and expertise to meet the heightened legal and regulatory standards.

Corporate responsibility

The 1990s saw a decade of too many companies focusing on the shareholder at the expense of other key stakeholders of business.

Corporate responsibility involves a company's responsible behavior toward all of its key stakeholders – investors, customers, employees, suppliers, and its communities. A responsible business always considers its impact on its varied stakeholders, seeking to achieve maximum balance.

It is important to note, that in addition to being the right thing to do, such behavior actually creates long-term value for the business.

Studies have shown that over the long term, companies that act responsibly toward their stakeholders improve their revenue, profits, share prices and workforces substantially faster than companies that don't.

Short-term vs. long-term

The 1990s also saw a dramatic shift from long-term shareholder value creation to short-term stock price appreciation as a means of generating wealth.

The individual investor's voice has become increasingly represented by institutions – pension plans, 401(k) plans and mutual funds – which intensify the pressure on corporations for a higher return over shorter periods.

It is time for the pendulum to swing back to achieve a better balance between the short and long term. We have a unique opportunity for policymakers, regulators, legislators, and business leaders to coalesce around a new paradigm.

Boards of directors must exercise leadership in abandoning short-term strategies that harm long-term value creation and leave it up to investors to choose whether that company meets their investment priorities and time frames. In contrast, some companies will elect to move from being publicly traded to privately owned.

Executive compensation

Executive compensation has become the subject of much public scrutiny. Two themes emerge: excessive amounts of executive compensation and pay for mediocre performance.

Executive compensation has grown significantly faster than compensation for the average worker, and some CEOs were compensated generously while their companies failed.

Clearly, CEOs face substantial risks in guiding their companies, and this should be reflected in the financial rewards. However, boards should play a lead role in readjusting the levels of compensation, which will lead to a better distribution between the lowest-paid worker and the CEO.

Pay should be based on performance, not overall stock market movement, with an emphasis on the long term. Stock options are important and should be linked and paid out based on long-term company performance. The same exercise rules should apply to executives, management and employees.

The bonds of trust and integrity between a business and its stakeholders are crucial. While clearly the actions of a few have jeopardized these bonds for many, there is hope for restoration. Boards of directors and CEOs will play an ever-increasing pivotal role in restoring this bond.

What we need now is courageous leadership.

Signers

Anthony Andersen, Retired Chairman & CEO, H. B. Fuller

Larry Benveniste, Dean, University of Minnesota, Carlson School of Management

Carl Bergquist, Chairman, President & CEO, The Berquist Company

Norman Bowie, Andersen Chair in Corporate Responsibility, University of Minnesota, Carlson School of Management

Mary Brainerd, President and CEO, HealthPartners, Inc.

Robert H. Carlson, Co-CEO, Reell

Thomas Colwell, CEO, Colwell Industries, Inc.

Judith Corson, Co-Founder and Former President, Custom Research

Gary Costley, President and CEO, International Multifoods

Jo Marie Dancik, Area Managing Partner, Ernst & Young LLP

Chuck Denny, Former Chairman & CEO, Telecommunications

Jon Eisele, Managing Partner, DeLoittle & Touche

Sidney Emery Jr., Chairman and CEO, MTS Systems

Ken Goodpaster, Koch Endowed Chair in Business Ethics, University of St. Thomas

Tom Holloran, Professor Emeritus, University of St. Thomas

Russell Huffer, President, Chairman and CEO, Apogee Enterprises, Inc.

Ron James, President and CEO, Center for Ethical Business Cultures

S.A. Johnson, Chairman, Hidden Creek Industries

Jay Kiedrowski, Executive Vice President, Institutional Investments, Wells Fargo Bank

David Koch, Chairman Emeritus, Graco, Inc.

Richard McFarland, Retired Chairman, RBC Dain Rauscher, Inc.

Richard (Pinky) McNamara, Owner and President, Activar Inc.

Kendrick Melrose, Chairman and CEO, The Toro Company

William Monahan, Chairman and CEO, ImationCorp.

Timothy Morin, Former President and CEO, Wizmo, Inc.

Jeffrey Noddle, Chairman and CEO, SUPERVALU INC.

Dale Olseth, Chairman & CEO, SurModics, Inc.

Paul Pesek, Chairman, Locus Medical Technology

Peter Pierce, Chairman, Lyle Signs, Inc.

Christopher Puto, Dean, University of St. Thomas, College of Business

James Renier, Former Chairman and CEO, Honeywell

James Secord, Former President and CEO, Lakewood Publications

John Solberg, President and CEO, Opus Northwest, LLC

Gerald Stenson, Executive Vice President, Wells Fargo Bank, N. A.

William Sweasy, Chairman, Red Wing Shoe Company

Tom Triplett, Attorney and Counselor

Kathryn Tunheim, President and General Manager, GCI Tunheim

Win Wallin, Chairman Emeritus, Medtronic, Inc.

Epilogue

We desperately need business leaders who have both convictions and the courage of those convictions.

Peter G. Peterson
(Senior Chairman/Cofounder of the Blackstone Group,
Newsweek, June 13, 2005)

According to the *Oxford English Dictionary*, "conscience" was originally understood as a common quality in which individuals shared: "a man or a people had more or less conscience," as persons or groups had more or less science, knowledge, intelligence, prudence, etc. The word came gradually to be used as an individual faculty or attribute, so that "*my conscience*" and "*your conscience*" were understood no longer as "our respective shares or amounts of the common quality *conscience*," but as "two distinct individual consciences, mine and yours."

In other words, "conscience" was originally a *cultural* attribute and only later came to be interpreted as a *personal* attribute, its most frequent meaning today. In many ways, this book has been an attempt to *return* the idea of conscience to its original meaning by offering a pathway from the personal mindsets of leaders to the corporate mindsets of their organizations.

Individual Conscience and Corporate Conscience

The debate over whether morality should be attributed to individuals or to organizations can be resolved once and for all if we come to appreciate that the two attributions are not mutually exclusive. I have argued that corporate leaders (individuals) have a *moral agenda*. Avoiding *teleopathy*, they are called to be architects of the consciences of their organizations. They must orient, institutionalize, and sustain a corporate culture (what we called Type 3 thinking) that takes seriously interests, rights, duties, and virtues in the business environment. And since "nobody gives what he/she doesn't have," the calling of corporate leaders is first and foremost a calling to personal awareness and personal integrity. Moral projection – from the conscience of the individual to the conscience of the corporation – is the natural corollary.

It is difficult to overstate the significance of this message for business leaders. For while it places enormous responsibilities on their shoulders, it also dignifies their calling. CEOs and other corporate executives are – like it or not – in the ethics business. Their role in society is anchored in moral values just like the roles of physicians, attorneys, educators, and other professionals.[1] Their compensation, in the end, is not merely a secular wage for adding economic value. True leaders add ethical value to "value-added."

Conscience: Both Authentic and Enlightened

Whether personal or corporate, conscience must eventually establish its credentials as both *authentic* and *enlightened*. Authenticity, as Bill George has made abundantly clear, is an essential ingredient in the character of effective leaders. But because even authentic consciences can be misguided, a second essential ingredient is enlightenment.[2] As I suggested in Chapter 3, enlightenment has to do with a disciplined application of the moral point of view in an administrative situation.

Enlightenment is about gaining access to what Joseph Ratzinger (now Pope Benedict XVI) called "an inner sense, *a capacity to recall*, so that the one whom it addresses, if he is not turned in on himself, hears its echo from within." This "capacity to recall" is what gives us hope of achieving something more than simply subjective opinion in the moral realm. The "recall" is, finally, an appeal to our shared human nature and our shared common good. It holds out the promise of discerning objectively wise (and avoiding unwise) courses of action. A *neglected* or *stifled* capacity to recall is what leads to "crimes of conviction" or, we might add in the wake of the corporate scandals, "crimes of arrogance."[3]

Remembering the Purpose of the Trip

The *capacity for recall* alluded to above is in the end what gives the corporate leader his or her true authority. And it resolves two paradoxes I mentioned earlier.[4] Call it a sense of mission, a vision, an understanding of the company's reason for being – this is what followers are really looking for. The power of position – over personnel, over budgets, over contracts – is secondary. Corporate leaders, like Bowen McCoy in the "Parable of the Sadhu," are called to *remember the purpose of the trip*: "Why were we so reluctant to try the lower path, the ambiguous trail? *Perhaps because we did not have a leader who could reveal the greater purpose of the trip to us.*"[5]

In a postmodern age in which moral relativism has become the unreflective order of the day, to speak of *truth* in connection with *ethics* may seem like overreaching. Before surrendering all confidence, however, we should remember that this is also an age in which terrorists flew airliners into the World Trade Center, killing thousands of innocent people. Our moral heartache signaled truth. And we should remember that this is an age in which corporate scandals ruined the lives and livelihoods of thousands of employees and shareholders. Again our moral heartache signaled truth.[6]

Overreaching is possible and humility is a valuable virtue in matters of ethics; but courage is a virtue just as valuable.[7] And it takes courage – the "courage of one's convictions" – to give voice to fundamental moral principles when ridicule or political correctness are invoked on the other side. Making moral judgments is part of the leadership territory.

There is, of course, room for disagreement among conscientious, reasonable persons – as there will be among conscientious, reasonable corporations. And the ethical discernment called for from persons and corporations leaves open possibilities of error, neglect, and rationalization. Yet the discussions of teleopathy and mindsets in

Chapters 1 and 2, as well as the reflections on Josiah Royce, Hannah Arendt, and Anthony DeMello in Chapter 3, all reinforce the importance of moral insight that reaches beyond personal sincerity toward truth.

So it comes to this. Whatever our politics may be, the proposition that there is "no capitalism without conscience" is a truth we would do well to acknowledge.[8] And if we acknowledge it, then the *formation and cultivation of conscience* becomes the most significant challenge of democratic capitalism. And the formation and cultivation of conscience is the function of the three academies discussed in Chapter 8.

Schools, corporations, and professional associations are, after families and churches, the principal shapers of moral values in our society. So if business schools, corporations, and professional associations abdicate their responsibilities for moral education, we should not be surprised to see new corporate scandals on a regular basis.[9]

Professional education at its best provides *perspective*, the kind of perspective that sees business in the context of humankind's search for meaning and happiness. Leaders with this type of education are more apt to appreciate "the greater purpose of the trip." They are more apt to be both authentic *and* enlightened.

T. S. Eliot once wrote about the nature of human community in a business civilization. A fragment from one of his poems written 75 years ago may offer a fitting conclusion for these reflections on conscience and corporate culture. My intention in this book has been to challenge both educators and business practitioners, seeming sometimes to be a stranger from the perspective of each audience. But sometimes the questions of strangers afford us perspective.

> When the Stranger says: "What is the meaning of this city?
> Do you huddle close together because you love each other?"
> What will you answer? "We all dwell together
> To make money from each other"? or "This is a community"?
> And the Stranger will depart and return to the desert.
> O my soul, be prepared for the coming of the Stranger,
> Be prepared for him who knows how to ask questions.[10]

Notes

Foreword

1 Thomas E. Holloran is a Senior Distinguished Fellow-School of Law and Professor Emeritus-College of Business at the University of St. Thomas, Minneapolis-St. Paul, Minnesota. He also is an honorary professor of Xi Be University, Xian, China, and has taught in the Soviet Union. He holds BS and JD degrees from the University of Minnesota.

He has been Chairman and CEO of Dain Rauscher (an investment banking firm and broker-dealer, formerly Inter-Regional Financial Group), President of Medtronic, Inc. (NYSE heart pacemaker manufacturer), and a practicing attorney. In addition to the Boards of Directors of Medtronic and Dain Rauscher, he has served on numerous other corporate boards.

He has held public office in Minnesota as the Mayor of Shorewood, the Chair of the Metropolitan Airports Commission and as Municipal Judge for the South Minnetonka communities. He serves or has served on numerous not-for-profit boards including the Archdiocese of St. Paul and Minneapolis, the Bush Foundation, the Center for Ethical Business Cultures, the Minneapolis Art Institute and the Walker Art Center.

Preface

1 These ideas were eventually published in Schön's *The Reflective Practitioner* (Basic Books, 1983).

2 See Michael Novak's book on the subject of vocation: *Business as a Calling: Work and the Examined Life* (Free Press, 1996). Also see Michael Naughton and Helen Alford's *Managing as if Faith Mattered* (Notre Dame Press, 2001).

3 I refer the reader here to my essay "Teaching and Learning Ethics by the Case Method," in Norman Bowie, ed., *The Blackwell Guide to Business Ethics* (Blackwell Publishers, 2002). It is reprinted as the Introduction to Goodpaster et al. *Business Ethics: Policies and Persons*, 4th edn. (McGraw-Hill, 2005).

4 Dostoevsky wrote that "a man cannot live without worshipping something." Glenn Tinder, reflecting on this point in his book *The Political Meaning of Christianity* (Louisiana State University Press, 1989, p. 51) remarks of professionals and institutions that "good customs and habits need a spiritual base; and if it is lacking, they will gradually – or perhaps suddenly, in some crisis – disappear. To what extent are we now living on moral savings accumulated over many centuries but no longer being replenished?" In the wake of the corporate scandals of the 1990s, culminating in the Enron and Arthur Andersen tragedies of 2001–2002, these words sound prophetic.

5 Recently, the Caux Principles have been supplemented with a *Self-Assessment and Improvement Process* (SAIP) for corporations, a process that can be compared with the Baldrige Process for Total Quality Management. See Goodpaster et al. "A Baldrige Process for Ethics?" *Science and Engineering Ethics*, 10(2), April 2004. I shall have more to say about the SAIP in Part II of this book.

6 James T. Laney, "The Education of the Heart," *Harvard Magazine*, September–October 1985, pp. 23–4.

7 In my article, "On Waking Up Spiritually," in Peter Vaill (ed.), *Beside Still Waters* (2007, forthcoming), I expand on this theme.

8 William J. Bennett, co-director of Empower America, remarked on the decline of decency in American culture in *Commentary* magazine, November 1995: "[W]e are reluctant to admit that much of what has gone wrong has not been done to us; we have done it to ourselves. It is self-delusion to think that the American people have been unwittingly and reluctantly drawn into a culture of permissiveness. . . . Rebuilding the national project depends [ultimately] on individual citizens living better and more decent lives. It does not require sainthood, moral perfection, or even moral excellence among citizens. It does require that we take seriously what too many Americans have come to neglect: our basic commitments as parents, spouses, neighbors, citizens, and people of faith. To accomplish these things, it would be no small help, as Aleksandr Solzhenitsyn and others have urged us, to remember God." (*The Wall Street Journal*, November 22, 1995, p. A10, *Notable & Quotable.*)

9 *The Heart Aroused: Poetry and the Preservation of the Soul in Corporate America*, (Doubleday 1994, p. 61).

Introduction

1 Columbia Accident Investigation Board, *Final Report*, vol. 1, p. 97, online at: http://caib.nasa.gov/news/report/pdf/vol1/full/caib_report_volume1.pdf [accessed October 10, 2005].

2 The tri-partite distinction here (private, public, and moral-cultural sectors) comes from Michael Novak, *The Spirit of Democratic Capitalism* (Madison Books, 1991).

3 Jeffrey E. Garten, *The Politics of Fortune: A New Agenda for Business Leaders* (Harvard Business School Press, 2002, p. 5).

4 Americans seem to have it in their blood to choose *contest* over *content* as they search for institutional wisdom. We prefer "checks and balances" to leadership that is unchecked and so potentially unbalanced. Perhaps the historical explanation lies in the rejection of monarchy and tyranny as perceived by our founders, and the bloodshed in the Revolutionary War that followed. In any case, built into our political and economic psyche there is deep caution about the public exercise of conscience, even as we have sought to protect it in the private arena. A difficult question is: Can conscience survive in a culture that first privatizes it and then expands the influence of the public sector? "First we shape our institutions," Winston Churchill is supposed to have said, "and then they shape us."

5 While the principal focus in this book is conscience in the arena of corporate or private sector cultures, readers can and should consider direct parallels with leadership challenges in the public and nonprofit sectors as well.

6 As we shall see, this theme is well-addressed by Bill George in his recent book *Authentic Leadership* (Jossey-Bass, 2003).

Part I   Introduction

1 J. L. Stocks, "Is There a Moral End?," *Proceedings of the Aristotelian Society*, Supp. Vol. VIII, 1930. Reprinted in D. Z. Phillips (ed.), *Morality and Purpose* (Routledge & Kegan Paul, 1969, p. 73).

2 *Random House Webster's Unabridged Dictionary*: "a statement or proposition that seems self-contradictory or absurd but in reality expresses a possible truth."

3 Lynn Sharp Paine, *Value Shift* (McGraw-Hill, 2003, p. 154).

4 *New York Times* (August 27, 2003).

Chapter 1

1 Since I begin with four illustrations that represent the tragic side of decision-making (two from 1986 and two from 2003), I should say at

263

the outset that such cases are not being presented as the *norm* in business. Opening this chapter on the dark side is simply a way of sketching the boundaries of the problem. The brighter side will make its appearance in due course! It bears mentioning, however, that in a July 2003 Zogby Poll of College Seniors, 56% agreed and 41% disagreed with the proposition that "The only real difference between executives at Enron and those at most other big companies, is that those at Enron got caught."

2 James B. Stewart and Daniel Hertzberg, "Unhappy Ending: The Wall Street Career of Martin Siegel Was a Dream Gone Wrong," *The Wall Street Journal*, February 17, 1987.

3 Ibid. The authors add: "More than anyone else so far implicated in the scandal, Mr. Siegel personified the American Dream."

4 Ibid.

5 Trudy E. Bell and Karl Esch, "The Fatal Flaw in Flight 51-L," *IEEE Spectrum*, February 1987, p. 48.

6 Ibid.

7 David Barboza, "From Enron Fast Track to Total Derailment," *New York Times*, October 3, 2002.

8 Ibid.

9 "As CEO, Jeff Skilling had set a goal of ridding Enron's balance sheet of poorly-performing or volatile assets. Did he decide at some point (well before his Congressional testimony) that it would be better not to know exactly how Mr. Fastow, his protege, was achieving his desired goal?" (Holman W. Jenkins Jr., "Business World: How Could They Have Done It?" *The Wall Street Journal*, August 28, 2002, p. A15.)

10 David Barboza, op. cit. Barboza goes on: "Those who know Andrew S. Fastow, the man at the center of the Enron scandal, say they often got the sense that he had something to prove."

11 The CAIB reported that "the physical cause of the loss of Columbia and its crew was a breach in the thermal protection system on the leading edge of the left wing. The breach was initiated by a piece of insulating foam that separated from the left bipod ramp of the external tank and struck the wing in the vicinity of the lower half of reinforced carbon-carbon Panel 8 at 81.9 seconds after launch. During re-entry, this breach in the thermal protection system allowed superheated air to penetrate the leading-edge insulation and progressively melt the aluminum structure of the left wing, resulting in a weakening of the structure until increasing aerodynamic forces caused loss of control, failure of the wing, and breakup of the orbiter." (*New York Times*, August 27, 2003.)

12 "Excerpts From Report of the Columbia Accident Investigation Board," *New York Times*, August 27, 2003.

13 David E. Sanger, "Inertia and Indecision at NASA," *New York Times*, August 27, 2003.

14 Ibid.

15 Matthew L. Wald with John Schwartz, "NASA Chief Promises a Shift in Attitude," *New York Times*, August 28, 2003.

16 See "moral projection, principle of," in P. Werhane and R. E. Freeman (eds.), *Blackwell Encyclopedic Dictionary of Business Ethics* (Blackwell, 1997, p. 432).

17 Full disclosure: I had the privilege/responsibility to be one of the judges that chose this essay as the winner, having been asked to do so by my Harvard faculty colleague (and then-Executive-Editor of *Harvard Business Review*) Kenneth Andrews.

18 Bowen McCoy, "The Parable of the Sadhu," *Harvard Business Review*, 1983, p. 106, (emphasis added). The article was re-published as a *Harvard Business Review Classic* in June–July 1997.

19 McCoy, 1983, p. 106.

20 "Enron chose Mr. Fastow as its chief financial officer in 1998, but only after considering several outside candidates. Former colleagues said he thought the process suggested a lack of confidence in him. 'I remember seeing him in his office that day,' said one former finance executive. 'He was just staring at his desk, *fixated*.' " (emphasis added). (Barboza, op. cit.)

21 The CAIB Report Synopsis of "Why the Accident Occurred" refers specifically to "the intense pressure the program was under to stay on schedule, driven largely by the self-imposed requirement to complete the International Space Station."

22 Saul Gellerman, "How 'Good' Managers Make Bad Ethical Choices," *Harvard Business Review*, 1987, p. 85. Gellerman is a former dean of the University of Dallas Graduate School of Management.

23 "A widely-noted contribution to the field was 'Ethical leadership and the psychology of decision making,' which appeared in the January 1996 edition of *Sloan Management Review*, by Harvard's Max Bazerman and Northwestern's David Messick." (Holman W. Jenkins Jr., "Business World: How Could They Have Done It?" *The Wall Street Journal*, August 28, 2002, p. A15).

24 Chapter 6 of the CAIB Report observes further that "Engineers who attended a [January 24, 2003] briefing indicated a belief that management focused on the answer – that analysis proved there was no safety-of-flight issue – rather than concerns about the large uncertainties that may have undermined the analysis that provided that answer."

25 Michael Maccoby, "The Corporate Climber Has to Find His Heart," *Fortune*, December 1976, p. 101.

26 Sylvia Ann Hewlett, in her book *When the Bough Breaks* (Basic Books, 1991), seems to be making a point about parenting not far from

Maccoby's point about the gamesman: "It seems that the aptitudes, skills, and talents people hone to be successful professionals may well backfire when they assume the role of parent. As *Fortune* magazine warned in a January 1990 issue, 'don't think that your brains, money or success will pave the way to parenting glory . . . the intensity and single-mindedness that make for corporate achievement are often the opposite of the qualities needed to be an effective parent'" (p. 86).

27 Maccoby's more recent thoughts on this subject can be read in his article "Narcissistic Leaders: The Incredible Pros, the Inevitable Cons," *Harvard Business Review*, January 2000.

28 David Whyte, *The Heart Aroused: Poetry and the Preservation of the Soul in Corporate America*, (Doubleday, 1994, p. 298). Whyte also says that "We can have fire in our approach only if our heart is in the work, and it is hard to put our heart in the work when most of what we feel is stress." (Ibid., p. 224).

29 John Ladd, "Morality and the Ideal of Rationality in Formal Organizations," *The Monist*, 1970, p. 507.

30 Ibid.

31 Barboza, op. cit.

32 Ibid.

33 *Columbia Accident Investigation Board Report*, August 26, 2003, (emphasis added).

34 "[T]here was rising pressure to play down risk and to place success – measured in terms of things like on-time launching of components for the space station – over safety." (John Schwartz and Matthew L. Wald, "Report on Loss of Shuttle Focuses on NASA Blunders," *New York Times*, August 27, 2003.)

35 Siegel and Fastow both seem to reflect the traits that Ron Daniel, former Managing Director of McKinsey & Co. seems to have thought were to be sought after: "The real competition out there isn't for clients, it's for people. . . . And we look to hire people who are first, very smart; second, insecure and thus driven by their insecurity; and third, competitive. Put together 3,000 of these egocentric, task-oriented, achievement-oriented people, and it produces an atmosphere of something less than humility. Yes, it's elitist. But don't you think there has to be room somewhere in this politically correct world for something like this?" (*Fortune Magazine*, November 1, 1993, p. 72.)

36 Trudy E. Bell and Karl Esch, op. cit., p. 48.

37 Recall in this connection the comments quoted earlier from one of the *Challenger* panel members: "It's the same damn thing," said Gen. Donald Kutyna of the Air Force, retired, a gadfly on the *Challenger* panel along with the physicist Richard Feynman. "They didn't learn a thing. We had nine O-rings fail, and they flew. These guys had seven

pieces of foam hit, and it still flew." (David E. Sanger, "Inertia and Indecision at NASA," *New York Times*, August 27, 2003.)

38 "Excerpts from Report of the Columbia Accident," *New York Times*, August 27, 2003.

39 As quoted in Bell and Esch, op. cit., p. 47.

40 *Blackwell Encyclopedic Dictionary of Business Ethics* (Blackwell, 1997, p. 627) and *Encyclopedia of Business Ethics and Society* (Sage, 2007).

41 "Teleo" (τελεο) in Greek meaning "goal, target, purpose" and "pathos" (παθος) meaning "disease, sickness." (Goodpaster, K. "Ethical Imperatives and Corporate Leadership," in K. R. Andrews (ed.), *Ethics in Practice* (Harvard Business School Press, 1991).) *Teleopathy* is now part of the management lexicon.

42 See David Whyte, op. cit., pp. 224–5, where he writes that "The very act of slowing into our own more natural rhythms may seem like a heart-stopping prospect, but there are some elegant lessons in the very reasons a heart may stop or start."

43 Jon Krakauer, *Into Thin Air: A Personal Account of the Mt. Everest Disaster* (Anchor-Doubleday, 1997, p. 233).

Chapter 2

1 As quoted in Judith Burns, "Is Sarbanes-Oxley Working?" Dow Jones Newswires, June 21, 2004. Cooper was replying to the question: "Is Sarbanes-Oxley enough?" Emphasis added.

2 *Random House Webster's Unabridged Dictionary.*

3 And eventually we will attribute "conscience" to both. See K. E. Goodpaster and J. B. Matthews, "Can a Corporation Have a Conscience?," *Harvard Business Review*, January–February 1982. Reprinted in *Harvard Business Review on Corporate Responsibility* (Harvard Business School Press, 2003, pp. 131–55).

4 Phillip Selznick, *Leadership in Administration: A Sociological Interpretation* (Harper & Row, 1957, pp. 38–9). Selznick goes on to link these attributes of character with the ways in which organizations become what he calls "institutions":

  1 The technical, rational, impersonal, task-oriented formal system (the "organization") is conditioned by the responsive interaction of persons and groups.

  2 In the course of time, this responsive interaction is patterned. A social structure is created. This patterning is *historical*, in that it reflects the specific experiences of the particular organization; it is *functional* in that it aids the organization to adapt itself to its internal

and external social environment; and it is *dynamic*, in that it generates new and active forces, especially internal interest groups made up of men committed to particular jobs or policies.

3 Organizations become institutions as they are *infused with value*, that is, prized not as tools alone but as sources of direct personal gratification and vehicles of group integrity. This infusion produces a distinct identity for the organization. Where institutionalization is well advanced, distinctive outlooks, habits, and other commitments are unified, coloring all aspects of organizational life and lending it a *social integration* that goes well beyond formal coordination and command (Ibid., pp. 39–40).

5 See T. W. Dunfee and D. C. Robertson, "Work-Related Ethical Attitudes," *Business and Professional Ethics Journal*, 3(2) (Winter 1984), pp. 25–40.

6 John Z. DeLorean and J. Patrick Wright, *On a Clear Day You Can See General Motors* (Smithmark Publications, 1979).

7 An amusing television commercial theme at the time of this writing refers to the land of "Perfect" and the value of Walgreen's Pharmacies if one does not happen to live in that land!

8 John Rawls, *A Theory of Justice* (Harvard University Press, 1971), p. 8: "I consider primarily what I call strict compliance as opposed to partial compliance theory (§§ 25, 39). The latter studies the principles that govern how we are to deal with injustice. It comprises such topics as the theory of punishment, the doctrine of just war, and the justification of the various ways of opposing unjust regimes, ranging from civil disobedience and conscientious objection to militant resistance and revolution. Also included here are questions of compensatory justice and of weighing one form of institutional injustice against another."

9 Ibid., p. 8.

10 Morton D. Davis, *Game Theory: A Nontechnical Introduction* (Basic Books, 1983, p. xvi).

11 William L. Weiss, CEO of Ameritech Corporation, remarked in a speech at the Harvard Business School on October 8, 1986 that "a mere manager tends to see the business as a system unto itself; but a leader sees it also as part of a larger world, a player in a larger game, where many constituencies – and especially customers – write the rules and referee the action."

12 See Aristotle's *Nichomachean Ethics*, book VI, ch. 7: "The wise man must not only know what follows from the first principles, but must also possess truth about the first principles. Therefore wisdom must be intuitive reason combined with scientific knowledge..." And further: "Nor is practical wisdom concerned with universals only – it must also recognize the particulars; for it is practical, and practice is

concerned with particulars. This is why some who do not know, and especially those who have experience, are more practical than others who know . . ."

13   Adam Smith, *The Wealth of Nations*, 1776, book 1, ch. 2, online at: http://www.adamsmith.org/smith/won-b1-c2.htm [accessed October 10, 2005].

14   "Profit and the Public Good," *The Economist*, January 22, 2005. Emphasis added. In the next chapter, we shall see that what Josiah Royce calls the "moral insight" – which is the basis for conscience and our sense of humanity – is unreliable, *intermittent* in relation to what he calls "the illusion of selfishness." In the Judeo-Christian tradition, this corresponds to humankind's "fallen" nature. That Adam Smith should want to structure the economic system to make it less dependent on human virtue is not, therefore, surprising. But whether it is *possible* to avoid what T. S. Eliot called "systems so perfect that nobody needs to be good" is a separate question to which we shall return.

15   "Profit and the Public Good," *The Economist*, January 22, 2005.

16   Rawls, op. cit., p. 8.

17   In the next chapter, we will examine two principles that give structure to the "values" side of *mindsets* depicted in Figure 2.1. This will help clarify their relevance to the idea of *conscience* in business ethics.

18   M. Scott Peck, *The Road Less Traveled* (Simon & Schuster, 1978). Special 25th Anniversary Edition, 2002.

19   In the next chapter, we shall examine one philosopher's account of this process as having a "second thought." Others have called the antidote to teleopathy as a kind of "second nature" overlaying our primitive or "first nature."

20   Lynn Sharp Paine, *Value Shift* (McGraw-Hill, 2003, p. 98).

21   Paul Lawrence and Davis Dyer, *Renewing American Industry* (Free Press, 1984, pp. 262–3. They continue: "Similarly, organizations, as such, do not expend effort to achieve efficiencies. People do. But when involved organization members strive in coordination with the efforts of others, we can fairly say that the organization is efficient as a production system. Treating organizations as production systems is probably the most venerable way of looking at them." Also relevant in connection with the idea of a "learning organization" is the work of Peter M. Senge, *The Fifth Discipline* (Doubleday, 1990).

22   Lynn Sharp Paine, op. cit., p. 145.

23   Bowen McCoy, "The Parable of the Sadhu," *Harvard Business Review* (June–July 1997, Classic Reprint). Emphasis added.

24   From William Harwood's CBS News program "Space Place" (aired July 22, 2003).

25   See K. E. Goodpaster, "Business Ethics and Stakeholder Analysis," *Business Ethics Quarterly*, January 2001, pp. 52–71. Also see K. E.

Goodpaster and T. E. Holloran, "In Defense of a Paradox," *Business Ethics Quarterly*, April 1994. Most recently: "Stakeholder Thinking: Beyond Paradox to Practicality," co-authored with Research Assistant T. D. Maines and Program Coordinator M. D. Rovang. Published in the Autumn 2002 edition of the *Journal of Corporate Citizenship* (pp. 93–111). Published independently in J. Andriof, S. Waddock, B. Husted, and S. S. Rahman (eds.), *Unfolding Stakeholder Thinking: Theory, Responsibility, and Engagement* (Greenleaf Publishing, 2002).

26 T. J. Peters and R. H. Waterman, *In Search of Excellence* (Harper & Row, 1982, p. 42).

27 Recall the title of John Ladd's classic article, "Morality and the Ideal of Rationality in Formal Organizations," discussed in Chapter 1.

28 See K. E. Goodpaster, "Business Ethics, Ideology, and the Naturalistic Fallacy," *Journal of Business Ethics*, 4(4), August 1985, pp. 227–32.

29 Paul Lawrence and Davis Dyer, *Renewing American Industry* (Free Press, 1984, p. 295).

30 Kenneth Andrews, *The Concept of Corporate Strategy* (Dow Jones–Irwin, 1971, p. 18).

31 Stephen R. Covey, *The Seven Habits of Highly Successful People* (Simon & Schuster, 1989); Jim Collins, *Good to Great* (HarperCollins, 2001); Peter Drucker, *The Essential Drucker* (HarperCollins, 2001); David M. Messick and Max H. Bazerman, "Ethical Leadership and the Psychology of Decision Making" *Sloan Management Review*, X, Winter 1996, pp. 9–22.

32 Charles Handy, "What's a Business For?," *Harvard Business Review*, December 2002.

33 *The Economist*, January 22, 2005.

34 One thinks of the intensity of war as a human undertaking, and our conviction even in this context to impose limits (the Geneva Convention).

Chapter 3

1 *The Blackwell Encyclopedic Dictionary of Business Ethics* (Blackwell Publishers, 1997, p. 133).

2 Hannah Arendt, "Thinking," *The New Yorker*, November 21, 1977, pp. 65–140; November 28, 1977, pp. 114–63; December 5, 1977, pp. 135–216.

3 Ibid. Arendt also remarked that: "When everybody is swept away unthinkingly by what everybody else does and believes in, those who think are drawn out of hiding because their refusal to join in is conspicuous and thereby becomes a kind of action. . . . and has a liberating effect on the faculty of judgment" (December 5, 1997, p. 196).

4 Anthony DeMello, S.J., *Awareness*, (Doubleday, 1990, p. 56).

5 Hannah Arendt, "Thinking," *The New Yorker*, December 5, 1977, p. 195. Indeed, DeMello's view is reminiscent of the views of the intuitionists in ethical theory at the beginning of the twentieth century. *Awareness* is an active, engaged, perspective on decision-making that resists "definition" – replacement by surrogates that claim to "automate" our moral judgment.

6 Josiah Royce, *The Religious Aspect of Philosophy* (Originally published in 1865; reprinted in 1965 by permission of Harper & Row, by Peter Smith, Gloucester, MA., pp. 155–6), emphasis added.

7 Will Durant, *The Story of Philosophy* (Simon and Schuster, 1926).

8 Immanuel Kant, *Fundamental Principles of the Metaphysics of Morals* (1785).

9 Alexis DeTocqueville, *Democracy in America* (1840). Further: "Nothing, in my opinion, is more deserving of our attention than the intellectual and moral associations of America. . . . Amongst the laws which rule human societies, there is one which seems to be more precise and clear than all others. If men are to remain civilized, or to become so, the art of associating together must grow and improve in the same ratio in which the equality of conditions is increased."

10 Philosopher Alan Gewirth describes morality as attending to transactions between *agents* and *recipients* "where what is affected is the recipient's freedom and well-being, and hence his capacity for action. . . . Such modes of affecting in transactions can be most readily recognized in their negative forms: when one person coerces another, hence preventing him from participating purposively or with well-being in the transaction." Gewirth, *Reason and Morality* (University of Chicago Press, 1978, p. 129).

11 The first approach is sometimes called *deontological* and is associated with the writings of Immanuel Kant. It tends to move from self to others with special attention to "partiality," aiming at the rational consent of one's fellow human beings. The second approach is sometimes called *teleological* (or *consequentialist*) and is associated with the writings of John Stuart Mill. It tends to move from self to others with special attention to "impartiality," to the impact of actions on the interests of one's fellow human beings.

12 Stephen Carter, in his book *God's Name in Vain: The Wrongs and Rights of Religion in Politics* (Basic Books, 2000) writes: "Preserving the ability of the faithful to put God first is precisely the purpose for which freedom of religion must exist," and "Politics needs morality, which means that politics needs religion." (p. 5). He goes on: "It is in the nature of religion to resist. It is in the nature of the state to battle against that resistance. A just state will therefore allow a broad range of religious freedom to ensure that its own hands are tied." (p. 176).

13 Jean Jacques Rousseau, *The Social Contract or Principles of Political Right* (1762), Chapter 6: "The Social Compact." Emphasis added.

14 Thomas Nagel, *The View from Nowhere* (Oxford University Press, 1986). Nagel adds: "The paradox is that this partial, perspectival respect for the interests of others should not give way to an agent-neutral respect free of perspective."

15 Thomas Nagel, *What Does It All Mean?* (Oxford university Press, 1987). Emphasis added.

16 Huntington, "The Clash of Civilizations?" *Foreign Affairs* (1993).

17 Indeed, this breakdown, far from being a sign of moral weakness, may actually be a sign of moral virtue. Paradox or not, our "failure" in extreme real world cases to identify or sympathize with certain parties may testify to our humanity.

18 Plato's writings emphasize the importance of "recollection" in acquiring knowledge, and in the present context, recollection is the only antidote to a kind of "moral forgetting."

19 Bowen McCoy, "The Parable of the Sadhu" (op. cit., p. 106).

20 Bowen McCoy, in his "Parable of the Sadhu," speaks of the role of the leader as reminding his people of "the purpose of the trip." I have argued that teleopathy, with its symptoms of fixation, rationalization, and detachment, actually *fosters* this forgetting.

21 Current efforts to identify, espouse, and implement a transcultural set of ethical values in international business hold promise largely because participating corporate leaders believe that non-arbitrary appeals beyond cultural norms are meaningful. I have in mind here the *Caux Principles*, developed in 1994 at the Caux Roundtable in Switzerland by business leaders from Asia, Europe, and North America. More on this subject later.

22 It is important to note, having discussed the views of Royce, Arendt, and DeMello, that there is considerable consensus around the *developmental* nature of conscience in human life. We shall look at this in connection with Piaget's account of conscience in children. Suffice it to say that the combination of the *polarities* at the core and multiple stages of *development* suggests that moral disagreement is not only to be *expected*, it may even be the norm. It also suggests that moral *agreement* may be more likely when such variables are taken into account.

23 Philosopher Thomas Nagel refers often to the *persistent* tension in ethics between emotion and reason, subjective and objective, partial and impartial viewpoints on the world and our place in it. "The real issue," he writes, "is the relative priority, in regard to action, of two ways of looking at the world. On the one hand there is the position that one's decisions should be tested ultimately from an external point of view, to which one appears as just one person among others. . . . This point of view claims priority by virtue of greater comprehensiveness.

... On the other hand there is the position that since an agent lives his life from where he is, even if he manages to achieve an impersonal view of his situation, whatever insights result from this detachment need to be made part of a personal view before they can influence decision and action." That this duality of perspective may be part of the human condition need not drive us to a retreat from reason. It might just as plausibly invite us to a deeper appreciation of Pascal's dictum, "The heart has reasons the reason knows not of."

24 As an old Christian hymn puts it: "Deep within, I will plant my law, not in stone but in your heart." Jeremiah 31:33; Ezekiel 36:26.

25 See William Dembski, *Intelligent Design* (InterVarsity Press, 1999).

26 Encyclical Letter *Dominum et Vivificantem* (18 May 1986), 43: AAS 78 (1986), 859. Also see Second Vatican Ecumenical Council, Pastoral Constitution on the Church in the Modern World "Gaudium et Spes," 16, and the Declaration on Religious Freedom "Dignitas Humanae," 3.

27 *The Moral Philosophers* (Oxford University Press, 1983, p. 249). Emphasis added.

28 As we contemplate this matter, we might reconsider the remark of political scientist Glenn Tinder, who warns that at the end of the twentieth century: "Our position is precarious, for good customs and habits need a spiritual base; and if it is lacking, they will gradually – or perhaps suddenly, in some crisis – disappear." Glenn Tinder, *The Political Meaning of Christianity* (Wipf and Stock, 2000, p. 51).

29 See James Mitchell, *The Ethical Advantage: Why Ethical Leadership is Good Business* (Center for Ethical Business Cultures at the University of St. Thomas, 2003).

30 *Wall Street Journal*, July 9, 2003. Emphasis added.

31 Philip Selznick, *Leadership in Administration: A Sociological Interpretation* (Harper & Row, 1957, p. 141).

32 Piaget, *The Moral Judgment of the Child* (London: Routledge & Kegan Paul, 1932, p. 402).

33 The third stage was for Piaget the beginning of true cooperation, and was the main goal of the educator (leader): "Cooperation suppresses both egocentrism and moral realism, and thus achieves an interiorization of rules. A new morality follows upon that of pure duty. Heteronomy steps aside to make way for a consciousness of good, of which the autonomy results from the acceptance of the norms of reciprocity." (Ibid., p. 404) Echoes here of Royce's *moral insight*, Arendt's *thoughtfulness*, DeMello's *awareness* and the reciprocity of the Golden Rule.

34 See "Dow Corning Corporation: The Breast Implant Controversy," in K. E. Goodpaster and L. L. Nash, *Policies and Persons: A Casebook in Business Ethics* (3rd edn., McGraw-Hill, 1998).

35 Note: the word "rationality" has many meanings, only some of which are at home in the present context. Sometimes "rational" can be

associated with "impartial," and this is *not* its meaning here. Rather, "rational" is here meant to invoke a "strategic plan of action" in a competitive system – a more "partial" perspective. For more on this distinction between "rationality" and "respect" see K. E. Goodpaster and J. B. Matthews, "Can a Corporation Have a Conscience?" *Harvard Business Review*, Jan–Feb 1982, republished in *Harvard Business Review on Corporate Responsibility* (Harvard Business School Press, 2003).

36 Michael Porter, *Competitive Advantage* (The Free Press, 1998, p. 1).

37 Philosophers have identified a number of basic frameworks for integrating rationality and respect. Some, for example, emphasize interests and employ cost–benefit analysis, while others emphasize rights and relate them to a social contract. Still others make use of a mixture of basic duties and obligations. I will expand on these avenues of ethical analysis later, but for now it is sufficient to focus on their shared foundations.

38 Sidgwick, *The Methods of Ethics* (Hackett Publishing Company; 7th edn., June 1, 1981). Emphasis added. Sidgwick's principle of "Rational Benevolence" corresponds to what I am here calling "respect," and his "Maxim of Prudence" corresponds to what I am here calling "rationality."

39 See Robert Axelrod, *The Evolution of Cooperation*. (Basic Books, 1985). Also see Goodpaster and Matthews, op. cit.

40 Francis Fukuyama, *Trust: The Social Virtues and the Creation of Prosperity* (The Free Press, 1995, pp. 27–8).

41 In Chapter 1, I explained this approach using the "Moral Projection Principle."

42 Note that the contrast with "moral" here is not with "immoral" but rather with something like "nonmoral" or "premoral."

43 Mary Midgley, *Heart and Mind* (St. Martin's Press, 1981, pp. 72, 75).

44 Piaget, op. cit., p. 386.

45 Selznick, op. cit., p. 38.

46 *Sloan Management Review*, (Winter 1996).

47 Ibid.

48 *Source*: Department of Defense Internet article review.

49 See Dawn Elm and Kenneth Goodpaster, "Rationality and Respect," a note on ethical decision-making. This note was originally part of an online *Introduction to Business Ethics* course published by *Coursewise Publishers* in 1999.

50 Holman W. Jenkins Jr., "Business World: How Could They Have Done It?" *Wall Street Journal* August 28, 2002, p. A15. Jenkins goes on: "Did a bacillus descend from space and make Enron senior employees in equal parts evil and stupid? Whatever else it was, the activities of Enron's finance department – people like Andrew Fastow and Michael Kopper, with the presumed if uncertain participation of CEO Jeff Skilling – amounted to a colossal misjudgment. Their company is

bankrupt instead of thriving. Its senior employees are jobless, their wealth is under attack and they face criminal prosecution and jail. Presumably these are not the results Enron executives intended."

51 Utilitarian Jeremy Bentham insisted "each to count for one, none for more than one."

52 See Goodpaster and Nash, op. cit., pp. 135–50.

53 See K. E. Goodpaster et al. *Business Ethics: Policies and Persons*, 4th edn. (McGraw-Hill, 2005), Part III.

54 It is true that individualistic rights-based claims usually involve reciprocal *duties* on the part of those who are called on to respect those rights. The avenue of *duty-based thinking*, however, refers not to these reciprocal duties but to duties anchored in *relationships*.

55 See Goodpaster et al., op. cit.

56 The "Seven Deadly Sins," by contrast, all involve vices or habits that are destructive of the self or of others. *Virtue-based thinking* is concerned as much with avoiding vices as with supporting virtues.

57 Kenneth L. Woodward, "What is Virtue?" *Newsweek*, June 13, 1994, pp. 38–9. Note that at the end of this passage, Woodward *may* be saying that virtue is ultimately justified in terms of the *common good* (interests, rights, duties?). On the other hand, he may be saying that a virtuous society would be its own reward, even if it did *not* result in the common good.

58 See "The Corporate Scandals of 2002," a set of essays on Enron, Andersen, WorldCom, and Tyco, written by T. Dean Maines under the supervision of Kenneth E. Goodpaster, University of St. Thomas.

59 Again, we imagine appeals to *universal identification* and *impartial generalization*.

60 We will explore the notion of "surrogates" further in the next chapter.

61 Fukuyama, *Trust: The Social Virtues and the Creation of Prosperity* (The Free Press, 1995, p. 11). Fukuyama writes: "Law, contract, and economic rationality provide a necessary but not sufficient basis for both the stability and prosperity of postindustrial societies; they must as well be leavened with reciprocity, moral obligation, duty toward community, and trust, which are based in habit rather than rational calculation. The latter are not anachronisms in a modern society but rather the *sine qua non* of the latter's success."

62 Lynn Sharp Paine, *Value Shift* (McGraw-Hill, 2003, p. 165).

Chapter 4

1 Jeffrey Garten, *The Politics of Fortune* (Harvard Business School Press, 2002, p. 139).

2 David Whyte, *The Heart Aroused: Poetry and the Preservation of the Soul in Corporate America* (Doubleday, 1994, p. 270).

3 We could add scores of similar stories based on well-researched case studies of business organizations. We could also discuss the widely quoted "Parable of the Sadhu" by Bowen McCoy (*Harvard Business Review*, 1983, 1997) in which an executive loses his sense of humanity on a Himalayan mountain-climbing expedition and leaves a man to die on the slope. Many companies ended up in scandal during the last quarter of the twentieth century due to goals or targets presented to management as overriding – to be met "come hell or high water."

4 Ron Daniel, former Managing Director, McKinsey & Co., *Fortune*, November 1, 1993, p. 72. We see from this example that teleopathy can afflict organizations as well as individuals!

5 See the note "An Introduction to the Sarbanes-Oxley Act of 2002," written by T. Dean Maines under my supervision, Spring 2003, published in K. E. Goodpaster, L. L. Nash, and H.-C. deBettignies *Business Ethics: Policies and Persons* (4th edn., McGraw-Hill Irwin, 2006).

6 Chris Lee and Ron Zemke, "The Search for Spirit in the Workplace," *Training*, June 1993, pp. 21–8: "It seems that mid-life crises combined with economic insecurity are persuading some boomers to return to their childhood religions, some to turn to unconventional churches and some to the various 12-step programs of the 'recovery' movement. . . . Besides boomers' mid-life crises and general economic insecurities, we might add to the list of contributing trends: downsizing and 'delayering' as a result of global competition, decisional and informational overload, social disintegration through crime, broken marriages and families, and fractured urban education systems."

7 Peters quoted in Lee and Zemke, op. cit., p. 26.

8 This case will be discussed at length in Part II, but for now we can note that RPM's "Direction Statement" opens with: "RPM is a team dedicated to the purpose of operating a business based on the practical application of Judeo-Christian values for the mutual benefit of: *co-workers and their families, customers, shareholders, suppliers, and community.* We are committed to provide an environment where there is no conflict between work and moral/ethical values or family responsibilities and where everyone is treated justly. The tradition of excellence at RPM has grown out of a commitment to excellence rooted in the character of our Creator. Instead of driving each other toward excellence, we strive to free each other to grow and express the desire for excellence that is within all of us." See K. E. Goodpaster, L. L. Nash, and H.-C. deBettignies, op. cit.

9 The remainder of the RPM Direction Statement is more conventional, ethically speaking: "By adhering to the following principles, we are challenged to work and make decisions consistent with God's purpose for creation according to our individual understanding: DO WHAT IS

RIGHT – We are committed to do what is right even when it does not seem to be profitable, expedient, or conventional; DO OUR BEST – In our understanding of excellence we embrace a commitment to continuous improvement in everything we do. It is our commitment to encourage, teach, equip, and free each other to do and become all that we were intended to be. TREAT OTHERS AS WE WOULD LIKE TO BE TREATED; SEEK INSPIRATIONAL WISDOM – by looking outside ourselves, especially with respect to decisions having far-reaching and unpredictable consequences, but we will act only when the action is confirmed unanimously by others concerned." Goodpaster et al., op. cit.

10 *American Law Institute Proceedings*, ERISA language on pension fund managers' responsibilities, etc. See K. E. Goodpaster, "Business Ethics and Stakeholder Analysis," *Business Ethics Quarterly*, 1(1), January 1991, pp. 52–71.

11 "For those who want to lobby for a more radical effacement or shift in the locus of the public/private boundary, there is opportunity for attack along the lines of unseating corporations from their entitlement to ordinary constitutional liberties. Some of the liberties that protect natural persons might not apply, or might apply less stringently, when corporations and other associations of various sorts are the claimants. The less heavily we weigh their liberty claims, the more we would be justified to encumber them with obligations. . . . I do not doubt that if we could see to origins, we would find what is public and what is private lying close to the heart of the human feelings that give rise to governments." From "Corporate Vices and Corporate Virtues: Do Public/Private Distinctions Matter?" *University of Pennsylvania Law Review*, 130(6), June 1982.

12 This is, of course, the now-classic argument of Milton Friedman in "The Social Responsibility of Business is to Increase Its Profits." *New York Times Magazine* (September 13, 1970), pp. 32–3, 122–6.

13 Peter Drucker, "The Age of Social Transformation," *The Atlantic Monthly*, November 1994, pp. 53–80.

14 The Sarbanes-Oxley Act may or may not be a benchmark that provides an exception to this rule.

15 "Profit and the Public Good," *The Economist*, January 22, 2005.

16 "The World According to CSR," *The Economist*, January 22, 2005.

17 "The Good Company," *The Economist*, January 22, 2005.

18 "Leaders: Bad Arguments Against the Good Company?" *Ethical Corporation*, January 31, 2005, online at: http://www.ethicalcorp.com.

19 "There is another danger too: namely, that CSR will distract attention from genuine problems of business ethics that do need to be addressed. These are not in short supply. To say that CSR reflects a mistaken analysis of how capitalism serves society *is certainly not to say that*

managers can be left to do as they please, nor to say that the behaviour of firms is nobody's concern but their own. There is indeed such a thing as 'business ethics': managers need to be clear about that, and to comprehend what it implies for their actions." (Emphasis added.) "The Good Company," *The Economist*, January 22, 2005.

20 Recall our discussion in Chapter 3 about "rationality" and "respect."

21 "The Ethics of Business" *The Economist*, January 22, 2005.

22 "Opinion," *The Economist*, January 22, 2005.

23 "Leaders: Bad Arguments Against the Good Company?" *Ethical Corporation*, January 31, 2005, online at: http://www.ethicalcorp.com. Elaborating on the point: "Government exists to intervene through public spending, taxes, and regulation where necessary to achieve social justice, or to correct market failures. *The Economist* acknowledges, however, citing the example of global warming, that governments are sometimes loath to pressure for change. Government weakness is worse than they describe. Globalisation prompts governments everywhere to race for the bottom."

24 Elaine Sternberg, *Just Business: Business Ethics in Action* (Oxford University Press, 2000).

25 "The Ethics of Business" *The Economist*, January 22, 2005.

26 Shoshana Zuboff, "A Starter Kit for Business Ethics," *Fast Company Magazine*, January 2005, p. R8.

27 "The Ethics of Business," *The Economist*, January 22, 2005.

28 Originally published on the website of *The Social Affairs Unit*, http://www.socialaffairsunit.co.uk, 5/6 Morley House, 314–322 Regent Street, London. Emphasis added.

29 "The Union of Concerned Executives," *The Economist*, January 22, 2005. The editors add: "When Robin Hood stole from the rich to give to the poor, he was still stealing. He might have been a good corporate citizen, but he was still a bandit – and less of one, arguably, than the vicariously charitable CEO, who is spending money taken not from strangers, but from people who have placed him in a position of trust to safeguard their property."

30 Boycotts and class action suits from consumers and strikes by employees represent similar kinds of stakeholder recourse when CEOs break trust. Voter recalls are the analogue in the public sector.

31 "Leaders: Bad Arguments Against the Good Company?" *Ethical Corporation*, January 31, 2005, online at: http://www.ethicalcorp.com.

32 Ibid. The editorial goes on: "The law protects shareholders because they have lent money to the company, but they are not alone in lending resources. Loyal consumers reserve for a company a space in their minds; employees lend their commitment beyond the job description; communities extend their toleration – the license to operate. Our anachronous legal conception of the company fails to acknowledge

these participants in the enterprise. *The Economist* reminds us that not everything that is legal is ethical. This anachronism is a case in point."

33   "Business Ethics and Stakeholder Analysis," *Business Ethics Quarterly*, 1(1), January 1991, pp. 52–71. "As an old Latin proverb has it, *nemo dat quod non habet*, which literally means 'nobody gives what he doesn't have.' Freely translating in this context we can say: No one can expect of an *agent* behavior that is ethically less responsible than what he would expect of himself. I cannot (ethically) *hire* done on my behalf what I would not (ethically) *do* myself."

34   Lynn Sharp Paine, *Value Shift* (McGraw-Hill, 2003, p. 156).

35   Ibid. Paine continues with her version of what I have called the *Nemo Dat Principle*: "Just as an agency relationship with shareholders does not cancel out managers' preexisting obligations, it does not insulate shareholders from responsibilities they would otherwise have if managing their capital themselves. If individuals have duties to use their property in ways that respect the legitimate claims of others, they do not escape these duties by hiring someone else to manage their property for them."

36   "Leaders: Bad Arguments Against the Good Company?" *Ethical Corporation*, January 31, 2005, online at: http://www.ethicalcorp.com.

37   Clarence Walton, *Archons and Acolytes: The New Power Elite* (New York: Rowman & Littlefield Publishers, 1998).

38   "The Union of Concerned Executives," *The Economist*, January 22, 2005. The editors go on: "Almost all CSR has at least some cost, after all, even if it is no more than a modest increase in the firm's bureaucratic overhead. That cost subtracts from social welfare in its own right. So the kind of CSR that merely goes through the motions, delivering no new resources to worthy causes, giving the firm's workers or customers no good reason to think more highly of it (perhaps the opposite), involves a net loss of welfare."

39   "The Ethics of Business," *The Economist*, January 22, 2005.

40   "Leaders: Bad Arguments Against the Good Company?" *Ethical Corporation*, 31 January, 2005, online at: http://www.ethicalcorp.com.

41   *Oxford English Dictionary: counterfeit* – adj. 1 (of a coin, writing, etc.) made in imitation; not genuine; forged. 2 (of a claimant etc.) pretended. – n. a forgery; an imitation. [Counterfeits or surrogates are in some ways like autopilots, external systems that free us from the tedium of having to pay attention.] They become substitutes for "guidance by awareness" or mindfulness; indeed they are tools for (temporary) thoughtlessness.

42   "Leaders: Bad Arguments Against the Good Company?" *Ethical Corporation*, January 31, 2005, online at: http://www.ethicalcorp.com.

43   Peter Drucker, op. cit.

44 See K. E. Goodpaster, "Ethical Imperatives and Corporate Leadership." This paper was first presented as a Ruffin Lecture in Business Ethics at the Darden School, University of Virginia, in April 1988. It was later published in Kenneth R. Andrews (ed.), *Ethics in Practice: Managing the Moral Corporation* (Harvard Business School Press, 1991).

45 Choruses from *The Rock*, VI (1934).

46 *Creating and Maintaining an Ethical Corporate Climate* (Woodstock Booklet, Georgetown University Press, 1990).

47 "Leaders: Bad Arguments Against the Good Company?" *Ethical Corporation*, January 31, 2005, online at: http://www.ethicalcorp.com.

48 Recall the question of Glenn Tinder. "To what extent are we now living on moral savings accumulated over many centuries but no longer being replenished?" Glenn Tinder, *The Political Meaning of Christianity*, p. 51. Tinder also remarks that Jews and Christians "will be deeply suspicious of the maxim that the invisible hand of the market is always to be trusted in preference to the visible hand of government. Such a maxim has a look of idolatry. The principle that only God, and never a human institution, should be relied on absolutely suggests a far more flexible and pragmatic approach to the issue." Ibid., p. 185.

49 Peter Drucker, op. cit.

50 For a much fuller discussion, see K. E. Goodpaster and T. E. Holloran, "Anatomy of Corporate Spiritual and Social Awareness: The Case of Medtronic, Inc.," *Proceedings of the Third International Symposium on Catholic Social Thought and Management Education*, Goa India (January 1999).

51 James Collins, "Level 5 Leadership," *Harvard Business Review*, 79(1), January 2001, p. 68.

52 Ibid. Collins adds: "We keep putting people in positions of power who lack the seed to become a Level 5 leader, and that is one major reason why there are so few companies that make a sustained and verifiable shift from good to great."

53 If we ask whether the awareness that comes from conscience is self-sacrificial, the answer might surprise us. It may be different from that usually intended by those who see sacrifice as destructive. Consider the words of British philosopher Richard Norman: "The sacrificing of one's own interests need not be a sacrificing of oneself to something external. My commitment to my friends or my children, to a person whom I love or a social movement in which I believe, may be a part of my own deepest being, so that when I devote myself to them, my overriding experience is not that of sacrificing myself but of fulfilling myself." (*The Moral Philosophers*, 1983).

54 In Minnesota and nationally, Dayton Hudson Corporation was perhaps best known for institutionalizing corporate community involvement, as was Honeywell, Inc., until the summer of 1999 when it was acquired

by Allied Signal of New Jersey. Honeywell's record of corporate community involvement was extraordinary in private–public partnerships for improving neighborhoods, increasing minority employment and work–family balance.

Part II   Introduction

1 Bowen McCoy, "The Parable of the Sadhu," *Harvard Business Review*, 1983.
2 Lynn Sharp Paine, *Value Shift* (McGraw-Hill, 2003, p. 194). Paine adds: "By a moral center, I don't mean just a code of conduct or list of aphorisms inscribe on a Lucite plaque, but rather a set of answers to the fundamental questions every moral actor, whether an individual or a company, must come to terms with."

Chapter 5

1 Quoted in Margaret Lulic, *Who We Could Be at Work* (Minneapolis: Blue Edge Press, 1994, p. 14). Wikstrom, no longer with Reell, eventually became co-CEO of the company with Robert Carlson.
2 In Chapter 7, I will enrich the Reell story to illustrate the dynamics (and challenges) of *sustaining* corporate values over time.
3 Source: *Random House Webster's Unabridged Dictionary.*
4 Charles Handy, "What's a Business For?" *Harvard Business Review*, December 2002.
5 Ibid. Handy adds: "We need to eat to live; food is a necessary condition of life. But if we lived mainly to eat, making food a sufficient or sole purpose of life, we would become gross."
6 Bill George, *Authentic Leadership* (Wiley & Sons, 2003, p. 110).
7 Jim Collins and Jerry Porras, *Built to Last* (HarperCollins, 1994, 1997).
8 Ibid., p. 47. Merck II went on: "I want to . . . express the principles which we in our company have endeavored to live up to . . . Here is how it sums up: We try to remember that medicine is for the patient. We try never to forget that medicine is for the people. It is not for the profits. The profits follow, and if we have remembered that, they have never failed to appear. The better we have remembered it, the larger they have been." (George Merck II as quoted in Collins and Porras, op. cit., p. 48).
9 Ibid., p. 49. "In some cases, like Sony, the ideology derives from the founding roots. In some cases, like Merck, it comes from the second generation. In other cases, like Ford, the ideology went dormant and was rekindled in later years. But in nearly all cases, we found evidence

of a core ideology that existed not merely as words but as a vital shaping force." (Ibid., p. 54)

10 Ibid., p. 58.

11 Ibid., p. 80.

12 Ibid. The authors add that they found no evidence "that the pledge, once stated, became anywhere near as pervasive a guiding document in Bristol-Myers. Whereas J&J employees spoke explicitly about the link between the credo and key decisions, we found no similar comments by Bristol-Myers employees."

13 David Jacobson, "Founding Fathers," *Stanford Magazine*, February 24, 2005. The author goes on: "The HP Way worked because it wasn't just a high-minded mission statement. It was reflected and reinforced by the down-to-earth character of the co-founders."

14 Ibid. Jacobson adds: "Ultimately, Hewlett and Packard believed innovation sprang from grander lures than good wages and benefits. It grew out of an organization where people felt they were scaling Maslow's pyramid of self-actualization, not just climbing the company ladder."

15 Jim Collins and Jerry Porras, op. cit., p. 56. Emphasis added. Collins and Porras add: "For HP, bigger was better *only within the context of making a contribution.*" (p. 58).

16 Peter Burrows, "The HP Way Out of a Morass," *Business Week Online*, February 14, 2005. Under the title of his article, Burrows writes: "The culture that ousted CEO Fiorina tried to change is also the one that turned the outfit into a tech powerhouse – and could do so again."

17 Therese Poletti and Dean Takahashi, "One year later, 'HP Way' no longer rules workplace," *SiliconValley.com* (posted Monday, April 14, 2003). Porras added: "What is the integrity of the place now compared to what it used to be? That is at the core of what HP has been about. When you start to throw that out . . . you know where the culture is going."

18 Peter Burrows, op. cit.

19 Ibid.

20 "Major Restructuring Expected at H-P," *Wall Street Journal Online*, July 15, 2005. On July 20, the details were released: 14,500 layoffs worldwide (out of 150,000 employees); freezing US defined-benefit plans, shifting new employees to 401(k) plans; merging the sales force into business units. Expected total savings were $1.9 billion annually, starting in fiscal 2007.

21 Jeffrey L. Cruikshank and David B. Sicilia, *The Engine That Could: 75 Years of Values-Driven Change at Cummins Engine Company* (Boston: HBS Press, 1997, p. 507).

22 Ibid., p. 508.

23 T. Dean Maines, "Company, Narrative, Virtue," unpublished manuscript, p. 10.

24 Michael Oneal, "Outsourcing: Pain and Profit," *Chicago Tribune*, April 4, 2004. Oneal goes on: "Columbus has adjusted to the new reality and remains a healthy, prosperous town. But the paternalism that once sustained it is no match for the incessant demands for cost-cutting at Cummins. Markets like China and India present rich new opportunities. To ignore them likely would put the company, and all its jobs, at risk."

25 Ibid. Solso followed in the CEO footsteps of giants J. Irwin Miller, Henry Schacht, and James Henderson.

26 Ibid.

27 As quoted in Michael Oneal, op. cit.

28 Pope John Paul II called this a "community of work" in his encyclical letter on capitalism, *Centessimus Annus* (1991).

29 Originally published on the website <http://www.socialaffairsunit.co.uk> of The Social Affairs Unit, 5/6 Morley House, 314–322 Regent Street, London. Anderson makes clear his antipathy for conventional mission statements in this passage: "'Mission' applied to corporations is a weasel word. It goes beyond another much more suitable word such as 'purpose', in that it suggests something vaguely good and high-minded. The company is patting itself on the back. And not just for its economic efficiency. 'Mission' has a moral ring. And we find more such moral language in the mission statements, words such as 'integrity', 'ethics' and 'good'. The overall effect is to claim some ethical status for the company. Already, if only in the use of language, the Board is echoing the stakeholder view of company obligation."

30 Bill George, op. cit., p. 105.

31 "Leaders: Bad Arguments Against the Good Company?" *Ethical Corporation*, January 31, 2005. Originally found online at: http://www.ethicalcorp.com.

32 Such a process may be relatively easy in a small organization because behavior is observable daily and communication is direct. But in a large divisionalized and diversified corporation, the task is much more complex.

33 See Chapter 2 "Mindsets and Culture."

34 Further questions include: In what circumstances are employees willing to follow conscience, even when it might be economically costly? In what circumstances is there a tendency toward teleopathy, toward putting results ahead of ethical concerns when conflicts occur? Are there company policies or practices that have unintended negative ethical implications? The objective initially is not so much to *solve problems* as to surface (descriptively) the contours of the organization's values-in-action. Eventually the objective is to align espoused values with values-in-action through *institutionalization*. More on this in Chapter 6.

35 Translated by David Wagoner, "Lost," in *Traveling Light: Collected and New Poems* (University of Illinois Press, 1999, p. 10) and quoted in David Whyte, *The Heart Aroused*, (Revised Edition, 2002, pp. 261–2).

36 Special thanks to Paul Erdahl, Vice President, Executive and Leadership Development at Medtronic, for sharing his time and experience for this section of the chapter.

37 Erdahl noted that while the scale of the survey would seem to invite an electronic administration process in this age of email and the Internet, he believes that the more conventional "paper and pencil" approach actually enhances the response rate.

38 Gantz Wiley Research, which consults with Medtronic on Global Voices, suggests a number of "follow-up" actions: determining results-based priorities, developing a communication plan, implementing action plans, and monitoring progress. Gantz Wiley also provides normed industry data on certain questions in the survey, about 30 out of the 70 questions (43%).

39 See article by Benjamin Schneider, Paul J. Hanges, D. Brent Smith, and Amy Nicole Salvaggio of the University of Maryland, "Which Comes First: Employee Attitudes or Organizational Financial and Market Performance?" *Journal of Applied Psychology*, 88(5), 2003.

40 Bill George, op. cit., pp. 155–6.

41 Details about the tools can be found at the websites of both Gantz Wiley Research and CEBC: <www.cebcglobal.org>. The work of CEBC is discussed at length in Chapter 8 of this book.

42 Bill George, op. cit., p. 62. George adds: "Companies that pursue their mission in a consistent and unrelenting manner will create greater shareholder value than anyone believes possible. The success of such companies as 3M, Wells Fargo, and Walgreen's has been well documented by Jim Collins in his two thoroughly researched books, *Built to Last* and *Good to Great*."

43 This point illustrates the limitations of "corporate governance" approaches to ethics, which tend to focus exclusively on the Board of Directors and senior management. The operating teams and employees throughout an organization are essential participants in orienting and maintaining the company's conscience. Corporate governance is a *necessary* factor, but it is not *sufficient*.

44 Handy, op. cit.

45 The material in this section was first presented at a conference on "Voluntary Codes of Conduct for Multinational Corporations: Promises and Challenges," Baruch College, City University of New York, May 12–15, 2004.

46 Today the Minnesota Center for Corporate Responsibility (MCCR) is known as the Center for Ethical Business Cultures (CEBC) and is formally affiliated with the University of St. Thomas. To obtain a copy

of the *Minnesota Principles*, contact the Center for Ethical Business Cultures (http://www.cebcglobal.org).

47 See R. Kaku, "The Path of Kyosei," *Harvard Business Review* 75(4), 1997, pp. 55–63.

48 Paul Cardinal Poupard, M. Haytham Kahyat, and Rabbi David Rosen. In the words of Rabbi Rosen: "Both the individual and the collective must stand before the Lord, and *servant leadership* must minister to both. You – the Caux Round Table – are acting out of the two principles that undergird our Abrahamic faith traditions."

49 For more about the history of the Caux Round Table and to see translations of the principles into 12 languages, see the CRT website: http://www.cauxroundtable.org. Also to be found on the CRT website are summaries of many other sets of business principles and ethical norms, along with indications of their content relationship with the CRT *Principles*.

50 *Value Shift: Why Companies Must Merge Social and Financial Imperatives to Achieve Superior Performance* (McGraw-Hill, 2003).

51 In a speech on November 30, 2004, Minneapolis, MN.

52 K. E. Goodpaster, "Benchmarking: Fulfilling the Aspirational Goals of the Principles," July 22, 1999.

53 The SAIP inventors included both practitioners and academics: Harry R. Halloran, American Refining Group; T. Dean Maines, University of St. Thomas; Charles M. Denny, ADC, Inc. (Retired); Kenneth E. Goodpaster, University of St. Thomas; Timothy T. Greene, *The Enlightened World Foundation*; Lee M. Kennedy, 3M; Clinton O. Larson, Honeywell, Inc. (Retired); Arnold M. Weimerskirch, Honeywell, Inc. (Retired).

54 See "A Baldrige Process for Ethics?" coauthored by K. E. Goodpaster, Research Associate T. Dean Maines, and Arnold Weimerskirch, 3M Thwaits Fellow in the University of St. Thomas School of Engineering, in the April 2004 issue of the journal *Science and Engineering Ethics*. Weimerskirch has been a member of the Baldrige examiners' committee and has therefore been able to contribute significantly to working out the parallels between the Baldrige process and the SAIP.

55 Ibid.

56 The story of one SAIP beta test in the US is recounted in a new case series, American Refining Group, Inc. (A)(B) and (C) which can be found in K. E. Goodpaster, L. L. Nash, and H.-C. deBettignies, *Business Ethics: Policies and Persons*, 4th edn. (McGraw-Hill, 2005).

57 Harvard Business School Press, 2002, p. 85. Garten continues: "These and similar suggestions no doubt sound mundane, mechanical, and perhaps Pollyanna-ish. A commission looking into possibilities for promoting more integrity in the business culture may have much better ideas. But the essential point should not be lost: The more complex

the markets become, the more the integrity of its leaders matters, and the less likely that higher prescriptive laws and regulations will really matter."

58 It is worth noting that in a recent (2004) test of the SAIP in Germany, the company involved utilized an external team of auditors from a local university and publicized its results within the local community. This suggests that the "weakness" associated with the privacy of the tool can be remedied in practice.

59 Garten, op. cit., p. 144.

60 The Sarbanes-Oxley Act was signed into law by President George W. Bush on July 30, 2002. The Act is named after Sen. Paul E. Sarbanes (D-Maryland) and Rep. Michael R. Oxley (R-Ohio), who helped shape the bill's content and guided it through Congress.

61 The Ad Hoc Advisory Group continues: "These proposed changes are intended to eliminate ambiguities revealed by twelve years of sentencing experience and to describe more fully those essential attributes of successful compliance programs revealed by many years of program development and testing. They are also designed to respond to the lessons learned through the experience of national corporate scandals over the last two years and to synchronize the organizational sentencing guidelines with new federal legislation and emerging public and private regulatory requirements."

62 As quoted in K. E. Goodpaster, T. D. Maines, and A. M. Weimerskirch, "Creating a Corporate Conscience," *Minneapolis Star-Tribune* (December 1, 2003).

63 *Report of the Ad Hoc Advisory Group on the Organizational Sentencing Guidelines* (October 7, 2003).

64 Lynn Sharp Paine, *Value Shift* (McGraw-Hill, 2003), p. 201.

65 Garten, op. cit., p. 142.

Chapter 6

1 Richard Tanner Pascale and Anthony G. Athos, *The Art of Japanese Management: Applications for American Executives* (Warner Books, 1981).

2 David Whyte, *The Heart Aroused: Poetry and the Preservation of the Soul in Corporate America* (NY: Doubleday, 1994, pp. 36–8).

3 As quoted in David Whyte, op. cit., p. 42, primary source is Burton Raffel, translator, *Beowulf* (New American Library, 1963).

4 "General Mills Warned," *St. Paul Pioneer Press*, February 4, 2004.

5 Bill George, *Authentic Leadership* (Wiley & Sons, 2003, p. 75).

6 "Values begin with telling the truth, internally and externally. Integrity must run deep in the fabric of an organization's culture. It guides the everyday actions of employees and is central to its business conduct. Transparency is an integral part of integrity. The truth, both successes

and failures, must be shared openly with the outside world." (Ibid., p. 71).

7 See "American Refining Group, Inc. (A)." Reprinted in K. E. Good-paster, L. L. Nash, and H.-C. deBettignies, *Business Ethics: Policies and Persons*, 4th edn. (McGraw-Hill, 2005, p. 101).

8 Source: Letter to author from Bill Lee, September 7, 1983.

9 Jeffrey L. Cruikshank and David B. Sicilia, *The Engine That Could: 75 Years of Values-Driven Change at Cummins Engine Company* (Boston: Harvard Business School Press, 1997, pp. 12–13).

10 Bill George, op. cit., p. 128.

11 Bill George, op. cit., p. 129.

12 Another "symbol" of conscience in the Medtronic culture is a *space*. Corporate headquarters and other facilities have a *meditation room* where workers can find a quiet moment removed from the stress of their jobs. The rooms have literature from the many religions practiced by the company's employees.

13 The Beliefs of Borg-Warner. *Harvard Business School Case Services*: 9-383-091.

14 Here is a sample comment from a patient who spoke at the holiday celebration in 1994, referring to herself and her twin sister, both of whom had Medtronic cardiac implants: "Everyone of you should walk down the hall with light feet because you are keeping us alive. You make such a difference for us with every Xerox you run, every waste basket you empty, and every defibrillator you polish."

15 Perhaps "mission skeptic" Digby Anderson, discussed in Chapter 5, could have celebrations at which particularly grateful shareholders might give testimonials! Or not.

16 Charles Handy, "What's a Business For?" *Harvard Business Review*, December 2002.

17 Alison Maitland, "Leading Companies Faulted on Ethics Training," <FT.com> (February 23, 2005).

18 *2004 Federal Sentencing Guidelines for Organizations*, Section 8B2.1(b)(4)(A).

19 Michael Hoffman, Dawn-Marie Driscoll, and Mark Rowe, "Effective Ethics Education of the Board," *Ethikos and Corporate Conduct Quarterly*, 18(4), January/February 2005, p. 2.

20 I concur with the authors of the following thoughtful observation: "In the board context, we will continue to use the term 'education' (in preference to 'training'), even though the amended Federal Sentencing Guidelines for Organizations (FSGOs) refer to the need to conduct effective training programs in which an organization's governing authority must participate. The reasoning bears repetition. Directors should perceive activities in this area as being part of their continuing education responsibilities. Moreover, use of the term education will

reinforce the board's sense of an opportunity to extend, refine and practice its thinking – and therefore improve its decision-making – rather than merely [receive] presentations." (Michael Hoffman, Dawn-Marie Driscoll, and Mark Rowe, "A Better Class of Board Ethics Education," *Ethikos and Corporate Conduct Quarterly*, 18(5), March/April 2005, p. 5.)

21 Bill, George, op. cit., pp. 74–5.

22 See "H. J. Heinz Company: The Administration of Policy (A)" (*Harvard Business School Case Services*, 9-382-034). Reprinted in K. E. Goodpaster, L. L. Nash, and H.-C. deBettignies, op. cit.

23 Malcolm Gladwell, "The Talent Myth: Are Smart People Overrated?" *The New Yorker* (July 22, 2002). Gladwell goes on: "The reasons for its collapse are complex, needless to say. But what if Enron failed not in spite of its talent mind-set but because of it? What if smart people are overrated?"

24 Ibid. Gladwell illustrates: "Lynda Clemmons, the so-called 'weather babe' who started Enron's weather derivatives business, jumped, in seven quick years, from trader to associate to manager to director and, finally, to head of her own business unit. How do you evaluate someone's performance in a system where no one is in a job long enough to allow such evaluation?"

25 Ibid. (Emphasis added.)

26 Charles Handy, op. cit. Handy adds "If the contemporary business with its foundation of human assets is to survive, it will have to find better ways to protect people from the demands of the jobs it gives them. Neglecting the environment may drive away customers, but neglecting people's lives may drive away key members of the workforce."

27 The richness in the application of ideas like "calling" and "vocation" to business life is well-described in Michael Novak's *Business as a Calling: Work and the Examined Life* (Free Press, 1996). Also see Michael Naughton and Helen Alford's *Managing as if Faith Mattered* (Notre Dame Press, 2001).

28 Remember philosopher Richard Norman's observation, quoted in Chapter 3, that "my commitment to my friends or my children, to a person whom I love or a social movement in which I believe, may be a part of my own deepest being, so that when I devote myself to them, my overriding experience is not that of *sacrificing* myself but of *fulfilling* myself." *The Moral Philosophers* (Oxford University Press, 1983, p. 249). Poet David Whyte once remarked that "the antidote to exhaustion is not *rest*; the antidote is *wholeheartedness*."

29 Win Swenson, in the November/December 2003 issue of *Ethikos and Corporate Conduct Quarterly*, described the proposed amendments to the FSGO and made an interesting observation: "While not without controversy, the Advisory Group found that 'culture,' 'values,' and

'ethics' were becoming increasingly visible in government policies (e.g., §406 of the Sarbanes-Oxley Act) and considered critical by some commentators." Later, in Chapter 8, I discuss the Supreme Court findings about the constitutionality of the Sentencing Guidelines and the practical implications of those findings for federal prosecutors, courts, and corporate compliance programs.

30 Bill George, op. cit., p. 85.

31 See "Dow Corning Corporation: Business Conduct and Global Values" (*Harvard Business School Case Services*, 9-385-018 and 019). Also see "Dow Corning Corporation: The Breast Implant Controversy" in K. E. Goodpaster, L. L. Nash, and H.-C. deBettignies, op. cit.

32 Kenneth Andrews, "Can the Best Corporations Be Made Moral?" *Harvard Business Review*, May–June 1973, pp. 57–64.

33 Bill George, op. cit., p. 62. George then adds: "These companies eventually get sold off or incorporated into a larger company, or they go into a long-term state of decline. It is a paradox that by focusing on pleasing shareholders they wind up pleasing no one – not their customers, their employees, their communities, and ultimately *not* their shareholders."

34 Copyright © 2003 by Kenneth E. Goodpaster, Clinton O. Larson, T. Dean Maines, and Arnold M. Weimerskirch. All rights reserved. Any use, copying, reproduction, further distribution, or modification without permission of the copyright holders is strictly prohibited.

Chapter 7

1 Philip Selznick, *Leadership in Administration: A Sociological Interpretation* (Harper & Row, 1957).

2 *Source*: My own one-on-one interviews with Reell employees.

3 Reell's 1992 *Direction Statement* (some excerpts):

"RPM is a team. Its purpose is to operate a business based on the practical application of Judeo-Christian values for the mutual benefit of: *team members, customers, shareholders, suppliers, and community.*"

"As a team, striving to follow the will of God, we currently manufacture wrap spring clutches and other rotary motion control devices for a world market. Our goal is to continually improve our ability to meet customer needs. How we accomplish our mission is important to us . . ."

"The tradition of excellence at RPM has grown out of a commitment to excellence rooted in the character of our Creator. Instead of driving each other toward excellence, we strive to free each other to grow and express the excellence that is within all of us. We strive to work and make decisions based on these guiding principles: *We Will Do What Is Right; We Will Do Our Best; We Will Treat Others As We Would Like To Be Treated; We Will Seek Inspirational Wisdom.*"

4 According to Reell's lawyer, "Both state and federal laws prohibit religious discrimination. At the state level, the Minnesota Human Rights Act prohibits a Minnesota employer from discriminating against employees with respect to 'hiring, tenure, compensation, terms, upgrading, conditions, facilities, or privileges of employment . . .' on the basis of religion, among other things. Title VII of the Civil Rights Act of 1964 also prohibits religious discrimination at the federal level."

5 "Reell Precision Manufacturing, Inc.: A Matter of Direction (A)(B)(C)(D) and (E)," in K. E. Goodpaster, L. L. Nash, and H.-C. deBettignies, *Business Ethics: Policies and Persons*, 4th edn. (McGraw-Hill, 2005, Exhibit 6).

6 For the new Reell (E1) and (E2) cases, written by T. Dean Maines under the supervision of Professors Michael Naughton and Kenneth Goodpaster, see K. E. Goodpaster, L. L. Nash, and H.-C. deBettignies, op. cit.

7 "Reell is a team united in the operation of a business based on the practical application of spiritual values to promote the growth of individuals and advance the common good for the benefit of co-workers and their families, customers, shareholders, suppliers, and community. Rooted in Judeo-Christian values, we welcome and draw on the richness of our spiritually diverse community. We are committed to provide an environment where there is harmony between work and our moral/ethical values and family responsibilities and where everyone is treated justly." (*Source*: Reell 2004 Direction Statement.)

8 "When religion presses back against the dominant culture, both are changed as a result of the encounter. One reason that the culture changes may be that we are constructed in a way that causes our souls to resonate to religious language, even when we prefer to avoid it. The spirituality of religion, for most Americans, fills a hole in the human soul that the more material aspects of our world leave agape." (Stephen Carter, *God's Name in Vain* (Basic Books, 2000, p. 172).)

9 Chester Barnard, *The Functions of the Executive* (Harvard University Press, 1938).

10 The "inward" manifestation of this possibility (but not the "outward" manifestation) may have been at work in the H. J. Heinz case, discussed in the previous chapter. Recall that the discovery of the unacceptable financial reporting practices did not come from *within* Heinz, but from an external Campbell Soup lawsuit. The values of the SEC and the IRS, however, did *not* represent what I am calling a "macrofit" with the values of Heinz.

11 Note that the congruence being sought here is quite compatible with – and may even call for – diversity along other dimensions, such as gender, age, ethnicity, etc. The key consideration is shared moral values. The Reell case, with which we opened this chapter, contains many of the dynamics under discussion here.

12 Military organizations make for an interesting set of case examples. Sometimes the high degree of fit is contributed by the nobility of the cause, but at other times, solely by the draconian nature of the discipline. M. Scott Peck offers a great deal of insight into this subject in his book *People of the Lie: The Hope for Healing Human Evil* (Simon & Schuster, 1983, p. 228).

13 Escher's fascination with nested figures has been pursued with sophistication in the past two decades by the fractal geometry of Harvard mathematician Benoit Mandelbrot. The notion of fractal "self-similarity" is described in K. E. Goodpaster, "Toward an Integrated Approach to Business Ethics," *Thought*, 60(237), June 1985, pp. 17–18.

14 I would argue that the US Federal Sentencing Guidelines for Organizations (FSGO) promulgated in 1991 and re-affirmed with some revisions in 2004, are – as regulatory schemes go – innovative in their effort to avoid what was a rather anarchic sentencing regime in the past, while avoiding the imposition of a rigid set of external rules. What the guidelines seek is a credible discipline for the *cultures* of the organizations being regulated. The constitutionality of their application in the US, of course, continues to be a problem. In the language introduced in this chapter, it can be described as a "macrofit" problem.

15 For more on "fractals," see K. E. Goodpaster, op. cit., pp. 161–80. Also see Benoit Mandelbrot, *The Fractal Geometry of Nature* (Freeman, 1983).

16 Some observers believe that the courts are departing from a *laissez faire* posture toward a more intrusive one on issues of free speech, privacy, and freedom of conscience. In a classic article that is still relevant today, David Ewing argued for "constitutionalizing" the corporation as an alternative (see "Civil Liberties in the Corporation," *New York State Bar Journal*, April 1978). Recent debates over employee Internet privacy and employee drug testing illustrate the strong forces on both sides of this issue.

17 Such statements are also, as we have seen, important tools for orientation and implementation.

18 Kenneth Andrews, "Can the Best Corporations Be Made Moral?" *Harvard Business Review*, May–June 1973, p. 60.

19 Rationality-oriented and respect-oriented values are discussed in Chapters 2 and 3.

20 Bill George, *Authentic Leadership* (John Wiley & Sons, 2003, p. 163).

21 "Lex Service Group (A)(B)(C) and (D)," in K. E. Goodpaster, L. L. Nash, and H.-C. deBettignies, op. cit., Part 2.

22 Bill George, *The Authentic Leader* (Wiley & Sons, 2003, p. 146).

23 K. E. Goodpaster, L. L. Nash, and H.-C. deBettignies, op. cit., Part 3.

24 Jeffrey Garten, *The Politics of Fortune* (Harvard Business School Press, 2002, p. 11) writes. "For business leaders in particular, the new paradigm of leadership must go beyond pleasing Wall Street and delivering ever higher profits on a quarterly basis. Besides considering all the stakeholders of a company – employees, customers, suppliers, communities – business leaders must also consider the concerns of society, such as a cleaner environment and a higher level of integrity in business dealings."

25 Energy, Power, and the Cree Nations (A) and (B), in K. E. Goodpaster, L. L. Nash, and H.-C. deBettignies, op. cit.

26 Ibid. Chief Primrose continued with emotion: "The issues are very complex – suicides occur in other communities including my own. . . . A recent opinion survey indicated that overall our membership is quite positive about our future. By the path that we have followed by developing a positive, cooperative relationship with the governments and Manitoba Hydro we have created a mood of optimism, not desolation or despair. . . . The potential agreement being discussed [with Northern States Power of Minnesota] will continue to enhance our socioeconomic opportunities. We are not being exploited by big corporations. The exploitation of our people is coming from groups that continue to suppress economic opportunities for my people."

27 Ibid.

28 During the 1970s and 1980s, the debate over the ethics of doing business in South Africa under *apartheid* revealed similar dynamics. Corporate signatories to the Sullivan Principles sought to avoid the hard choice between disinvesting entirely and contributing to what most regarded as social injustice. They sought instead to influence the *apartheid* policy of the government. Dresser Industries decided after much controversy that it could not or would not seek such influence. IBM, on the other hand, took a different approach. Although it refused for many years to close down its operations in South Africa, it reaffirmed a policy of working for social change from within, both independently and through its commitment to the Sullivan principles. In 1986, IBM sold its subsidiary, but continued to sell products through the newly independent South African company. Other companies pulled out entirely, believing that their continued business activity there only served to reinforce the *status quo*. See "Dresser Industries and South Africa," in K. E. Goodpaster, J. B. Matthews, and L. L. Nash *Policies and Person: A Casebook in Business Ethics* (McGraw-Hill, 1985, pp. 430–47) and "The ICCR and the Debate over South African Disinvestment," (*Harvard Business School Case Services*, 9-386-149).

29 See "Velsicol Chemical Corporation (A)," (*Harvard Business School Case Services*, 9-385-021).

30 For the full text of the AdvaMed code, see: http://www.advamed.org.

31 Philip Selznick, op. cit.

32 See the note "The Corporate Scandals of 2002 (B): Arthur Andersen" and "An Introduction to the Sarbanes-Oxley Act of 2002," written by T. Dean Maines under my supervision, Spring 2003, published in K. E. Goodpaster, L. L. Nash, and H.-C. deBettignies, op. cit.

33 See K. E. Goodpaster, L. L. Nash, and H.-C. deBettignies, op. cit.

34 Is the Reell case a less "politically correct" analogue to this case, only with freedom of religion rather than free speech as its pivot?

35 An example of early research along these lines is the work of psycho-analyst Michael Maccoby. In *The Gamesman: The New Corporate Leaders* (Simon and Schuster, 1976), Maccoby argues that certain moral character traits are selected against by the "psychostructures" of many corporations, affecting the cultures of the organizations themselves.

36 "Dayton Hudson Corporation: Conscience and Control (A)(B)(C)" in K. E. Goodpaster, L. L. Nash, and H.-C. deBettignies, op. cit.

37 Ibid., Case (C), Exhibit 1.

38 November 29, 1984. Emphasis added.

39 Jeffrey Garten, *The Politics of Fortune* (Harvard Business School Press, 2002, p. 152).

Chapter 8

1 This theme was well-addressed by Bill George in his recent book *Authentic Leadership* (Jossey-Bass, 2003).

2 More precisely: "Can you tell me, Socrates, whether virtue is acquired by teaching or by practice; or if neither by teaching nor practice, then whether it comes to man by nature or in what other way?"

3 Parts of this chapter are drawn from a visiting lecture entitled "Business Ethics: From Classroom to Corporation" that I presented at the University of Dayton, October 25–26, 2000. Other parts are drawn from "Teaching and Learning Ethics by the Case Method" in Norman Bowie (ed.), *Blackwell's Guide to Business Ethics* (Blackwell Publishers, 2002, pp. 117–41).

4 The Caux Round Table, as we have seen in Chapter 5, is an NGO that has espoused a set of transcultural ethical principles for business. A group of practitioners and scholars then developed a self-assessment and improvement process (SAIP) based on the Caux *Principles* analogous to the Baldrige process for quality management.

5 Robert J. Shiller, "How Wall Street Learns to Look the Other Way," *Wall Street Journal* Op-Ed, February 8, 2005.

6   *The Prince*, Chapter 15, "Of the Things for which Men, and Especially Princes, Are Praised or Blamed." Machiavelli writes: "A man who wishes to make a profession of goodness in everything must necessarily come to grief among so many who are not good. Therefore it is necessary for a prince, who wishes to maintain himself, to learn how not to be good, and to use this knowledge and not use it, according to the necessity of the case."

7   Jim Collins, *Built to Last*, p. 55. Collins continues: "They have tended to pursue a cluster of objectives, of which making money is only one – and not necessarily the primary one. Indeed, for many of the visionary companies, business has historically been more than an economic activity, more than just a way to make money. Through the history of most of the visionary companies we saw a core ideology that transcended purely economic considerations. And – this is the key point – they have had core ideology *to a greater degree than the comparison companies in our study.*"

8   Ethics Education Task Force of *AACSB International*, "Ethics Education in Business Schools," February 3, 2004.

9   Ibid.

10 Recall our discussion of "mindsets" and their structures in Chapter 2.

11 University of St. Thomas, 1990.

12 More on "compartmentalizing" later in this section on the first academy.

13 Robert J. Shiller, op. cit.

14 Warren G. Bennis and James O'Toole, "How Business Schools Lost Their Way," (*Harvard Business Review Online*, May 2005).

15 In the next section (The Second Academy), e-learning as it relates to ethics is a particularly useful method, precisely because large corporations are usually geographically dispersed and are therefore frequently unable to offer "synchronous" learning activities.

16 Robert J. Shiller, op. cit.

17 Ethics Education Task Force of *AACSB International*, op. cit.

18 Sam Goldwyn is reputed to have said, "For your information, let me ask you a question." Such "informative" questions have a role in both student evaluations and faculty surveys.

19 Ethics Education Task Force of *AACSB International*, op. cit.

20 Warren G. Bennis and James O'Toole, op. cit.

21 Jeffrey E. Garten, Dean, Yale School of Management, *The Politics of Fortune: A New Agenda for Business Leaders* (Harvard Business School Press, 2002, p. 174).

22 Ibid.

23 *Enterprise Learning: A Spending Summary* by Gary Gabelhouse, CEO, Fairfield Research Inc.

24 By "insourced," I mean hired in from local academic institutions for company-specific versions of seminars, workshops, or classes.

25 Keith Darcy, interim executive director of the US Ethics Officer Association, quoted in "Ethics Officers – a growing breed?" *Ethical Corporation*, originally online February 7, 2005, www.ethicalcorp.com.

26 Material in this and the following two sections is drawn from "A Brief Note on Corporate Ethics Officers" prepared in 1998 by Research Assistant Hassan Valji, and revised in 2004 by Research Associate T. Dean Maines, under the supervision of Kenneth E. Goodpaster, University of St. Thomas.

27 Itamar Sittenfeld, "Federal sentencing guidelines for organizations," *Internal Auditor*, 53(2), 1996, p. 58.

28 Paul E. Fiorelli, "Why Comply? Directors face heightened personal liability after Caremark," *Business Horizons*, 41(4), 1998, p. 50.

29 Edward S. Petry Jr. and Fred Tietz, "Can Ethics Officers Improve Office Ethics?" *Business and Society Review*, 82, 1992, p. 21.

30 See www.corporatecompliance.org.

31 K. E. Goodpaster and J. B. Matthews, Jr., "Can a Corporation Have a Conscience?" *Harvard Business Review on Corporate Responsibility* (Boston: Harvard Business School Publishing, 2003, pp. 131–55).

32 See "Ethics Officers – a growing breed?" *Ethical Corporation*, originally online February 7, 2005, www.ethicalcorp.com.

33 Keith Darcy, interim executive director of the US Ethics Officer Association, as quoted in "Ethics Officers – a growing breed?" *Ethical Corporation*, originally online February 7, 2005, www.ethicalcorp.com.

34 Alison Maitland, "Leading companies faulted on ethics training," *Financial Times*, February 23, 2005. Originally found at www.financialtimes.com.

35 Ibid. The report said that "the same argument was used a decade ago to restrict investment in safety training that was now regarded as a standard aspect of business."

36 "High Court's sentencing ruling will cause inconsistent sentences, DOJ official warns," *Criminal Law Reporter*, 76(15), p. 263.

37 One Washington DC attorney is quoted as warning companies not to view the High Court decision as a reason to alter their compliance programs: "The reason to implement a compliance program is to avoid having law enforcement problems in the first place, not to pray for a reduced sentence in the event of a criminal conviction." "High Court's sentencing ruling will cause inconsistent sentences, DOJ official warns," *Criminal Law Reporter*, 76(15), p. 264.

38 Ibid. Additionally, Swenson said, "the organizational guidelines, unlike their controversial counterparts for sentencing individuals, are widely viewed as creating a good model for corporate sentencing which means that judges won't want to deviate from them."

39 "High Court's sentencing ruling will cause inconsistent sentences, DOJ official warns," *Criminal Law Reporter*, 76(15), p. 264.

40 I refer here to both "outsourced" seminars and programs and custom programs within the organization.

41 Jeffrey E. Garten, Dean, Yale School of Management, *The Politics of Fortune: A New Agenda for Business Leaders* (Harvard Business School Press, 2002, p. 174).

42 See W. Michael Hoffman, Dawn-Marie Driscoll, and Mark Rowe, "Effective Ethics Education of the Board," *Ethikos*, 18(4–5), 2005.

43 David Whyte, *The Heart Aroused: Poetry and the Preservation of the Soul in Corporate America* (NY: Doubleday, 1994, p. 23). Later in the book, Whyte adds: "We can have fire in our approach only if our heart is in the work, and it is hard to put our heart in the work when most of what we feel is stress. The very act of slowing into our own more natural rhythms may seem like a heart-stopping prospect, but there are some elegant lessons in the very reasons a heart may stop or start." (pp. 224–5).

44 Anthony DeMello, SJ, "Presence," *One Minute Wisdom* (Doubleday, 1985, p. 12).

45 Parker J. Palmer, "A Model for Right Action", in *The Active Life* (Harper & Row, 1992, pp. 55–8), taken from Thomas Merton, "The Woodcarver," *The Way of Chuang Tzu* (New Directions Publishing Corporation, 1965, pp. 110–11).

46 Palmer: "When I ask Chinese scholars what would have happened if Khing had failed to produce a bell stand acceptable to the prince, they usually answer with a sweeping movement of the forefinger across the front of the throat. Khing was under considerable pressure to do the job and to do it right, on penalty of his life." Ibid.

47 Recall from Chapter 6 the warning issued by Charles Handy: "If the contemporary business with its foundation of human assets is to survive, it will have to find better ways to protect people from the demands of the jobs it gives them. Neglecting the environment may drive away customers, but neglecting people's lives may drive away key members of the workforce." Handy, "What's a Business For?" *Harvard Business Review*, Nov–Dec, 2002.

48 Warren G. Bennis and James O'Toole, op. cit.

49 The *Random House Unabridged Dictionary* defines it this way: "profession, *n.* a vocation requiring knowledge of some department of learning or science: *the profession of teaching.* Cf. learned profession."

50 Wilfred Bockelman, *The Culture of Corporate Citizenship: Minnesota's Business Legacy for the Global Future, Commissioned by the Center for Ethical Business Cultures* (MN: Galde Press, 1999).

51 Robert Bellah, with Richard Madsen, William M. Sullivan, Ann Swidler, Steven M. Tipton, *Habits of the Heart – Individualism and Commitment in American Life* (University of California Press, 1985, p. 290), emphasis added.

52 Warren G. Bennis and James O'Toole, op. cit.

53 Examples abroad: The Prince of Wales International Business Leaders Forum (IBLF), Business in the Community (BITC) in the UK, the CSR Academy in Europe. Lately, these business-related NGOs are being referred to in the nomenclature of the United Nations' Global Compact as "civil society."

54 Even in what some would call its "politically corrected" modern version, approved by the American Medical Association, the Hippocratic Oath communicates moral commitment:

"You do solemnly swear, each by whatever he or she holds most sacred:

- That you will be loyal to the Profession of Medicine and just and generous to its members.
- That you will lead your lives and practice your art in uprightness and honor.
- That into whatsoever house you shall enter, it shall be for the good of the sick to the utmost of your power, your holding yourselves far aloof from wrong, from corruption, from the tempting of others to vice.
- That you will exercise your art solely for the cure of your patients, and will give no drug, perform no operation, for a criminal purpose, even if solicited, far less suggest it.
- That whatsoever you shall see or hear of the lives of men or women which is not fitting to be spoken, you will keep inviolably secret.

These things do you swear. Let each bow the head in sign of acquiescence. And now, if you will be true to this, your oath, may prosperity and good repute be ever yours; the opposite, if you shall prove yourselves forsworn."

55 See the ISBEE website at http://www.ISBEE.org. ISBEE cooperates with regional and national networks of business ethics around the globe: the Society for Business Ethics (North America), the European Business Ethics Network (EBEN), the Japan Society for Business Ethics Studies (JABES), the Latin American Business Ethics Network (ALENE), and the African Business Ethics Network (BEN-Africa). It actively supports the creation of business ethics networks, particularly in developing countries.

56 ISBEE has also helped sponsor regional conferences in São Paulo, Brazil (1998), Shanghai, China (2002), and Prague, Czech Republic (2003).

57 One particularly relevant research report was *Deriving Value from Corporate Values*, which seeks to clarify how companies define corporate values, to expand on research about the relationship of values to business performance, and to identify best practices for managing corporate

values. "The report is based on a major study of corporate values, including the results of surveys of senior executives at 365 companies in 30 countries in five regions, almost one-third of whom are CEOs or board members."

58 The Aspen Institute website: http://www.aspeninstitute.org.

59 Warren G. Bennis and James O'Toole, op. cit.

60 See http://www.cebcglobal.org (the website of the Center for Ethical Business Cultures).

61 Further information can be found at the CEBC website. As mentioned in Chapter 5, the CEBC Integrity Survey™ is a 28-question stand-alone employee survey tool used to obtain an in-depth assessment of an organization's ethical environment. The CEBC Integrity QuickCheck™, a subset of the CEBC Integrity Survey, is a five-question instrument which can be used as a standalone assessment or added to an existing employee survey. It provides a high-level overview of an organization's ethical landscape. The tools use the surveying expertise of Gantz Wiley Research. Results of the CEBC Integrity Survey and Integrity QuickCheck can be benchmarked against WorkTrends, an annual study and normative database, and can be analyzed using the principles of the Gantz Wiley Research High Performance Model™.

62 The book's promotional material asks: "How did Minnesota – a distant, isolated American state – and its Twin Cities business community become known world-wide for the citizenship and integrity of its corporations and corporate leaders? Natives sometimes weary of reminders of Minnesota's reputation, but the fact remains that leaders from cities across the United States and delegations from Europe, Asia and the Americas keep singing Minnesota's praise and asking – how did you do it?"

63 Robert N. Bellah,, "Professions Under Siege: Can Ethical Autonomy Survive?" *Logos*, 1(3), Fall 1997, pp. 31–50.

64 James T. Laney, "The Education of the Heart," *Harvard Magazine*, September–October 1985, pp. 23–4.

65 Published Sunday, April 13, 2003 in the Minneapolis *Star Tribune*.

Epilogue

1 "Other professional schools have carved out standards that are appropriate for their various professions; now business schools must have the courage to do the same." Warren G. Bennis and James O'Toole, "How Business Schools Lost Their Way," *Harvard Business Review Online*, May 2005.

2 Nicholas Dent, in his article on "conscience" in the *Routledge Encyclopedia of Philosophy Online*, implies that authenticity is not enough when

he writes: "We are told that some Nazis saw carrying out the extermination programme as a matter of conscience . . . In reply, it can be said that only consciences which are 'enlightened' require respect. The question whether conscience can be enlightened, or fallible and perverted, leads on to a second strand in thinking about conscience."

3 Ratzinger Report, "Conscience and Truth," presented at the 10th Workshop for Bishops, February 1991, Dallas, Texas. Ratzinger continues: "It is never wrong to follow the convictions one has arrived at – in fact, one must do so. But it can very well be wrong to have come to such askew convictions in the first place, by having stifled the protest of [conscience]. . . . For this reason, criminals of conviction like Hitler and Stalin are guilty."

4 See the discussion of the paradox of legitimacy in the introduction to Part I and in Chapter 4. The paradox of paternalism is discussed in Chapter 7.

5 Bowen McCoy, "The Parable of the Sadhu," *Harvard Business Review*, 1983, p. 106, emphasis added. Re-published as a *Harvard Business Review Classic* in June–July 1997.

6 Jeffrey Garten, *The Politics of Fortune* (Harvard Business School Press, 2002, p. 26): "A strong argument can be made that September 11, 2001, has changed the environment in which business leaders will now operate – indeed, that the terrorist attacks have changed society's expectation of what leaders can be. I also believe that the Enron debacle was the culmination of a long era of personal greed and commercial excess, and that the public is ready for the pendulum to swing back to more fundamental and traditional values. Americans may well have entered a period in which the notions of patriotism and community spirit are back in a way not seen since the early days of the Cold War."

7 Mary Midgley, *Heart and Mind* (St. Martin's Press, 1981, pp. 72, 75). Recall from Chapter 3 Midgley's observation that "Moral judgment is not a luxury, not a perverse indulgence of the self-righteous. It is a necessity. . . . Morally as well as physically, there is only one world, and we all have to live in it."

8 President George W. Bush in a speech on Wall Street, July 2002. In relation to what I have called the three academies, Bush said: "Our schools of business must be principled teachers of right and wrong, *and not surrender to moral confusion and relativism.* Our leaders of business must set high and clear expectations of conduct, demonstrated by their own conduct."

9 See Warren G. Bennis and James O'Toole, "How Business Schools Lost Their Way," *Harvard Business Review Online*, May 2005. The authors insist that "Other professional schools have carved out standards that are appropriate for their various professions; now business schools

must have the courage to do the same." They then quote Thomas Lindsay, former provost of the University of Dallas:

> [B]usiness education in this country is devoted overwhelmingly to technical training. This is ironic, because even before Enron, studies showed that executives who fail – financially as well as morally – rarely do so from a lack of expertise. Rather, they fail because they lack interpersonal skills and practical wisdom; what Aristotle called prudence. Aristotle taught that genuine leadership consisted in the ability to identify and serve the common good. To do so requires much more than technical training. It requires an education in moral reasoning, which must include history, philosophy, literature, theology, and logic.

Lindsay is further quoted as estimating that before the recent scandals, business students spent "95% of their time learning how to calculate with a view to maximizing wealth. Just 5% of their time . . . is spent developing their moral capacities."

10 Excerpt from T. S. Eliot, "Choruses from 'The Rock'" (1934), *Collected Poems 1909–1962* (Harcourt Brace and Company, 1963, p. 154). Copyright 1936 by Harcourt, Inc., copyright © 1964, 1963 by T. S. Eliot, reprinted by permission of the publisher.

Index